A-Z STOKE-O

G000123911

CONTENT[S]

Key to Map Pages	2-3
Large Scale Centres	4-7
Map Pages	8-49

Index
Hosp
of Inte...

REFERENCE

Motorway	M6	Map Continuation	12 · 4
A Road	A50	Car Park (Selected)	P
Under Construction		Church or Chapel	†
B Road	B5040	Fire Station	■
Dual Carriageway		Hospital	⊞
One Way Street	→	House Numbers A and B Roads only	128 460
Traffic flow on A Roads is also indicated by a heavy line on the driver's left.	→	Information Centre	🄸
Restricted Access		National Grid Reference	350
Pedestrianized Road		Police Station	▲
Track		Post Office	★
Footpath		Toilet	▽
		with facilities for the Disabled	▽
Residential Walkway		Educational Establishment	
Railway	Station / Tunnel / Level Crossing / Heritage Station	Hospital, Hospice or Health Centre	
		Industrial Building	
Built-up Area	GLOVER ST	Leisure & Recreational Facility	
		Place of Interest	
Local Authority Boundary		Public Building	
Posttown Boundary		Shopping Centre or Market	
Postcode Boundary within Posttown		Other Selected Buildings	

SCALE

Map Pages 8-49
1:19,000   3⅓ inches (8.47 cm) to 1 mile, 5.26 cm to 1km

0   ¼   ½ Mile
0   250   500   750 Metres

Map Pages 4-7
1:7920   8 inches (20.32 cm) to 1 mile, 12.63 cm to 1km

0   ⅛   ¼ Mile
0   100   200   300   400 Metres

Copyright of Geographers' A-Z Map Company Limited

Head Office:
Fairfield Road, Borough Green, Sevenoaks, Kent TN15 8PP
Telephone 01732 781000 (General Enquiries & Trade Sales)
Showrooms:
44 Gray's Inn Road, London WC1X 8HX
Telephone 020 7440 9500 (Retail Sales)
www.a-zmaps.co.uk

Ordnance Survey® This product includes mapping data licensed from Ordnance Survey® with the permission of the Controller of Her Majesty's Stationery Office.
© Crown Copyright 2002. Licence number 100017302
Edition 4 2002
Copyright © Geographers' A-Z Map Co. Ltd. 2002

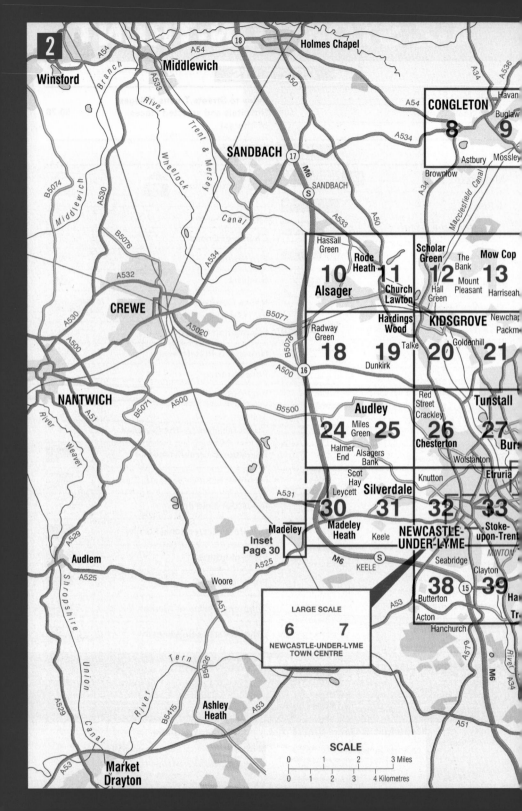

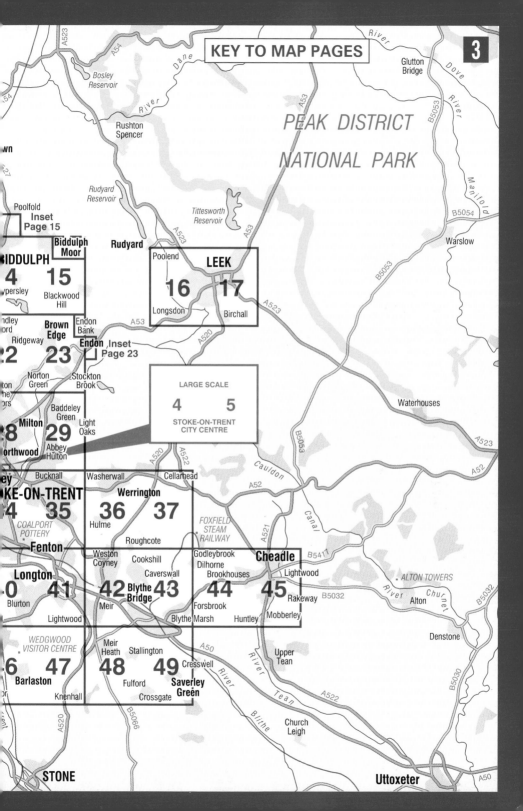

River

Glutton
Bridge

Dane

A54

*Bosley
Reservoir*

A523

PEAK DISTRICT

B5053

River

NATIONAL PARK

River

Rushton
Spencer

A53

Manifold

B5054

*Rudyard
Reservoir*

A523

Warslow

Poolfold
**Inset
Page 15**

*Tittesworth
Reservoir*

A53

**Biddulph
Moor**

Rudyard

B5053

BIDDULPH

Poolend

LEEK

4

15

16

17

persley

Blackwood
Hill

Longsdon

Birchall

A523

Waterhouses

Endon
Bank

**Brown
Edge**

A520

A523

ndley
ord

Ridgeway

2

23

Endon **Inset
Page 23**

Norton
Green

Stockton
Brook

LARGE SCALE

ton
he
ors

Baddeley
Green

4   **5**

Milton

**STOKE-ON-TRENT
CITY CENTRE**

8

29

Light
Oaks

Waterhouses

rthwood

Abbey
Hulton

A52

Bucknall

Washerwall

Cellarhead

Cauldon

ey

A520

A522

A52

OKE-ON-TRENT

Werrington

A521

Canal

4

35

36

37

*COALPORT
POTTERY*

Hulme

*FOXFIELD
STEAM
RAILWAY*

B5053

Fenton

Roughcote

Weston
Coyney

Cookshill

Godleybrook
Dilhorne
Brookhouses

Cheadle

B5411

Longton

Caverswall

Lightwood

ALTON TOWERS

B5032

0

41

42

43

44

45

Alton

Blurton

*Blythe
Bridge*

Rakeway

B5032

River

Churnet

Meir

Forsbrook

Mobberley

Lightwood

Blythe Marsh

Huntley

Denstone

Meir
Heath

Stallington

A50

Upper
Tean

*WEDGWOOD
VISITOR CENTRE*

Cresswell

B5030

6

47

48

49

Knenhall

Fulford

**Saverley
Green**

A522

River

Barlaston

Crossgate

A50

Church
Leigh

Tean

A520

B5066

Blithe

STONE

Uttoxeter

A50

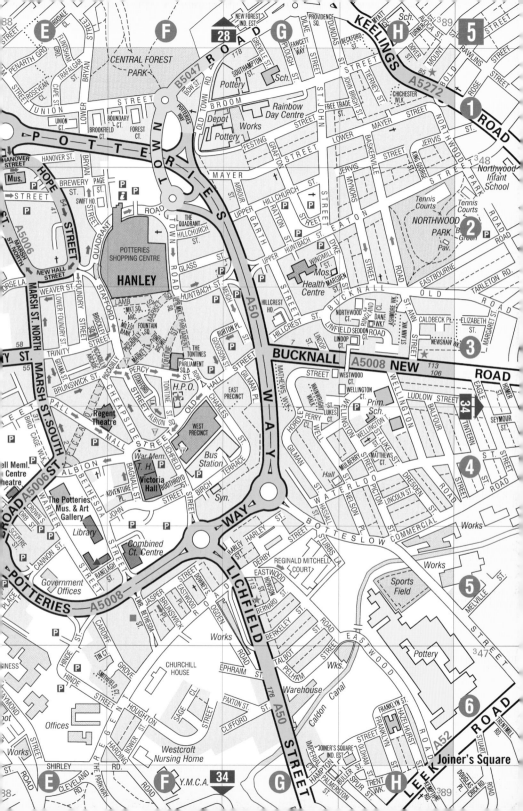

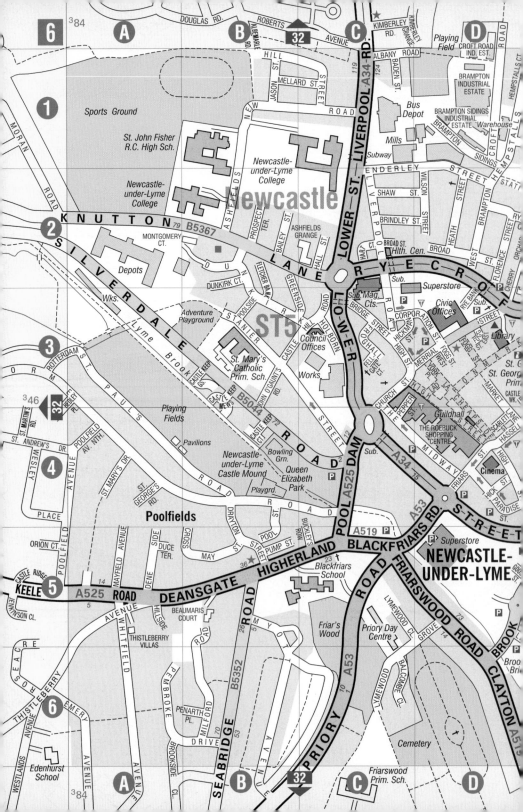

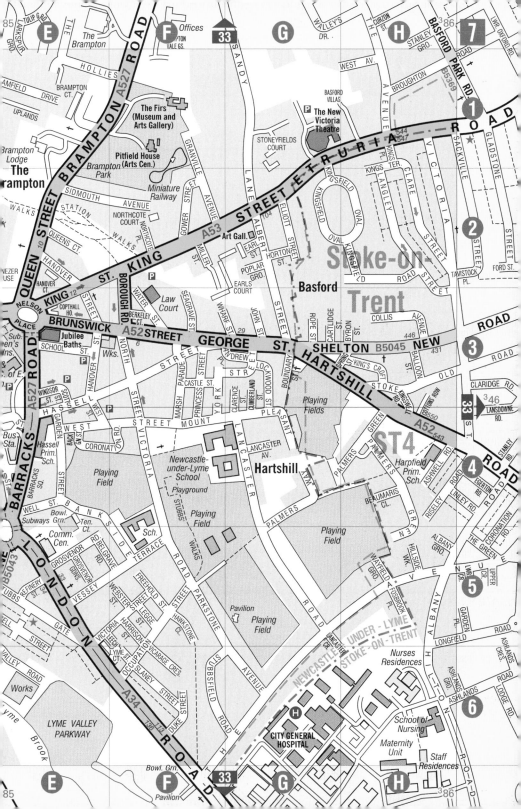

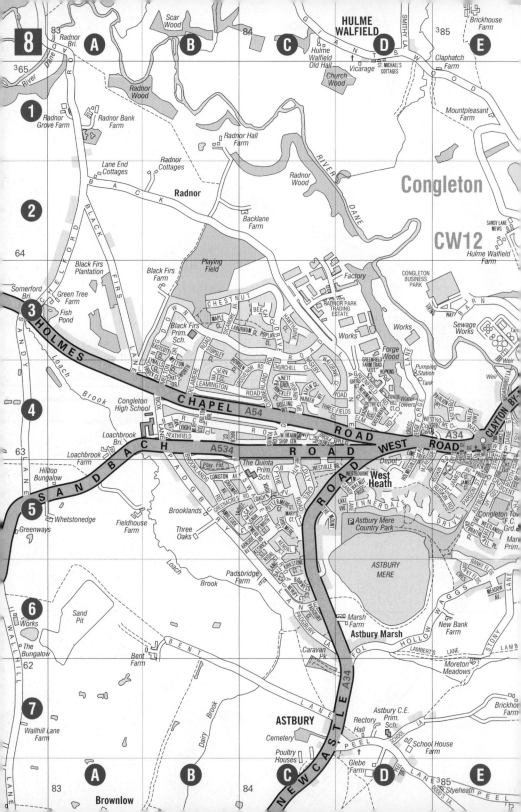

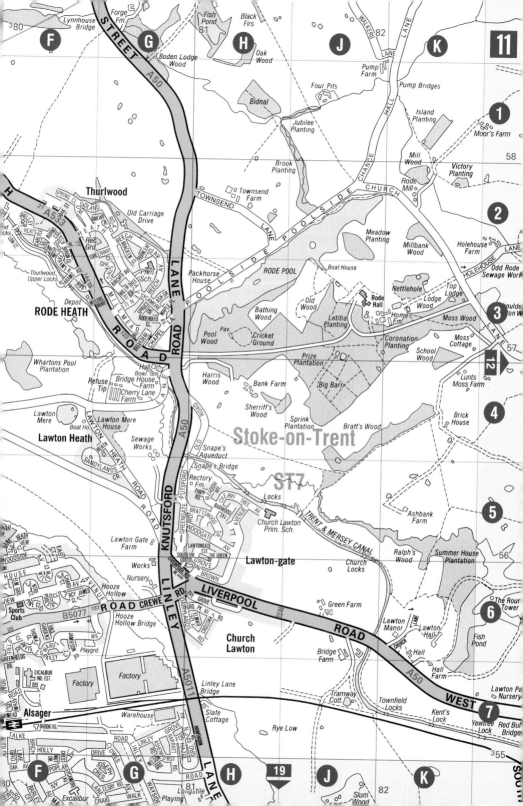

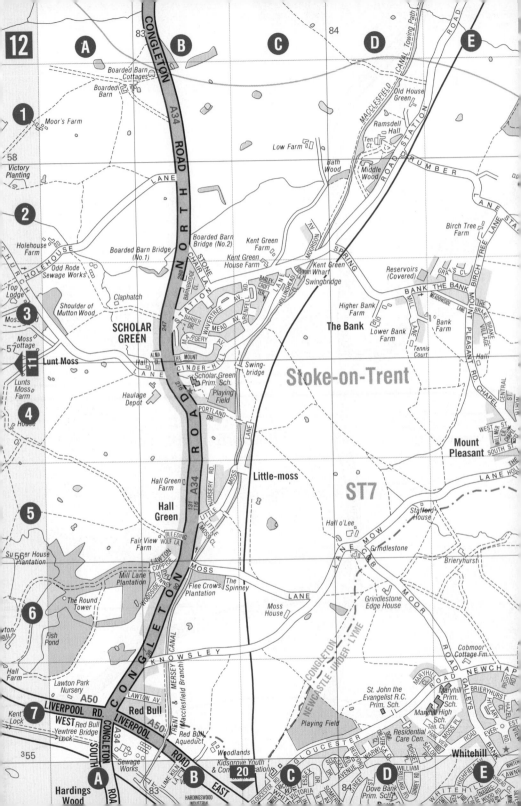

Grid references: A B C D E (top and bottom), 1–7 (left side)

12

Congleton Road North
A34

Boarded Barn Cottages
Boarded Barn
Moor's Farm
Victory Planting
58
83

Holehouse Farm
Odd Rode Sewage Works
Top Lodge
Boarded Barn Bridge (No.1)
Claphatch
Shoulder of Mutton Wood
SCHOLAR GREEN
Moss Cottage
57
Lunt Moss
Lunts Moss Farm
House

Boarded Barn Bridge (No.2)
Kent Green Farm
Kent Green House Farm
Low Farm

Bath Wood
Middle Wood
Old House Green
Ramsdell Hall
Ten Ct.

Macclesfield Canal Towing Path

84

Kent Green Wharf
Kent Green
Swingbridge
Higher Bank Farm
Lower Bank Farm
The Bank

Reservoirs (Covered)
Birch Tree Farm

BANK THE BANK
Bank Farm
Tennis Court
Hall

Stoke-on-Trent

Haulage Depot
Scholar Green Prim. Sch.
Playing Field
Swingbridge
Portland Dr.

Hall Green Farm
Hall Green
Little-moss

Mount Pleasant

ST7

Fair View Farm
Bleeding Wolf La.
Super House Plantation
56

Mill Lane Plantation
The Round Tower
Fish Pond
Hall Farm

Flee Crows Plantation
The Spinney
Moss House
Hall o'Lee
Grindlestone

Stafford House
Grindlestone Edge House
Brieryhurst

Cobmoor Cottage Fm.
NEWCHAP
GALLEYS
Brieryhurst

Lawton Park Nursery
A50
Red Bull
Liverpool Rd West
Kent Lock
Red Bull Yewtree Bridge Lock
Liverpool Rd
A50
Red Bull Aqueduct

St. John the Evangelist R.C. Prim. Sch.
Playing Field
Maryhill Prim. Sch.
Maryhill High Sch.
Residential Care Cen.
Whitehill

Sewage Works
Kidsgrove Youth & Community Station
Woodlands
20

Hardings Wood
355
83
84

Congleton Road South
A34
Knowsley
Trent & Mersey Canal (Macclesfield Branch)
Lawton Av.
Congleton Road East
Gloucester Rd
Dove Bank Prim. Sch.
Whitehill

11

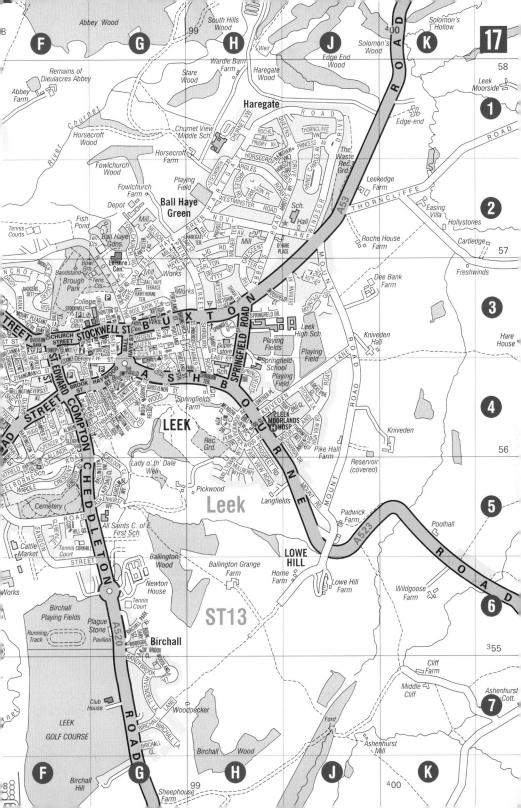

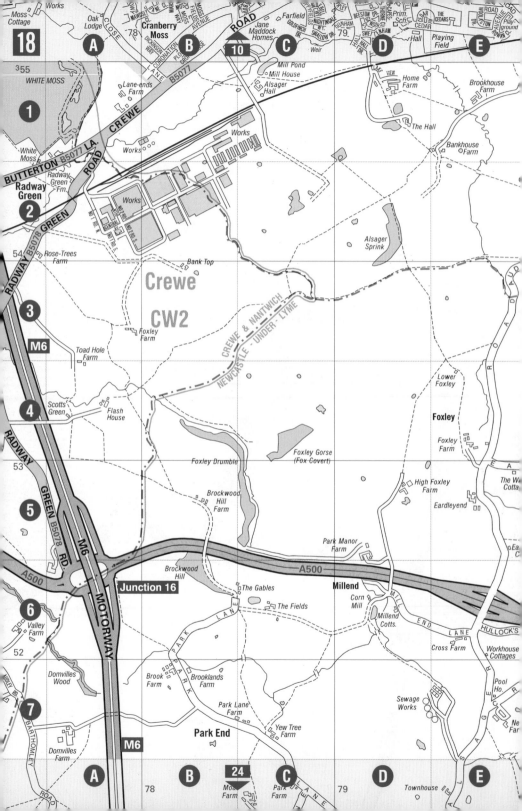

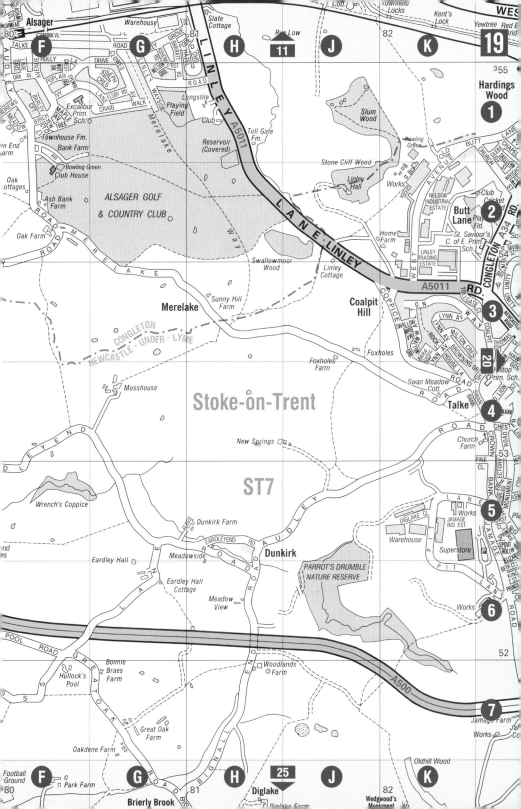

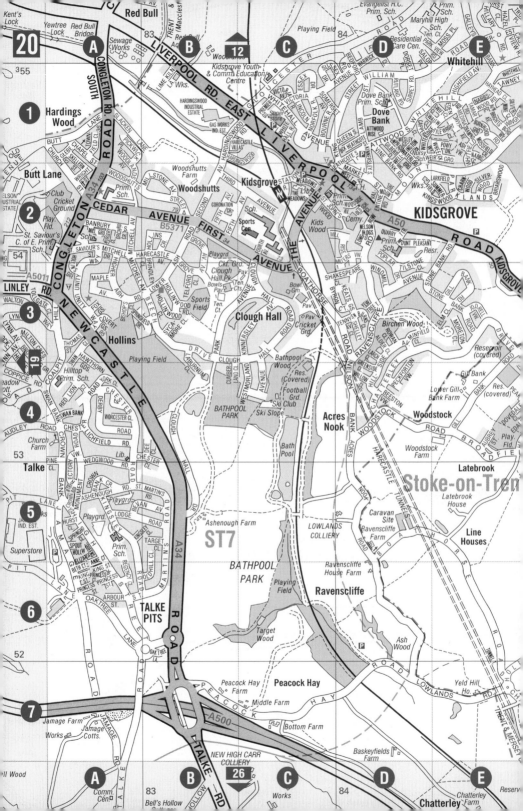

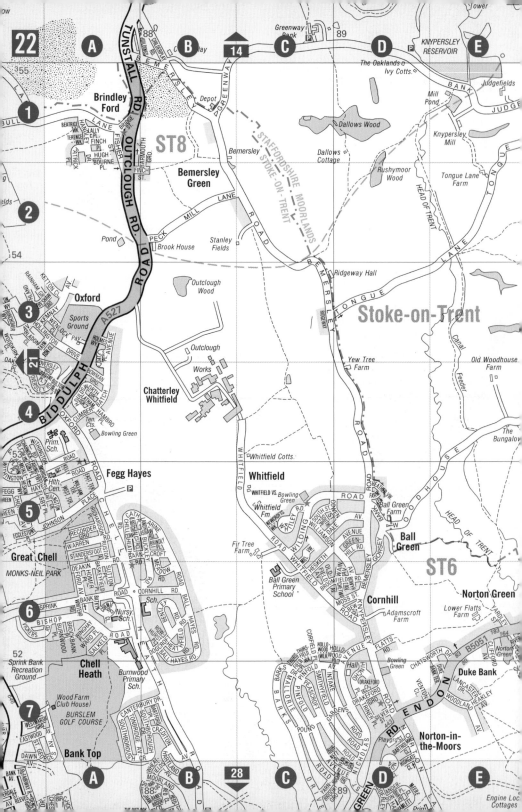

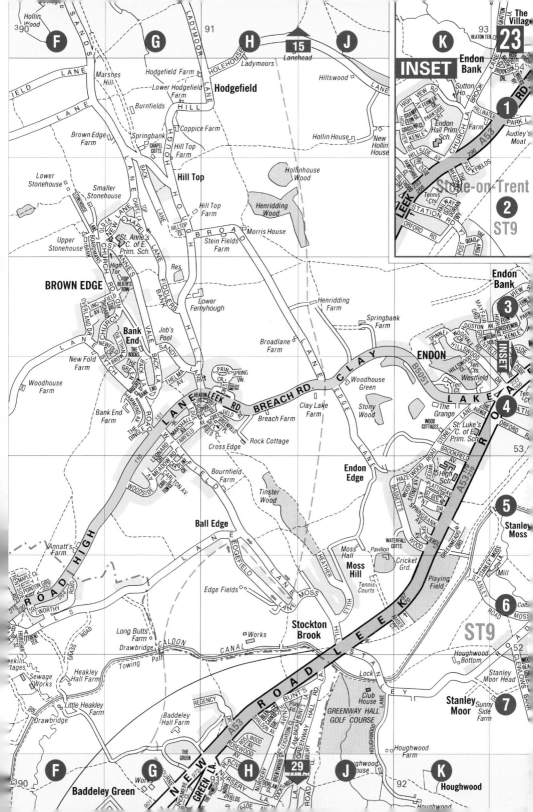

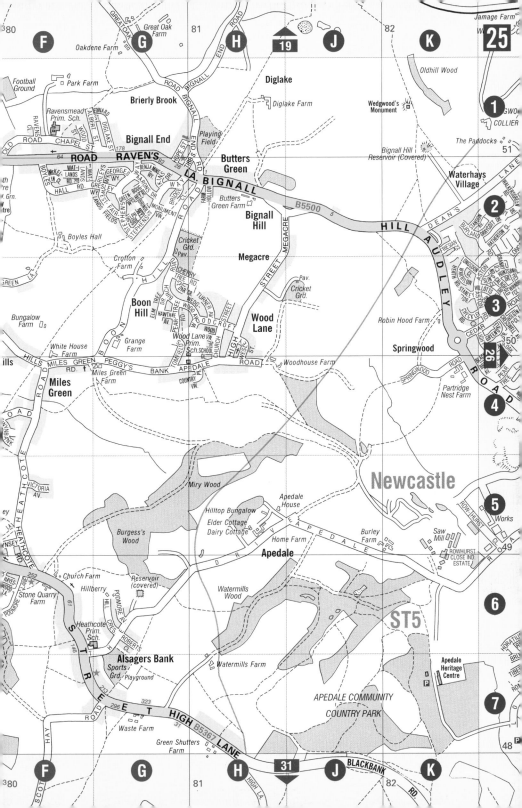

380   81   82

Jamage Farm
GWO
COLLIER

Oldhill Wood

1

Oakdene Farm
Great Oak Farm
Football Ground
Park Farm

Diglake

Diglake Farm
Wedgwood's Monument

The Paddocks
51

Brierly Brook

Ravensmead Prim. Sch.
RAVENS MEAD
EDWARD
DIGLAKE ST
ALBERT ST
WOOD ST
CHAPEL ST
178
OLD ROAD
ROAD
64 RAVEN'S
MCKEL
WAT LANDS
BOYLES RD.
HALL RD.
GRESLEY AV.
WY
LANDS
FIELDS
STEPHENS
GREEN BANK RD.
BENJAMINS
GEORGE
BRIELYS
GRESLEY
WY

Bignall End

Butters Green

Playing Field

BIGNALL END RD.
HOPE ST
WALL

Butters Green Farm

Bignall Hill Reservoir (Covered)
Waterhays Village

2

Boyles Hall
Crofton Farm

Cricket Grd.
Pav.

Bignall Hill

Megacre

Pav.
Cricket Grd.

HILL
AUDLEY
B5500 5
DEAN'S LANE

3

Bungalow Farm

Boon Hill

Grange Farm

White House Farm

CHERRY TREE RD.
HAWTHORN AV.
PEAR TREE
WEDG.
WOOD
Wood Lane Prim. Sch.
SCHOOL
HIGH ST
WOODCROFT
WEST ST
CHURCH ST

Wood Lane

Robin Hood Farm

Springwood

Partridge Nest Farm

26
350

4

Hills
HILLS
MILES GREEN RD.
PEGGY'S BANK
Miles Green Farm
APEDALE
COUNTRY VW.
ROAD
Woodhouse Farm

SPRINGWOOD ROAD

CEDAR GREENW
PEAR TREE

Miles Green

BOON HILL ROAD

Miry Wood

Apedale House

Newcastle

5
Works

HEATHCOTE RD.
VICTORIA AV.

Hilltop Bungalow
Elder Cottage
Dairy Cottage
Home Farm

Burley Farm

Saw Mill

ROWHURST CLOSE IND. ESTATE
49

Burgess's Wood

Church Farm
Hillberry
252

Reservoir (covered)

Apedale

ST5

6

Stone Quarry Farm
HAYES LANE
61
Heathcote Prim. Sch.
PODMORE AV.
HILL CRES.
ROBERTS CL.

Watermills Wood

HORATIU
BRU
TIBER

Apedale Heritage Centre
P

7

Alsagers Bank
Sports Grd.
Playground
243

Watermills Farm

APEDALE COMMUNITY COUNTRY PARK

STREET
146
323
296
HIGH LANE B5367
31
Waste Farm
Green Shutters Farm

HAY
SCOT

31

J   BLACKBANK

48
P

380   81   82   RD.

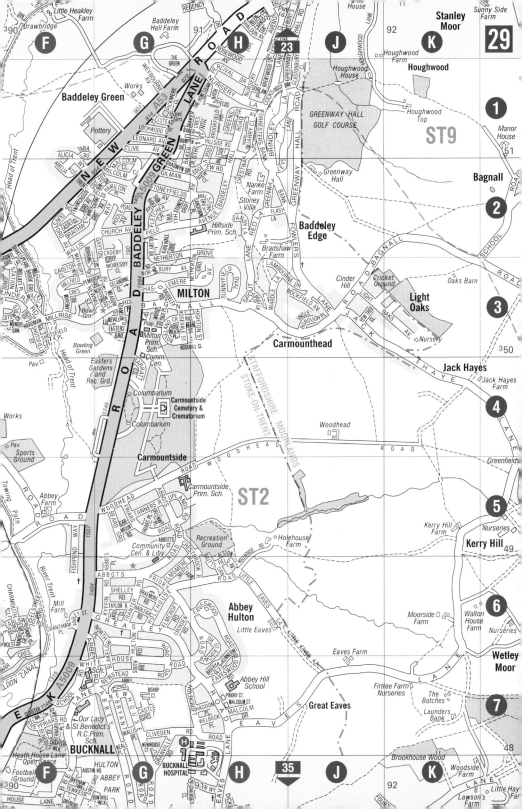

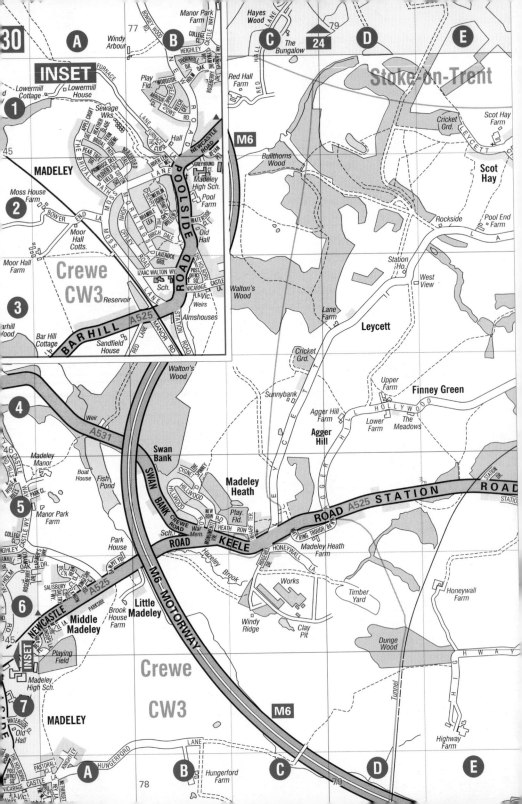

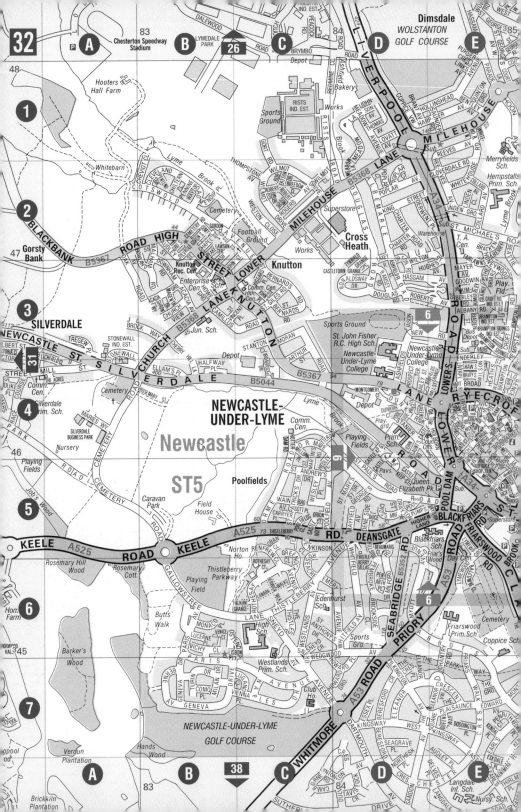

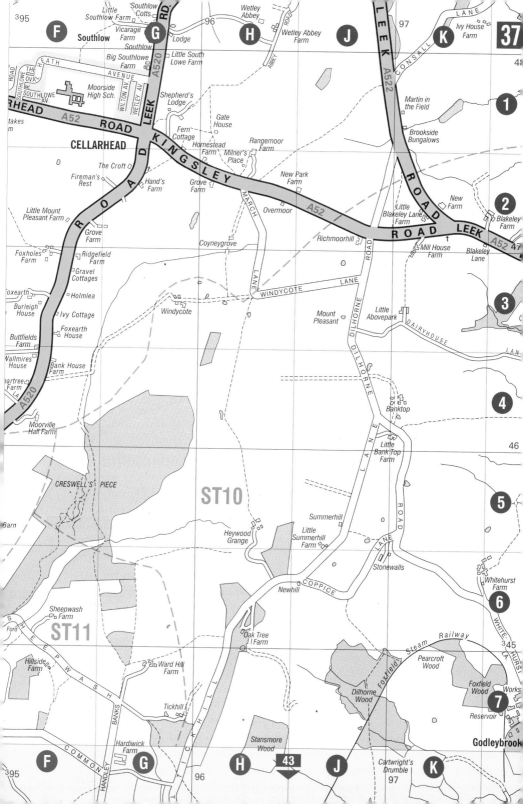

48

42

A **B** **C** **D** **E**

Lightwood

Pittsburgh House

1

Meir Heath

Stoke-on-Trent

Warehouse

Works

Works

Playing Field

Pav.

Spring Prim

Stallington Grange

2

Stoke-on-Trent

Stafford B5029

3

Windmill Hill

ST3

Diamond Plantation

Stallington

Stallington Hall Farm

Stallington Farm

Nursery

47

Chestnut Farm

The Poplars Farm

Nursy

Ravenswood

Rabbit Warren

4

Dale House

Leadendale

Leadendale Farm

Blacklake Plantation

Cricket Ground

Club House

Blacklake Farm

Reservoir (Covered)

Baker's Cottage

Sports Ground

Leadendale

Nursery

Leyden House

Football Ground

Blacklake Plantation

Fulford Dale Farm

Fulfor Mand

5

Blacklake Farm

Parkside Poultry Farm

6

Stone

School House

Schoolhouse Wood

Moddershall Grange

Greenacres

Woodside Cottage

Broom's Farm

ST15

Longbank

Manor Farm

Stallington Heath

Nursery

7

Knenhall

Squirrels Leap

Moddershall Oaks

Idlerocks Farm

Idlerocks

Reservoir (covered)

Fulfo

Crossgate

Field Farm

Spot Acre

A **B** **C** **D** **E**

INDEX

Including Streets, Places & Areas, Hospitals & Hospices, Industrial Estates,
Selected Flats & Walkways, Stations and Selected Places of Interest.

HOW TO USE THIS INDEX

1. Each street name is followed by its Posttown or Postal Locality and then by its map reference; e.g. Abbey Grn. Rd. *Leek* ....1E **16** is in the Leek Posttown and is to be found in square 1E on page **16**. The page number being shown in bold type.

2. A strict alphabetical order is followed in which Av., Rd., St., etc. (though abbreviated) are read in full and as part of the street name; e.g. Alanley Clo. appears after Alan Dale but before Alan Rd.

3. Streets and a selection of flats and walkways too small to be shown on the maps, appear in the index in *Italics* with the thoroughfare to which it is connected shown in brackets; e.g. *Axbridge Wlk. Stoke ....3B 28 (off Kinver St.)*

4. Places and areas are shown in the index in **blue type** and the map reference is to the actual map square in which the town centre or area is located and not to the place name shown on the map; e.g. **Alsager. 6E 10**

5. An example of a selected place of interest is Apedale Heritage Cen. 7K 25

6. An example of a hospital or hospice is BRADWELL HOSPITAL. 5D 26

7. An example of a station is **ALSAGER STATION. RAIL 7F 11**

8. Map references shown in brackets; e.g. Adventure Pl. *Stoke* ....2B **34** (4F **5**) refer to entries that also appear on the large scale pages **4-7**.

GENERAL ABBREVIATIONS

All : Alley
App : Approach
Arc : Arcade
Av : Avenue
Bk : Back
Boulevd : Boulevard
Bri : Bridge
B'way : Broadway
Bldgs : Buildings
Bus : Business
Cvn : Caravan
Cen : Centre
Chu : Church
Chyd : Churchyard
Circ : Circle
Cir : Circus
Clo : Close
Comn : Common
Cotts : Cottages

Ct : Court
Cres : Crescent
Cft : Croft
Dri : Drive
E : East
Embkmt : Embankment
Est : Estate
Fld : Field
Gdns : Gardens
Gth : Garth
Ga : Gate
Gt : Great
Grn : Green
Gro : Grove
Ho : House
Ind : Industrial
Info : Information
Junct : Junction
La : Lane

Lit : Little
Lwr : Lower
Mc : Mac
Mnr : Manor
Mans : Mansions
Mkt : Market
Mdw : Meadow
M : Mews
Mt : Mount
Mus : Museum
N : North
Pal : Palace
Pde : Parade
Pk : Park
Pas : Passage
Pl : Place
Quad : Quadrant
Res : Residential
Ri : Rise

Rd : Road
Shop : Shopping
S : South
Sq : Square
Sta : Station
St : Street
Ter : Terrace
Trad : Trading
Up : Upper
Va : Vale
Vw : View
Vs : Villas
Vis : Visitors
Wlk : Walk
W : West
Yd : Yard

POSTTOWN AND POSTAL LOCALITY ABBREVIATIONS

Act : Acton
Als : Alsager
Als B : Alsagers Bank
Ash B : Ash Bank
A'bry : Astbury
A'ly : Audley
Bad G : Baddeley Green
Bag : Bagnall
B'stn : Barlaston
B'ly : Barthomley
B'ton : Betchton
Bet : Betley
Bid : Biddulph
Bid M : Biddulph Moor
Big E : Bignall End
B Bri : Blythe Bridge
B Frd : Brindley Ford
Brn E : Brown Edge
Brn L : Brown Lees
B'lw : Brownlow
Bug : Buglawton
Bur : Burslem
But : Butterton
Cav : Caverswall
C'dle : Cheadle
Ches : Chesterton
Chu L : Church Lawton

Cong : Congleton
C'wll : Cresswell
Dil : Dilhorne
Dray : Draycott
Dres : Dresden
Eat T : Eaton Bank Trad. Est.
End : Endon
Fen I : Fenton Ind. Est.
For : Forsbrook
Ful : Fulford
Gil H : Gillow Heath
Halm : Halmerend
Han : Hanchurch
Har : Harriseahead
Has G : Hassall Green
Hav : Havannah
Hem H : Hem Heath
High B : High Carr Bus. Pk.
Hot I : Hot Lane Ind. Est.
Hul : Hulme
Hul W : Hulme Walfield
Join I : Joiners Square Ind. Est.
K'le : Keele
Ker : Kermincham
Kid : Kidsgrove
King : Kingsley
Knen : Knenhall

Knut : Knutton
Knyp : Knypersley
Lask E : Lask Edge
Leek : Leek
Ley : Leycett
L Oaks : Light Oaks
Long H : Longbridge Hayes
Long : Longsdon
L'tn : Longton
Lyme B : Lymedale Bus. Pk.
Mad : Madeley
Mad H : Madeley Heath
Meir H : Meir Heath
Mor : Moreton
Mow C : Mow Cop
New : Newcastle
N'cpl : Newchapel
Pac : Packmoor
P East : Parkhouse Ind. Est. E.
P West : Parkhouse Ind. Est. W.
Park : Parklands
Port : Porthill
Rad G : Radway Green
Red S : Red Street
Rode H : Rode Heath
Rook : Rookery
R'gh C : Rough Close

Row I : Rowhurst Ind. Est.
Rud : Rudyard
Sand : Sandyford
Sav G : Saverley Green
Sch G : Scholar Green
S Hay : Scot Hay
Sil : Silverdale
Smal : Smallthorne
S Grn : Sneyd Green
Som : Somerford
Spot A : Spot Acre
Stoc B : Stockton Brook
Stoke : Stoke-on-Trent
Stone : Stone
Tal : Talke
Tal P : Talke Pits
Thor : Thorncliffe
*Tittensor
Tren : Trentham
T Vale : Trent Vale
Tun : Tunstall
Werr : Werrington
W Coy : Weston Coyney
Wet R : Wetley Rocks
Wol : Wolstanton

A

Aarons Dri. *Big E* 2G **25**
Abberley Ho. *New* 5F **27**

Abbey Ct. *Stoke* 7G **29**
Abbey Grn. Rd. *Leek* 1E **16**
Abbey Hulton. 6H **29**
Abbey La. *Stoke* 1F **35**
Abbey Rd. *Stoke* 6F **29**

Abbey Rd. *Wet R* 1H **37**
Abbey St. *New* 4K **31**
Abbey St. *Stoke* 6F **29**
Abbots Pl. *Stoke* 6G **29**
Abbots Rd. *Stoke* 5G **29**

Abbot's Way. *New* 6D **32**
Abbot's Clo. *Cong* 7K **9**
Abbotts Ct. *Stoke* 5G **29**
Abbotts Dri. *Stoke* 4D **28**
Abbott's Rd. *Leek* 3H **17**

Abercorn St. *Stoke* 1E **40**
Aberford Gro. *Stoke* 7D **28**
Abingdon Way. *Stoke* 7A **40**
Acacia Av. *New* 3B **32**
Acacia Gdns. *Kid* 7F **13**
Acacia Gro. *New* 3B **32**
Achilles Way. *Stoke* 4E **34**
Acorn Ri. *Stoke* 6J **41**
Acres Nook. 4D **20**
Acres Nook Rd. *Stoke* 4D **20**
Acres, The. *New* 4A **32**
Acreswood Rd. *Stoke* 2A **28**
Acton. 6A **38**
Acton La. *Act* 7A **38**
Acton St. *Stoke* 6C **28**
Acton Way. *Chu L* 4E **10**
Adams Av. *Stoke* 6G **21**
Adams Gro. *Leek* 5C **16**
Adams St. *New* 1F **33**
Adams St. *Stoke* 7D **34**
Adamthwaite Clo. *B Bri* 7E **42**
Adamthwaite Dri. *B Bri* 6E **42**
Adderley Green. 7J **35**
Adderley Pl. *B'stn* 4E **46**
Adderley Rd. *Stoke* 1D **28**
Addington Way. *Stoke* 1J **41**
Addison St. *Stoke* 6C **28**
Adelaide St. *Stoke* 5K **27**
Adkins St. *Stoke* 5B **28**
Adrian St. *Stoke* 7D **34**
Adventure Pl. *Stoke* . .2B **34** (4F **5**)
Aegean Clo. *Stoke* 6B **40**
Agger Hill. 4C **30**
Agger Hill. *Ley* 5C **30**
Ainsdale Clo. *Stoke* 5J **41**
Ainsley Clo. *Stoke* 6G **29**
Ainsworth St. *Stoke* 1B **40**
Aintree Clo. *Stoke* 7A **40**
Aitken St. *Stoke* 4H **27**
Ajax Way. *Stoke* 4E **34**
Akesmoor La. *Gil H* 3J **13**
Alanbrooke Gro. *Stoke* 5K **41**
Alan Dale. *Werr* 1C **36**
Alanley Clo. *Stoke* 3C **28**
Alan Rd. *Stoke* 2H **35**
Alastair Rd. *Stoke* 2J **39**
Albany Gro. *Stoke* . . .5G **33** (5H **7**)
Albany Rd. *New* 3E **32** (1C **6**)
Albany Rd. *Stoke* 5G **33** (5H **7**)
Albany St. *Stoke* 4F **21**
Albemarle Rd. *New* . . .2D **32** (1B **6**)
Alberta St. *Stoke* 4H **41**
Albert Av. *Stoke* 3K **41**
Albert Pl. *Cong* 3H **9**
                              (Havannah St.)
Albert Pl. *Cong* 5G **9**
                                   (High St.)
Albert Pl. *Stoke* 5G **41**
Albert Rd. *Stoke* 1A **46**
Albert Sq. *Stoke* 7D **34**
Albert St. *Bid* 2B **14**
Albert St. *Big E* 1F **25**
Albert St. *Ches* 5B **26**
Albert St. *Leek* 3F **17**
Albert St. *New* 4G **33** (2G **7**)
Albert St. *Sil* 3K **31**
Albert St. *Stoke* 1H **41**
Albert Ter. *New* 7F **27**
Albion St. *Stoke* 2B **34** (4F **5**)
Albion St. *Leek* 4F **17**
Albion St. *Stoke* 2B **34** (4E **5**)
Alcester Clo. *Stoke* 5A **22**
Aldbury Rd. *Stoke* 5D **40**
Aldeburgh Dri. *New* 4E **38**
Alder Clo. *Kid* 3D **20**
Alderflat Dri. *Stoke* 7C **40**
Alder Gro. *New* 4A **26**
Alderhay La. *Rook* 6F **13**
Alderney Clo. *New* 2B **38**
Alderney Cres. *Stoke* 3E **40**
Aldersea Clo. *Stoke* 3H **27**
Alders Rd. *Bid M* 1G **15**
Alderton Gro. *Stoke* 1C **48**
Alder Wlk. *Stoke* 2H **39**
Aldrin Clo. *Stoke* 7D **42**
Alexandra Rd. *New* 7F **27**
Alexandra Rd. *Stoke* 4K **41**

Alford Dri. *Stoke* 2B **36**
Alfred St. *Stoke* 6D **34**
Alfreton Rd. *Stoke* 7F **35**
Algar Rd. *Stoke* 7H **33**
Alicia Way. *Stoke* 1F **29**
Allenby Sq. *Stoke* 2H **39**
Allendale Wlk. *Stoke* 5D **40**
Allensmore Av. *Stoke* 1G **41**
Allen St. *C'dle* 4H **45**
Allen St. *Stoke* 5H **33**
Allensway. *New* 2B **38**
Allerton Rd. *Stoke* 7J **39**
All Saints Rd. *Stoke* 1K **39**
Alma Clo. *Sch G* 3B **12**
Almar Pl. *Stoke* 6K **21**
Alma St. *Leek* 3E **16**
Alma St. *Stoke* 7C **34**
Almond Gro. *Stoke* 3D **40**
Almond Pl. *New* 3A **26**
Alsager. 6E **10**
Alsager Leisure Cen. 6C **10**
Alsager Rd. *A'ly* 5E **18**
Alsagers Bank. 7G **25**
ALSAGER STATION. RAIL . . .7F **11**
Alsop St. *Leek* 4F **17**
Alstonfield Av. *Stoke* 6H **29**
Althorpe Pl. *New* 3C **38**
Althrop Gro. *Stoke* 3J **41**
Alton Clo. *New* 4J **31**
Alton Gro. *Stoke* 6J **35**
Alwyn Cres. *Stoke* 4C **28**
Amber Ct. *Stoc B* 6K **23**
Amberfield Clo. *Stoke* 2K **41**
Amblecote Dri. *Stoke* 2K **41**
Ambleside Pl. *Cong* 5B **8**
Ambleside Pl. *Stoke* 1K **27**
Ambrose Pl. *Stoke* 4J **21**
Amelia Clo. *Bad G* 2F **29**
America St. *Stoke* 1G **27**
Amicable St. *Stoke* 5J **27**
Amison St. *Stoke* 2J **41**
Ampthill Pl. *Stoke* 5J **39**
Ancaster St. *Stoke* 4G **21**
Anchor Ind. Est.
   Stoke 2H **41**
Anchor Pl. *Stoke* 2H **41**
Anchor Rd. *Stoke* 2H **41**
Anchor Ter. *Stoke* 2H **41**
Anderson Pl. *Stoke* 1D **28**
Andover Clo. *Stoke* 7H **35**
Andrew Mulligan Clo.
   Stoke 6F **21**
Andrew Pl. *New* 4F **33** (3G **7**)
Andrew St. *Stoke* 4F **21**
Anglesey Dri. *Stoke* 3F **41**
Angle St. *Leek* 3E **16**
Angus Clo. *Stoke* 2H **35**
Annan Clo. *Cong* 6J **9**
Anna Wlk. *Stoke* 5J **27**
Anne Ct. *Tal P* 5A **20**
Anne St. *Stoke* 4F **21**
Annette Rd. *Stoke* 7G **35**
Ansmede Gro. *Stoke* 5E **40**
Anson Rd. *Stoke* 6A **42**
Anthony Gro. *Stoke* 3A **48**
Anthony Pl. *Stoke* 2J **41**
Antrobus St. *Cong* 4F **9**
Apedale. 5J **25**
Apedale Community Country Pk.
   . . . . .7J **25**
Apedale Heritage Cen. 7K **25**
Apedale Rd. *Big E* 4G **25**
Apedale Rd. *New & Ches* 5J **25**
Apley Pl. *Stoke* 6J **39**
Apollo Wlk. *Stoke* 3B **28**
Apple Clo. *Cong* 4D **8**
Applecroft. *Mad* 1A **30**
Applecroft. *New* 3B **26**
Appledore Gro. *Stoke* 3H **21**
Appleford Pl. *Stoke* 5D **40**
Applegarth Clo. *Stoke* 7G **35**
Appleton Clo. *Bid* 4D **14**
Appleton Clo. *Cong* 7G **9**
Applewood Cres. *Stoke* 6D **42**
Aqueduct St. *Stoke* 6A **34**
Aquinas St. *Stoke* 6K **33**

Arbour Clo. *Mad* 1B **30**
Arbourfield Dri. *Stoke* 3F **35**
Arbour St. *Stoke* 1C **34** (2G **5**)
Arbour St. *Tal P* 6A **20**
Arclid Ct. *Cong* 4H **9**
Arclid Way. *Stoke* 3G **35**
Arctic Pl. *Stoke* 6A **40**
Arden Clo. *Leek* 4J **17**
Arden Ct. *Cong* 7K **9**
Argles Rd. *Leek* 2H **17**
Argosy Clo. *Stoke* 7C **42**
Argyle St. *Stoke* 3A **34** (6C **4**)
Argyll Clo. *B Bri* 1F **49**
Argyll Rd. *Stoke* 4J **41**
Aries Clo. *Stoke* 5J **21**
Arkwright Gro. *Stoke* 4E **28**
Arlington Way. *Stoke* 7B **42**
Armshead. 1C **36**
Armshead Rd. *Werr* 1C **36**
Armstrong Grn. *Stoke* 5B **28**
Arnold Gro. *New* 4E **26**
Arnside Av. *Cong* 5C **8**
Arran Dri. *Pac* 3J **21**
Arrowsmith Dri. *Als* 7C **10**
Arthur Cotton Ct. *Stoke* 3K **27**
Arthur St. *Leek* 3G **17**
Arthur St. *New* 3C **32**
Arthur St. *Stoke* 1H **27**
Arundel Dri. *C'dle* 3J **45**
Arundel Way. *Stoke* 7H **35**
Ascot Clo. *Cong* 3F **9**
Ashbank. 2A **36**
Ash Bank Rd. *Stoke & Werr*. . .2K **35**
Ashbourne Dri. *New* 4H **31**
Ashbourne Gro. *Stoke* 7B **28**
Ashbourne Rd. *C'dle* 3H **45**
Ashbourne Rd. *Leek* 4G **17**
Ashburton St. *Stoke* 5A **28**
Ashby Cres. *Stoke* 5E **40**
Ash Clo. *C'dle* 4J **45**
Ashcombe Grn. *Stoke* 5E **40**
Ashcombe Way. *Leek* 5G **17**
Ashcott Wlk. *Stoke* 4H **35**
Ashcroft Av. *Stoke* 3H **39**
Ashcroft Clo. *New* 6D **26**
Ashcroft Gro. *New* 6E **26**
Ashcroft Oval. *New* 6E **26**
Ashcroft Pl. *New* 6E **26**
Ashcroft Rd. *New* 6D **26**
Ashdale Clo. *Als* 5D **10**
Ashdale Ri. *New* 3E **38**
Ashdale Rd. *Leek* 3J **17**
Ashdale Rd. *Stoke* 1B **40**
Ashendene Gro. *Stoke* 6J **39**
Ashenhurst Rd. *Als* 7G **11**
Ashenhurst Way. *Leek* 5G **17**
Ashenough Rd. *Tal P* 5A **20**
Ashfield Ct. *Stoke* 3D **32**
Ashfields Grange. *New*
   . . . . .4E **32** (2B **6**)
Ashfields New Rd.
   New 4D **32** (2B **6**)
                            (in two parts)
Ashfield Sq. *Stoke* 3F **35**
Ashford St. *Stoke* 5A **34**
Ash Grn. Clo. *Stoke* 7K **39**
Ash Gro. *Ash B* 2A **36**
Ash Gro. *B'stn* 6C **46**
Ash Gro. *B Bri* 6D **42**
Ash Gro. *Cong* 4C **8**
Ash Gro. *New* 3J **31**
Ash Gro. *Rode H* 3G **11**
Ashlands Av. *Stoke* 5H **33**
Ashlands Cres. *Stoke*
   . . . . .6H **33** (5H **7**)
Ashlands Gro. *Stoke* . .6H **33** (6H **7**)
Ashlands Rd. *Stoke* . . .6H **33** (6H **7**)
Ashlar Clo. *Stoke* 3K **21**
Ashley Gro. *New* 1F **33**
Ashman St. *Stoke* 2B **28**
Ashmead Clo. *Als* 7F **11**
Ashmead M. *Als* 7F **11**
Ashmore's La. *Als* 7E **10**
Ashmore Wlk. *Stoke* 3H **5**
Ashover Gro. *Stoke* 3H **21**

Ashridge Av. *New* 4E **38**
Ashridge Gro. *Stoke* 1J **41**
Ashton Clo. *Cong* 6K **9**
Ashton Ct. *New* 4F **39**
Ashton Ct. *Werr* 2B **36**
Ash Tree Hill. *C'dle* 4F **45**
Ashurst Gro. *Stoke* 7C **42**
Ash Vw. *Kid* 1E **20**
Ash Way. *New* 2C **38**
Ash Way. *Stoke* 2A **36**
Ashwell Rd. *Stoke* 5G **33** (4H **7**)
Ashwood. *Stoke* 1G **41**
Ashwood Gro. *B Bri* 1H **49**
Ashwood Ter. *Stoke* 1H **41**
                              (off Ashwood)
Ashworth St. *Stoke* 7C **34**
Askern Clo. *Stoke* 5K **41**
Aspen Clo. *Har* 7H **13**
Asquith Clo. *Bid* 2C **14**
Astbury. 7D **8**
Astbury Clo. *Kid* 7F **13**
Astbury La. Ends. *Cong* 7G **9**
Astbury Marsh. 6D **8**
Astbury Mere Country Pk. 5D **8**
Astbury St. *Cong* 5E **8**
Aster Clo. *Stoke* 7C **36**
Aston Rd. *New* 3K **25**
Astro Gro. *Stoke* 2F **41**
Athelstan St. *Stoke* 1G **27**
Athena Rd. *Stoke* 7E **28**
Atherstone Rd. *Stoke* 7K **39**
Athlone St. *Stoke* 2C **28**
Atholl Rd. *Stoke* 5J **41**
Atkin Clo. *Cong* 4C **8**
Atlam Clo. *Stoke* 2F **35**
Atlantic Gro. *Stoke* 6A **40**
Atlas St. *Stoke* 1D **40**
Attlee Rd. *C'dle* 4G **45**
Attwood Ri. *Kid* 1D **20**
Attwood St. *Kid* 1D **20**
Aubrey St. *Stoke* 4E **20**
Auckland St. *Stoke* 5K **27**
Auden Pl. *Stoke* 3J **41**
Audley. 2E **24**
Audley Pl. *New* 7E **32**
Audley Rd.
   Als & Tal P 7F **11**
Audley Rd. *B'ly* 7A **18**
Audley Rd. *Big E* 5H **19**
Audley Rd. *New* 2K **25**
Audley St. *New* 2B **32**
Audley St. *Stoke* 1G **27**
Audley Theatre. 2E **24**
Austen Clo. *C'dle* 4F **45**
Austin Ho. *Stoke* 1F **35**
Austin St. *Stoke* 3C **34**
Austwick Gro. *Stoke* 1H **39**
Aveling Grn. *Stoke* 4E **28**
Aveling Rd. *Stoke* 4E **28**
Avenue Rd. *Stoke* 4A **34**
Avenue, The. *Als* 6D **10**
Avenue, The. *B Bri* 7H **43**
Avenue, The. *End* 4K **23**
Avenue, The. *Kid* 2C **20**
Avenue, The. *New* 3G **33** (1H **7**)
Avenue, The. *Stoc B* 7K **23**
Avion Clo. *Stoke* 7D **42**
Avoca St. *Stoke* 7C **28** (1H **5**)
Avon Clo. *Kid* 1E **20**
Avon Clo. *New* 2E **38**
Avon Ct. *Als* 5D **10**
Avondale St. *Stoke* 4G **27**
Avon Dri. *Cong* 6H **9**
Avon Gro. *C'dle* 5H **45**
Avonside Av. *Stoke* 7J **21**
Avonwick Gro. *Stoke* 6F **29**
Axbridge Wlk. *Stoke* 3B **28**
                             (off Kinver St.)
Axon Cres. *Stoke* 3C **42**
Aylesbury Rd. *Stoke* 3G **35**
Aynsley Av. *New* 3E **38**
Aynsley Clo. *C'dle* 5G **45**
Aynsley Hall. *Stoke* 6B **34**
Aynsley Rd. *Stoke* 4A **34**
Aynsley's Dri. *B Bri* 7F **43**
Ayreshire Gro. *Stoke* 5J **41**
Ayr Rd. *C'dle* 1H **45**

Ayrshire Way—Berry La.

Ayrshire Way. Cong 6J 9
Ayshford St. Stoke 3G 41

B

Bk. Brook St. Brn L 5K 13
Bk. Bunt's La. Stoc B 7H 23
Bk. Cross La. Cong 7J 9
Bk. Ford Grn. Rd. Stoke 2C 28
Bk. Garden St. New 5F 33 (4E 7)
Bk. Heathcote St. Kid 1D 20
Back La. Brn E 4G 23
(Bank End)
Back La. Brn E 2G 23
(Hill Top)
Back La. Cong 2A 8
Back La. Leek 3E 16
Bk. Park St. Cong 5G 9
Bk. River St. Cong 4F 9
Baddeley Edge. 2H 29
Baddeley Green. 1F 29
Baddeley Grn. La. Stoke 2G 29
Baddeley Hall Rd. Stoke 2H 29
Baddeley Rd. Stoke 3G 29
Baddeley St. C'dle 4H 45
Baddeley St. Stoke 3J 27
Baden Rd. Stoke 3B 28
Baden St. New 3E 32 (1C 6)
Badger Gro. Stoke 7D 42
Badgers Brow. Stoke 2D 34
Badgers Ri. Leek 3F 17
Badgers Sett. Leek 3F 17
Badnall Clo. Leek 3E 16
Badnall St. Leek 3E 16
Baggott Pl. New 5C 32
Bagnall. 2K 29
Bagnall Rd. L Oaks 3J 29
Bagnall Rd. Stoke 3G 29
Bagnall St. Stoke 2B 34 (4F 5)
Bagot Gro. Stoke 4E 28
Bailey Ct. Als 7F 11
Bailey Cres. Cong 3J 9
Bailey Rd. Stoke 2D 40
Bailey's Bank. Bid 1J 15
Bailey's Hill. 1F 15
Bailey St. New 4D 32 (2B 6)
Bailey St. Stoke 4J 33
Bainbridge Rd. Stoke 7K 39
Bains Gro. New 4C 26
Baker Cres. Stoke 1G 29
Baker Cres. N. Stoke 1H 29
Baker Cres. S. Stoke 1G 29
Baker St. Stoke 7D 34
Bakers Vs., The. Cong 5F 9
Bakewell Clo. New 4J 31
Bakewell St. Stoke 1J 39
Bala Gro. C'dle 2J 45
Balcombe Clo. New 6E 32 (6C 6)
Balfour Gro. Bid 2D 14
Balfour St. Stoke 2C 34 (4H 5)
Ball Edge. 5H 23
Ball Green. 5D 22
Ball Haye Green. 2G 17
Ball Haye Grn. Leek 3G 17
Ball Haye Rd. Leek 3G 17
Ball Hayes Rd. Stoke 6B 22
Ball Haye St. Leek 3G 17
Ball Haye Ter. Leek 3G 17
Ballington Gdns. Leek 4G 17
(in two parts)
Ballington Vw. Leek 5G 17
Ballinson Rd. Stoke 5D 40
Balliol St. Stoke 6K 33
Ball La. Leek 3F 17
Ball La. Stoke 6F 23
Balloon St. Stoke 4G 33 (3H 7)
Ball's Yd. New 5E 32 (3D 6)
Balmoral Clo. Stoke 4K 39
Balmoral Dri. C'dle 5E 44
Baltic Clo. Stoke 7A 40
Bamber Pl. New 6C 26
Bamber St. Stoke 5A 34
Bambury St. Stoke 7G 35
Bamford Gro. Stoke 7A 28
Banbury Gro. Bid 3B 14
Banbury St. Tal 2A 20
Bancroft La. B Bri 1G 49
Bank Ct. Kid 1D 20
(off Attwood St.)
Bank End. 3G 23
Bank End. Brn E 4G 23
Bankfield Gro. S Hay 2F 31
(in two parts)
Bankfield Rd. Stoke 6A 42
Bank Hall Rd. Stoke 2A 28
Bankhouse Dri. Cong 3J 9
Bank Ho. Dri. New 3H 33
Bankhouse Rd. For 6J 43
Bankhouse Rd. Stoke 6J 39
Banks Clo. Cong 4E 8
Bankside. New 5F 33 (4E 7)
Bankside Ct. Als 5F 11
Banksman Rd. Stoke 6J 35
Bank St. C'dle 3G 45
Bank St. Cong 5G 9
Bank St. Rook 6F 13
Bank St. Stoke 7G 21
Bank, The. 3E 12
Bank, The. Sch G 3E 12
Bank Top. 7A 22
Bank Top Av. Stoke 1K 27
Banky Brook Clo. Stoke 1B 28
Banky Fields. Cong 6E 8
Banky Fields Cres. Cong 6E 8
Baptist St. Stoke 4J 27
Barber Dri. Sch G 3B 12
Barber Pl. Stoke 5J 21
Barber Rd. Stoke 5J 21
Barber's Sq. New 1G 33
Barber St. Stoke 3J 27
Barbridge Rd. New 2A 26
Barbrook Av. Stoke 2K 41
Barclay St. Stoke 1H 41
Bardsey Wlk. Stoke 3F 41
Barford Rd. New 3C 38
Barford St. Stoke 3G 41
Bargrave Dri. New 4E 26
Bargrave St. Stoke 4J 35
Barhill Rd. Mad 3A 30
Barker Ho. Stoke 6E 40
Barker St. New 6C 26
Barker St. Stoke 3J 41
Barks Dri. Stoke 7C 22
Barlaston. 6D 46
Barlaston Common. 3K 47
Barlaston Old Rd. Stoke 1A 46
Barlaston Rd. Stoke 7E 40
BARLASTON STATION. RAIL 6C 46
Barley Cft. Als 1F 19
Barleycroft. C'dle 5H 45
Barleycroft Ter. Sch G 3C 12
Barleyfields. A'ly 2E 24
Barleyfields. Stoke 1B 28
Barleyford Dri. Stoke 7J 35
Barlow St. Stoke 3H 41
Barlstone Av. B Bri 1G 49
Barmouth Clo. Knyp 4D 14
Barmouth Gro. B Frd 1B 22
Barnbridge Clo. Sch G 3B 12
Barn Ct. New 3F 39
Barncroft Rd. Stoke 5A 22
Barnes Way. Stoke 5H 41
Barnett Gro. Cong 4C 8
Barnett Gro. Stoke 6J 21
Barnfield. Stoke 7J 33
Barnfield Rd. Stoke 5K 27
Barnfields. 5E 16
Barnfields Clo. Leek 5E 16
Barnfields Ind. Est. Leek 5E 16
(Barnfields Rd.)
Barnfields Ind. Est. Leek 6E 16
(Sunnyhills Rd.)
Barnfields Rd. Leek 5E 16
Barngate St. Leek 3E 16
Barnlea Gro. Stoke 2B 48
Barn Rd. Cong 3E 8
Barnsdale Clo. Stoke 2A 46
Barnwell Gro. Stoke 5K 39
Baron St. Stoke 1F 41
Barracks Rd. New 5F 33 (4E 7)
Barracks Sq. New 5F 33 (4E 7)
Barracks Way. Leek 3E 16
Barrage Rd. Bid M 4G 15
Barratt Rd. Als 7G 11
Barrett Cres. Stoke 6K 27
Barrett Dri. Stoke 6K 27
Barrie Gdns. Tal 3K 19
Barrington Ct. New 2G 33
Barry Av. Stoke 2F 35
Bartholomew Rd. Stoke 6A 42
Barthomley Rd. A'ly 7A 18
Barthomley Rd. Stoke 6C 28
Bartlem St. Stoke 1J 41
Barton Cres. Stoke 3H 27
Barton Rd. Cong 5H 9
Barwood Av. Chu L 5H 11
Basford. 4H 33 (3G 7)
Basford Pk. Rd. New 1G 33 (1H 7)
Basford Vs. New 1G 7
Basildon Gro. Stoke 4H 41
Baskerville Rd. Stoke 7C 28 (1H 5)
Baskeyfield Pl. Stoke 6A 22
Basnett's Wood. End 5K 23
Bassett Clo. C'dle 3G 45
Bassilow Rd. Stoke 6E 34
Bateman Av. Brn L 5A 14
Bath Rd. New 3G 31
Baths Pas. Stoke 2G 41
(off Strand, The)
Baths Rd. Stoke 2G 41
Bath St. Leek 3G 17
Bath St. Stoke 6K 33
Bath St. W Coy 1C 42
Bath Ter. Stoke 7K 33
Bathurst St. Stoke 2H 41
Bath Vale. 4K 9
Batkin Clo. Stoke 6A 22
Batten Clo. Stoke 7D 42
Battison Cres. Stoke 4H 41
Baulk La. Ful 7F 49
Bayham Wlk. Stoke 1F 35
Baytree Clo. Stoke 6E 28
Beaconsfield. New 5F 27
Beaconsfield Dri. Stoke 5D 40
Beadnell Gro. Stoke 5H 41
Beard Gro. Stoke 5G 29
Beasley. 5C 26
Beasley Av. New 6C 26
Beasley Pl. New 5C 26
Beatrice Clo. Stoke 4K 39
Beatrice Wlk. B Frd 1A 22
Beattie Av. New 2E 32
Beatty Dri. Cong 3J 9
Beatty Rd. Leek 3H 17
Beaufort Av. Werr 2B 36
Beaufort Rd. Stoke 4H 41
Beaulieu Clo. Werr 2C 36
Beaumaris Clo. Stoke 5G 33 (4H 7)
Beaumaris Ct. New 5D 32 (5A 6)
Beaumont Clo. Bid 2J 15
Beaumont Ct. New 3C 38
(off Bridle Path, The)
Beaumont Rd. Stoke 1H 27
Beaver Clo. Stoke 2H 39
Beaver Dri. C'dle 3E 44
(in two parts)
Beckenham Clo. Stoke 6D 42
Beckett Av. Stoke 5C 42
Beckfield Clo. Bid M 1G 15
Beckford St. Stoke 7C 28 (1H 5)
Beck Rd. Mad 6A 30
Beckton St. Stoke 1H 27
Bedale Pl. Stoke 5D 40
Bedcroft. B'stn 5E 46
Beddow Way. Stoke 5J 21
Bedford Cres. New 2F 39
Bedford Gro. Als 5C 10
Bedford Rd. Kid 7D 12
Bedford Rd. Stoke 3A 34 (6C 4)
Bedford St. Stoke 3K 33 (6B 4)
(in two parts)
Beech Av. Rode H 2G 11
Beech Clo. Bid M 1G 15
Beech Clo. C'dle 4J 45
Beech Clo. Cong 3C 8
Beech Clo. Leek 7D 16
Beech Ct. B Bri 7E 42
Beechcroft. B'stn 5E 46
Beech Cft. Mad 1B 30
Beech Dri. Kid 3B 20
Beeches Row. Stoke 6G 21
Beeches, The. New 5F 27
Beechfield Rd. Stoke 1A 46
Beechfields. B'stn 5E 46
Beech Gro. Leek 3D 16
Beech Gro. New 1F 33
Beech Gro. Stoke 1B 40
Beechmont Gro. Stoke 6E 28
Beech Rd. Stoke 5E 40
Beech St. Stoke 3H 41
Beechwood Clo. B Bri 1G 49
Beechwood Clo. New 5F 39
Beechwood Dri. Als 6C 10
Beeston Dri. Als 7D 10
Beeston St. Stoke 1H 41
Beeston Vw. Kid 4D 20
Beggars La. Leek 5D 16
Belfast Clo. Stoke 2A 28
Belfield Av. New 1F 33
Belford Pl. Stoke 4J 33
Belgrave Av. Als 5E 10
Belgrave Av. Cong 4E 8
Belgrave Av. Stoke 4G 41
Belgrave Cres. Stoke 5H 41
Belgrave Rd. New 5F 33 (5E 7)
Belgrave Rd. Stoke 5H 41
Bell Av. Stoke 4J 41
Bellefield Vw. New 2F 33
(off High St.)
Bellerton La. Stoke 2D 28
Belle Vue. Leek 3E 16
Belle Vue Rd. Leek 3E 16
Bell Ho. Stoke 7E 40
Bellingham Gro. Stoke 6C 28
Bell La. B'stn 3D 46
Bellringer Clo. Bid 3B 14
Bellringer Rd. Stoke 7C 40
Bell's Hollow. New 2B 26
Bellwood Clo. Stoke 2B 48
Belmont Rd. Stoke 2K 33 (4A 4)
Belsay Clo. Stoke 2H 41
Belvedere Rd. Stoke 5K 39
Belvedere Ter. Rode H 3G 11
Belvoir Av. Stoke 2B 46
Bemersley Green. 2B 22
Bemersley Rd.
B Frd & Brn E 7B 14
Benedict Pl. Stoke 7F 29
Benfleet Pl. Stoke 3F 41
Bengal Gro. Stoke 6B 40
Bengry Rd. Stoke 4K 41
Benjamins Way. Big E 2G 25
Bennett Pl. New 5E 26
Bennett Precinct. Stoke 3G 41
(off Strand, The)
Bennett St. Stoke 5H 27
Bennion St. Stoke 3H 41
Benson St. Stoke 6J 21
Bentilee. 4J 35
Bent La. A'bry 6B 8
Bentley Av. New 1E 32
Bentley Rd. Stoke 6B 22
Berdmore St. Stoke 1F 41
Beresford Cres. New 7D 32
Beresford Dale. Mad 1A 30
Beresford St. Stoke 4A 34
Beresford Trad. Est. Stoke 6G 21
Bergamot Dri. Stoke 1B 48
Berkeley Av. Als 5E 10
Berkeley Ct. New 4F 33 (3F 7)
Berkeley St. Stoke 2C 34 (5G 5)
Berkshire Dri. Cong 3F 9
Berkshire Gro. New 1F 39
Bernard Gro. Stoke 3A 48
Bernard St. Stoke 2C 34 (5G 5)
Berne Av. New 7B 32
Berryfield Gro. Stoke 2A 42
Berry Hill. 3F 35
Berry Hill Greenway. Stoke 3G 35
Berryhill-Normacot Greenway.
Stoke 7J 35
Berry Hill Rd. Stoke 4C 34
(in two parts)
Berryhill Village. Stoke 4F 35
Berry La. Stoke 3H 41

52 A-Z Stoke

Berry St. *Stoke* 6A **34**
Berwick Rd. *Stoke* 4D **28**
Berwick Wlk. *New* 6C **32**
Best St. *Stoke* 1E **40**
Beswick Clo. *C'dle* 5G **45**
Beswick Rd. *Stoke* 6J **21**
Betchton Ct. *Cong* 4H **9**
Betchton La. *Chu L* 2D **10**
Bethell Rd. *Stoke* 5C **28**
Bethesda Rd. *Stoke* 3C **34**
Bethesda St. *Stoke* . . .2B **34** (4E **5**)
Betley Pl. *New* 7F **33**
Bettany Rd. *Stoke* 5K **27**
Bevan Av. *Tal P* 5A **20**
Bevandean Clo. *Stoke* 2B **46**
Bevan Pl. *Mad* 1B **30**
Beveridge Clo. *Stoke* 4C **42**
Beverley Cres. *For* 6H **43**
Beverley Dri. *Stoke* 3G **35**
Beville St. *Stoke* 7D **34**
Bevin La. *Stoke* 2F **35**
Bewcastle Gro. *Stoke* 7B **42**
Bew St. *Stoke* 6D **22**
Bexhill Gro. *Stoke* 6E **28**
Bexley St. *Stoke* 7A **28** (1D **4**)
Bibby St. *Rode H* 3F **11**
Bida La. *Cong* 7K **9**
Biddulph. 2B **14**
Biddulph Grange Gardens.
. . . . .1K **15**
(National Trust)
Biddulph Moor. 1G **15**
Biddulph Rd. *Cong* 6J **9**
Biddulph Rd. *Har* 4H **13**
Biddulph Rd. *Stoke* 5K **21**
Biddulph St. *Cong* 7K **9**
Biddulph Valley Leisure Cen.
. . . . .1C **14**
Bignall End. 1G **25**
Bignall End Rd. *Big E* 1H **25**
Bignall Hill. 2H **25**
Bignall Hill. *Big E* 2H **25**
Bigsbury Wlk. *Stoke* 5K **27**
(off Swainsley Clo.)
Billinge St. *Stoke* 4H **27**
Bilton St. *Stoke* 7K **33**
Birchall. 6G **17**
Birchall Av. *Stoke* 6F **21**
Birchall Clo. *Leek* 7G **17**
Birchall La. *Leek* 7G **17**
Birchall Pk. Av. *Leek* 6G **17**
Bircham Wlk. *New* 4E **38**
Birch Av. *Als* 1F **19**
Birch Av. *Knyp* 4K **13**
Birch Ct. *Cong* 4B **8**
Birch Dale. *Mad* 2B **30**
Birchdown Av. *Stoke* 1A **28**
Birchenfields La. *Dil* 1C **44**
Birchenwood Countryside Pk.
. . . . .1F **21**
Birchenwood Rd. *Stoke* 3H **21**
Birches Head. 7D **28**
Birches Head Rd. *Stoke* 7C **28**
Birches, The. *C'dle* 3G **45**
(off Royal Wlk.)
Birches, The. *C'dle* 4G **45**
(Lid La.)
Birches Way. *Kid* 1E **20**
Birchfield Av. *Rode H* 3G **11**
Birchfield Rd. *Stoke* 7H **29**
Birchgate. *Stoke* 1H **35**
Birchgate Gro. *Stoke* 1H **35**
Birch Grn. Gro. *Stoke* 5D **28**
Birch Gro. *For* 7H **43**
Birch Gro. *Stoke* 3B **48**
Birch Ho. Rd. *New* 4A **26**
Birchlands Rd. *Stoke* 6E **28**
Birchover Way. *Stoke* 3K **21**
Birch Rd. *Big E* 3G **25**
Birch Rd. *Cong* 4B **8**
Birch St. *Stoke* 7D **28**
Birch Ter. *Stoke* 2B **34** (4F **5**)
Birch Tree La. *Sch G* 3E **12**
Birch Wlk. *Stoke* 5F **41**
Bird Cage Wlk. *Stoke* . .2B **34** (4E **5**)
Bird Rd. *Stoke* 4C **42**

Birkdale Dri. *Kid* 7F **13**
Birkholme Dri. *Stoke* 2B **48**
Birks St. *Stoke* 1A **40**
Birrell St. *Stoke* 1E **40**
Biscay Gro. *Stoke* 6B **40**
Bishop Ct. *Stoke* 7G **29**
Bishop Rd. *Stoke* 6K **21**
Bishop's Clo. *Tal* 3A **20**
Bishop St. *Stoke* 1F **41**
Bitterne Pl. *Stoke* 5J **35**
Bittern La. *C'dle* 3H **45**
Black Bank. 1H **31**
Blackbank Rd. *New* 1H **31**
Blackbird Way. *Bid* 2D **14**
Blackbird Way. *Pac* 2J **21**
Blackbrook Av. *New* 4A **26**
Black Firs La. *Som* 2A **8**
Blackfriars Rd. *New* 5E **32** (5C **6**)
Blackheath Clo. *Stoke* 3J **41**
Black Horse La. *Stoke*
. . . . .1A **34** (3D **4**)
Blacklake Dri. *Stoke* 3B **48**
Blackshaw Clo. *Cong* 6K **9**
Blackthorn Pl. *New* 4B **26**
Blackwell's Row. *Stoke* 6A **28**
Blackwood Hill. 5K **15**
Blackwood Pl. *Stoke* 2K **41**
Bladon Av. *New* 3E **38**
Bladon Clo. *Stoke* 3K **21**
Bladon Cres. *Als* 5D **10**
Blakelow Rd. *Stoke* 7G **29**
Blakeney Av. *New* 3E **38**
Blake St. *Cong* 5E **8**
Blake St. *Stoke* 4J **27**
Blanchard Clo. *Stoke* 7D **42**
Blantyre St. *Stoke* 4H **41**
Blantyre Wlk. *Stoke* 4H **41**
Blatchford Clo. *Stoke* 4C **42**
Bleak Pl. *Stoke* 5K **27**
Bleakridge Av. *New* 4E **26**
Bleak St. *New* 2G **33**
Bleeding Wolf La. *Sch G* 5B **12**
Blencarn Gro. *Stoc B* 7H **23**
Blenheim Ct. *Als* 5E **10**
Blenheim St. *Stoke* 1C **40**
Bleriot Clo. *Stoke* 7D **42**
Blithe Vw. *B Bri* 1G **49**
Blithfield Clo. *Werr* 3B **36**
Bluebell Clo. *Bid* 3C **14**
Bluebell Dri. *New* 2D **38**
Bluebell Way. *Als* 7C **10**
Bluestone Av. *Stoke* 2A **28**
Blunt St. *New* 1F **33**
Blurton. 4E **40**
Blurton Priory. *Stoke* 6E **40**
Blurton Rd. *B'stn* 5F **47**
Blurton Rd. *Stoke* 2D **40**
Blythe Av. *Cong* 5C **8**
Blythe Av. *Stoke* 2B **48**
Blythe Bridge. 7G **43**
Blythe Bri. Rd. *Cav* 4F **43**
BLYTHE BRIDGE STATION. RAIL
. . . . .7G **43**
Blythe Clo. *B Bri* 7E **42**
Blythe Lodge. *B Bri* 7F **43**
(off Grindley La.)
Blythe Marsh. 7H **43**
Blythe Mt. Pk. *B Bri* 7H **43**
Blythe Rd. *For* 7H **43**
Blythe Vw. *Sav G* 5H **49**
Boardmans Bank. *Brn E* 2F **23**
Boathorse Rd. *Kid* 3C **20**
Boathorse Rd. *Stoke* 5D **20**
Bodmin Wlk. *Smal* 3C **28**
Bogs La. *B Bri* 1G **49**
Bolberry Clo. *New* 4A **26**
Bolina Gro. *Stoke* 7G **35**
Bold St. *Stoke* 7D **28** (1H **5**)
Bollin Clo. *Als* 7A **10**
Bollin Dri. *Cong* 6H **9**
Bollin Gro. *Bid* 1D **14**
Bolney Gro. *Stoke* 7E **28**
Bolsover Clo. *Stoke* 3K **21**
Bolton Pl. *Stoke* 6A **42**
Boma Rd. *Stoke* 6J **39**
Bondfield Way. *Stoke* 4C **42**
Bond St. *Stoke* 7G **21**

Bonnard Clo. *Stoke* 1D **48**
Bonner Clo. *Stoke* 1H **39**
Boon Av. *Stoke* 7K **33**
Boon Hill. 3G **25**
Boon Hill Rd. *Big E* 3G **25**
Boothen. 1A **40**
Boothen Grn. *Stoke* 1A **40**
Boothen Old Rd. *Stoke* 1A **40**
Boothen Pk. *Stoke* 7A **34**
Boothen Rd. *Stoke* 7A **34**
Boothenwood Ter. *Stoke* 1K **39**
Boothroyd St. *Stoke* . . .2B **34** (4F **5**)
Booth St. *A'ly* 3E **24**
Booth St. *Cong* 5E **8**
Booth St. *New* 6C **26**
Booth St. *Stoke* 7A **34**
Bordeaux Rd. *Stoke* 6B **42**
Bordeaux Wlk. *New* 3C **38**
Borough Rd. *Cong* 4H **9**
Borough Rd. *New* 4F **33** (2F **7**)
Borrowdale Rd. *Stoke* 1D **28**
Boscombe Gro. *Stoke* 2B **46**
Bosinney Clo. *Stoke* 1G **41**
Bosley Gro. *Stoke* 4F **21**
Bosley Vw. *Cong* 6K **9**
Boston Clo. *Stoke* 7F **21**
Boswell St. *Stoke* 3J **33**
Botany Bay Rd. *Stoke* 7D **28**
Botesworth Gdns. *Stoke* 3G **27**
Botteslow St. *Stoke* 2C **34** (5G **5**)
Boughey Rd. *Big E* 2G **25**
Boughey Rd. *Stoke* 5B **34**
Bosinney Clo. *Stoke* 7K **33**
Boulevard, The. *Stoke* 1H **27**
(off High St.)
Boulevard, The. *Stoke* 1H **27**
(Scotia Rd.)
Boulton St. *New* 6F **27**
Boulton St. *Stoke* 7C **28**
Boundary. 4B **44**
Boundary Clo. *Leek* 6G **17**
Boundary Ct. *Stoke* 1F **5**
Boundary La. *Cong* 7J **9**
Boundary St. *New* 4G **33** (3G **7**)
Boundary St. *Stoke* 7A **28** (1D **4**)
Boundary Vw. *C'dle* 4E **44**
Bourne Cotts. *Stoke* 4H **41**
Bourne Pl. *Leek* 3D **16**
Bourne Rd. *Kid* 1C **20**
Bournes Bank. *Stoke* 4J **27**
Bournes Bank S. *Stoke* 4J **27**
Bourne St. *Mow C* 3G **13**
Bourne St. *Stoke* 4J **27**
Bouverie Pde. *Stoke* 5E **28**
Bowden Clo. *Cong* 4B **8**
Bowden St. *Stoke* 3A **28**
Bower End La. *Mad* 2A **30**
Bower St. *Stoke* 3B **34** (6F **5**)
Bowfell Gro. *Stoke* 6G **35**
Bowhill La. *A'ly* 6A **24**
Bowland Av. *New* 2B **32**
Bowlers Clo. *Stoke* 6K **27**
Bowman Gro. *Stoke* 4A **22**
Bowman Ho. *Stoke* 6A **42**
Bowmead Clo. *Stoke* 1B **46**
Bowmere Clo. *Bid* 1B **14**
Bowness Ct. *Cong* 6C **8**
Bowness St. *Stoke* 7A **28**
Bowsey Wood Rd. *Mad* 1B **30**
Bowstead St. *Stoke* 6A **34**
Bow St. *Stoke* 7B **28** (1H **5**)
Bowyer Av. *Stoke* 6D **22**
Box La. *Cong* 4B **8**
Box La. *Stoke* 4A **42**
Boxwood Pl. *New* 4A **26**
Boyles Hall Rd. *Big E* 2F **25**
Brabazon Clo. *Stoke* 7D **42**
Brackenberry. *New* 2E **32**
Bracken Clo. *Rode H* 2G **11**
Bracken Clo. *Stoke* 2A **48**
Bracken Clo. *T'sor* 6A **46**
Bracken Dale. *Leek* 5C **16**
Brackenfield Av. *Stoke* 4H **35**
Brackens, The. *New* 4E **38**
Bracken St. *Stoke* 2D **40**
Brackley Av. *Stoke* 3A **28**
Bradbury Clo. *Stoke* 1D **48**

Bradbury Gdns. *Cong* 7H **9**
Braddocks Hay. 2D **14**
Bradeley. 1B **28**
Bradeley Village. *Stoke* 1A **28**
Bradford Ter. *Stoke* 6D **28**
Bradwell. 5D **26**
Bradwell Ct. *Cong* 5H **9**
Bradwell Grange. *New* 6E **26**
Bradwell Gro. *Cong* 5H **9**
BRADWELL HOSPITAL. 5D **26**
Bradwell La. *New* 4C **26**
Bradwell Lodge. *New* 6F **27**
Bradwell St. *Stoke* 4G **27**
Braemar Clo. *Stoke* 2J **35**
Braemore Rd. *Stoke* 6G **29**
Braithwell Dri. *Stoke* 2F **29**
Brakespeare St. *Stoke* 4F **21**
Brake, The. *Sch G* 3E **12**
Brake Village. *Sch G* 3E **12**
Bramble Lea. *Mad* 2B **30**
Brambles Ct. *Bid* 3C **14**
Brambles, The. *New* 4F **39**
Bramfield Rd. *New* 3F **33** (1E **7**)
Bramley Clo. *C'dle* 4H **45**
Bramley Pl. *Stoke* 3H **39**
Brammall Dri. *B Bri* 7F **43**
Brammer St. *Stoke* 1B **28**
Brampton Clo. *End* 1K **23**
Brampton Ct. *New* 3F **33** (1E **7**)
Brampton Gdns. *New* 2F **33**
Brampton Ind. Est. *New*
. . . . .3E **32** (1D **6**)
Brampton Rd. *New* 3F **33** (1E **7**)
Brampton Sidings. *New*
. . . . .3E **32** (1D **6**)
Brampton Sidings Ind. Est.
New 3E **32** (1D **6**)
Brampton, The. 3F **33** (1E **7**)
Brampton Va. Gdns. *New* 7F **33**
Brampton Wlk. *Stoke* 5H **41**
Bramshaws Acre. *C'dle* 4H **45**
Brandon Gro. *Stoke* 6J **39**
Branson Av. *Stoke* 3K **41**
Bransty Gro. *Stoke* 2B **46**
Brant Av. *New* 1D **32**
Brassington Way. *Stoke* 4H **35**
Brattice Pl. *Stoke* 6J **35**
Brattswood Dri. *Chu L* 5H **11**
Braystones Clo. *Stoke* 3H **21**
Breach Rd. *Brn E* 4H **23**
Bream Way. *Stoke* 2A **28**
Brecon Way. *Stoke* 3H **35**
Breedon Clo. *New* 2C **32**
Breeze Av. *Stoke* 7H **21**
Brendale Clo. *Stoke* 5K **39**
Brentnor Clo. *Stoke* 3A **42**
Brentwood Dri. *Werr* 1C **36**
Brentwood Gro. *Stoc B* 1H **29**
Brentwood Gro. *Werr* 1C **36**
Brereton Pl. *Stoke* 3H **27**
Bretherton Pl. *Stoke* 5K **21**
Brewery St. *Stoke* 1B **34** (2E **5**)
Brewester Rd. *Stoke* 2E **34**
Brianson Av. *Stoke* 5B **28**
Briarbank Clo. *Stoke* 5J **39**
Briars, The. *New* 3E **32**
Briarswood. *Kid* 2E **20**
Briarwood Pl. *Stoke* 5C **42**
Brickfield Pl. *Stoke* 1H **41**
Brick Ho. St. *Stoke* 4J **27**
Brick Kiln La. *P West* 5B **26**
Brick Kiln La. *Stoke* 3H **33**
Bridal Path, The. *Mad* 1A **30**
Bridestone Cen. *Cong* 4F **9**
Bridestowe Clo. *Stoke* 7B **42**
Bridge Clo. *Big E* 2G **25**
Bridge Ct. *Stoke* 3H **39**
Bridge Cft. *Stoke* 5A **22**
Bridge Ind. Est. *Stoke* 5A **28**
Bridge Pl. *Stoke* 2E **16**
Bridge Rd. *Stoke* 3H **39**
Bridge Row. *Cong* 3H **9**
Bridge St. *B Frd* 1A **22**
Bridge St. *Cong* 5E **8**
Bridge St. *New* 4E **32** (3C **6**)
Bridge St. *Sil* 4K **31**
Bridgett Clo. *Stoke* 1H **39**

Bridgewater Clo. *Cong* 6K **9**
Bridgewater St. *Stoke* 4G **27**
Bridgewood St. *Stoke* 3H **41**
Bridgnorth Gro. *New* 2B **26**
Bridgwood Rd. *B Bri & For* . . .7H **43**
Bridle Path. *Dres* 5H **41**
(off Peel St.)
Bridle Path. *Stoke* 2B **36**
Bridle Path, The. *New* 3C **38**
Brierley Rd. *Cong* 6K **9**
Brierley St. *Stoke* 3B **28**
Brierly Brook. 1G **25**
Brieryhurst Clo. *Stoke* 7H **29**
Brieryhurst Rd. *Kid* 7E **12**
Brightgreen St. *Stoke* 7J **35**
Brighton St. *Stoke* 6K **33**
Brighton, The. *New* 3J **31**
Brights Av. *Kid* 1E **20**
Bright St. *Stoke* 5B **42**
Brindiwell Gro. *Stoke* 1B **46**
Brindley Clo. *Tal* 3B **20**
Brindley Ford. 1A **22**
Brindley La. *L Oaks* 1H **29**
Brindley Mill. 2E **16**
Brindley Pl. *Stoke* 5B **22**
Brindley St. *New* 4E **32** (2C **6**)
Brindleys Way. *Big E* 2G **25**
Brindley Way. *Cong* 6K **9**
Brindon Clo. *Stoke* 3C **42**
Brinscall Grn. *Stoke* 4K **21**
(off Charnock Pl.)
Brinsley Av. *Stoke* 7K **39**
Brisley Hill. *Stoke* 7J **33**
Bristol St. *New* 7G **27**
Britannia Pk. Ind. Est.
Stoke 5A **28**
Britannia St. *Leek* 4E **16**
Brittain Av. *New* 5B **26**
Brittle Pl. *Stoke* 2C **28**
Britton St. *Stoke* 4J **33**
Brixham Clo. *Stoke* 4E **34**
Broadfield Rd. *Stoke* 4E **20**
Broadhurst La. *Cong* 4E **8**
Broadhurst St. *Stoke* 3A **28**
Broad La. *Brn E* 2H **23**
Broadlawns Dri. *Stoke* 7G **35**
Broad Meadow. 6B **26**
Broadmeadow Ct. *Ches* 6B **26**
Broadmine St. *Stoke* 7D **34**
Broadoak Way. *Stoke* 5D **40**
Broad St. *Leek* 4F **17**
Broad St. *New* 4E **32** (2C **6**)
(in two parts)
Broad St. *Stoke* 3A **34** (6D **4**)
Broadway. *Stoke* 4A **42**
Broadway Ct. *Stoke* 5A **42**
Broadway Pl. *Stoke* 4A **42**
Brockbank Pl. *Stoke* 6A **22**
Brocklehurst Way. *Stoke* 5D **28**
Brockley Sq. *Stoke* 1B **34** (3E **5**)
Brocksford St. *Stoke* 1F **41**
Brock Way. *New* 3A **32**
Brocton Wlk. *Stoke* 5D **40**
Brogan St. *Stoke* 7E **34**
Bromford Pl. *Stoke* 3A **34** (6C **4**)
Bromley Ct. *Stoke* 7A **28** (1C **4**)
Bromley Farm. 5H **9**
Bromley Hough. *Stoke* 1J **39**
Bromley Rd. *Cong* 5G **9**
Bromley St. *Stoke* 7K **27** (1B **4**)
Brompton Dri. *Stoke* 1G **29**
Bromsberrow Way. *Stoke* 7B **42**
Bromsgrove Pl. *Stoke* 3F **41**
Bronant Wlk. *Stoke* 5K **27**
(off Leonora St.)
Bronte Gro. *Stoke* 2F **29**
Brook Clo. *B Bri* 7H **43**
Brook Clo. *End* 1K **23**
Brookes Ct. *Stoke* 7D **34**
Brookfield Av. *End* 4K **23**
Brookfield Ct. *Stoke* 1E **5**
Brookfield Dri. *Als* 5D **10**
Brookfield Rd. *Stoke* 1H **29**
Brookfield Rd. *T Vale* 1H **39**
Brook Gdns. *Bid* 1C **14**
Brookgate. *For* 6J **43**
Brookhouse Dri. *B'stn* 5B **46**

Brookhouse La. *Cong* 4J **9**
(in two parts)
Brookhouse La. *Stoke* 2J **35**
Brookhouse Rd. *Als* 7E **10**
Brookhouse Rd. *C'dle* 3D **44**
Brookhouse Rd. *New* 3C **26**
Brookhouse Rd. *Stoke* 4B **42**
Brookhouses. 4E **44**
Brookhouses Ind. Est. *C'dle* . . .4E **44**
Brookhouse Way. *C'dle* 4E **44**
Brookland Av. *Stoke* 5F **41**
Brooklands Cotts. *Stoke* 3H **21**
Brooklands Rd. *Cong* 5B **8**
Brooklands Rd. *Stoke* 6J **21**
Brook La. *End* 1K **23**
Brook La. *New* 6E **32** (6D **6**)
Brookmead Gro. *Stoke* 7G **35**
Brook Pl. *New* 1F **39**
Brook Pl. *Stoke* 4J **33**
Brook Rd. *Stoke* 7K **39**
Brookside. *Stoke* 4G **27**
Brookside Clo. *New* 6D **32** (6A **6**)
Brookside Ct. *C'dle* 3E **44**
Brookside Dri. *End* 1K **23**
Brookside Dri. *Stoke* 4D **40**
Brookside Ind. Est. *Stoke* 4G **27**
Brook St. *Brn L* 5K **13**
Brook St. *Cong* 4G **9**
Brook St. *Leek* 4F **17**
Brook St. *Sil* 3K **31**
Brook St. *Stoke* 6A **34**
Brookview Dri. *Stoke* 3A **42**
Brookwood Clo. *New* 3D **38**
Brookwood Dri. *Stoke* 3B **42**
Broome Hill. *New* 5F **39**
Broomfield Pl. N.
Stoke 2K **33** (4B **4**)
Broomfield Pl. S.
Stoke 2K **33** (5B **4**)
Broomfield Rd. *Stoke* 6C **22**
Broomfields. *Bid M* 1G **15**
Broomhill St. *Stoke* 7F **21**
Broom St. *Stoke* 7C **28** (1F **5**)
Brough Clo. *Leek* 3F **17**
Brough La. *Stoke* 7A **40**
Brough Pk. Leisure Cen. 3G **17**
Broughton Cres. *B'stn* 5D **46**
Broughton Rd. *New* . . .3G **33** (1H **7**)
Broughton Rd. *Stoke* 2E **34**
Brownfield Rd. *Stoke* 4B **42**
Brown Av. *Chu L* 6H **11**
Brown Edge. 4G **23**
Brownhill Rd. *Brn E* 4G **23**
Brownhills Bus. Pk. *Stoke* 2G **27**
Brownhills Rd. *Stoke* 3G **27**
Browning Clo. *C'dle* 4F **45**
Browning Gro. *Tal* 3K **19**
Browning Rd. *Stoke* 4E **40**
Brown Lees. 7B **14**
Brown Lees Ind. Est. *Brn L* 6A **14**
Brown Lees Rd. *Brn L* 5A **14**
Brown Lees Rd. *Har* 6J **13**
Brownley Rd. *Stoke* 3C **28**
Brownlow. 7A **8**
Brownsea Pl. *Stoke* 2D **40**
Brown St. *Cong* 4G **9**
Brown St. *Stoke* 4K **27**
Brundall Oval. *Stoke* 3J **35**
Brunel Wlk. *Stoke* 2H **41**
Brunswick Ind. Est. *Stoke* 4G **27**
Brunswick Pl. *Stoke* . . .2B **34** (5F **5**)
Brunswick St. *Cong* 4H **9**
Brunswick St. *Leek* 3G **17**
Brunswick St. *New* 4F **33** (3E **7**)
Brunswick St. *Stoke* . . .1B **34** (3E **5**)
Brunt St. *Stoke* 5G **27**
Brutus Rd. *New* 7A **26**
Bryan St. *Stoke* 1B **34** (1E **5**)
Bryant Rd. *Stoke* 7G **29**
Brymbo Rd. *New* 7C **26**
Buccleuch Rd. *Stoke* 4J **41**
Buckingham Cres. *Stoke* 5K **39**
Buckland Gro. *Stoke* 2B **46**
Buckley Rd. *Stoke* 5B **22**
Buckley's Row. *New* 5E **32** (4C **6**)

Buckmaster Av. *New* 7F **33**
Bucknall. 7F **29**
BUCKNALL HOSPITAL. 7G **29**
Bucknall New Rd.
Stoke 1C **34** (3G **5**)
Bucknall Old Rd.
Stoke 1C **34** (3G **5**)
Bucknall Rd. *Stoke* 1D **34**
Bude Clo. *Als* 7C **10**
Buglawton. 2K **9**
Buller St. *Stoke* 3C **34** (6H **5**)
Bull La. *B Frd* 1K **21**
Bullocks Ho. Rd. *Har* 7H **13**
Bulstrode St. *Stoke* 4H **27**
Bunny Hill. *New* 1F **39**
Bunts La. *Cong* 6G **9**
Bunt's La. *Stoc B* 7H **23**
Burford Av. *New* 3A **26**
Burford Way. *Stoke* 4F **35**
Burgess St. *Stoke* 5H **27**
Burgundy Gro. *Stoke* 6B **42**
Burland Rd. *New* 2K **25**
Burleigh Gro. *New* 2G **33**
Burlidge Rd. *Stoke* 5K **21**
Burlington Av. *New* 2G **33**
Burmarsh Wlk. *Stoke* 5J **27**
Burnaby Rd. *Stoke* 5F **21**
Burnett Pl. *Stoke* 7C **22**
Burnham St. *Stoke* 1F **41**
Burnhays Rd. *Stoke* 2J **27**
Burnley St. *Stoke* 6C **28**
Burns Clo. *Kid* 3D **20**
Burns Clo. *Rode H* 2F **11**
Burnside Clo. *Stoke* 7B **42**
Burns Rd. *Cong* 5J **9**
Burns Row. *Stoke* 4C **42**
Burnwood Ct. *Stoke* 2C **28**
Burnwood Gro. *Kid* 1E **20**
Burnwood Pl. *Stoke* 6A **22**
Burrington Dri. *Stoke* 2A **46**
Burslem. 5G **9**
Burslem Enterprise Cen.
Stoke 4K **27**
Burslem Greenway. *Stoke* 3J **27**
Burslem Walkway. *Stoke* 3J **27**
Bursley Rd. *Stoke* 5K **27**
Bursley Way. *New* 4D **26**
Burton Cres. *Stoke* 5D **28**
Burton Pl. *Stoke* 1B **34** (3F **5**)
Burton St. *Leek* 4E **16**
Burt St. *Stoke* 3C **42**
Bute St. *Stoke* 2F **41**
Butler St. *Stoke* 7A **34**
Butterfield Pl. *Stoke* 1H **27**
Buttermere Clo. *Stoke* 4H **27**
Buttermere Ct. *Cong* 5C **8**
Butters Green. 2H **25**
Butterton. 4B **38**
Butterton La. *But* 3A **38**
Butterton La. *Rad G* 2A **18**
Butt St. *Stoke* 3E **16**
Butts Grn. *Stoke* 6H **29**
Butts, The. *Als* 6E **10**
Buxton Av. *New* 3H **31**
Buxton Old Rd. *Cong* 3H **9**
Buxton Rd. *Cong* 3H **9**
Buxton Rd. *Leek* 3G **17**
Buxton St. *Stoke* 5C **28**
Byatt's Gro. *Stoke* 4F **41**
Bycars La. *Stoke* 3J **27**
Bycars Rd. *Stoke* 3J **27**
Bylands Pl. *New* 2D **38**
Byrom St. *Leek* 3E **16**
Byron Clo. *C'dle* 4E **44**
Byron Clo. *Rode H* 2F **11**
Byron Ct. *Kid* 3C **20**
Byron St. *Stoke* 4G **33** (3H **7**)
Bywater Gro. *Stoke* 7J **35**

C

Cadeby Gro. *Stoke* 2G **29**
Cadman Cres. *Stoke* 1D **28**
Cairn Clo. *Stoke* 2J **35**
Caistor Clo. *Stoke* 3F **29**

Caldbeck Pl. *Stoke* 1C **34** (3H **5**)
Caldew Gro. *Stoke* 2B **46**
Caldy Rd. *Als* 6D **10**
Caledonia Rd. *Stoke* 4A **34**
California Bus. Pk. *Stoke* 1A **40**
California St. *Stoke* 3F **41**
Callender Pl. *Stoke* 4K **27**
Callow Hill La. *C'dle* 3A **44**
Calrofold Dri. *New* 3A **26**
Calvary Cres. *Stoke* 5J **35**
Calverley St. *Stoke* 4J **41**
Calver St. *Stoke* 1G **27**
Calvert Gro. *New* 5E **26**
Camberwell Gro. *Stoke* 1B **46**
Camborne Clo. *Cong* 7G **9**
Camborne Cres. *New* 1C **38**
Cambrian Way. *Stoke* 1H **35**
Cambridge Clo. *Bid* 1B **14**
Cambridge Ct. *New* 1G **39**
Cambridge Dri. *New* 1G **39**
Cambridge St. *Stoke* . . .2A **34** (5D **4**)
Camden St. *Stoke* 2D **40**
Camellia Clo. *Stoke* 4H **33**
Camelot Clo. *Stoke* 3B **46**
Camillus Rd. *New* 3B **32**
Camoys Ct. *Stoke* 5K **27**
Camoys Rd. *Stoke* 5K **27**
Campbell Av. *Leek* 5E **16**
Campbell Clo. *Cong* 3J **9**
Campbell Pl. *Stoke* 6A **34**
Campbell Rd. *Stoke* 2A **40**
Campbell Ter. *Stoke* 6D **28**
Campion Av. *New* 2G **33**
Camp Rd. *Stoke* 3B **28**
Canal La. *Stoke* 3G **27**
Canal M., The. *Stoke* 1B **46**
Canal Rd. *Cong* 5G **9**
Canal Side. *B'stn* 6C **46**
Canal Side. *Stoke* 6E **22**
Canal St. *Cong* 5G **9**
Canal St. *Stoke* 4G **27**
Canary Rd. *Stoke* 6J **35**
Canberra Cres. *Stoke* 7D **42**
Canning St. *Stoke* 1E **40**
Cannon Pl. *Stoke* 3A **34** (5D **4**)
Cannon St. *Stoke* 2B **34** (5E **5**)
Canterbury Dri. *Stoke* 7A **22**
Canvey Gro. *Stoke* 7C **42**
Capesthorne Clo. *Als* 7D **10**
Capesthorne Clo. *Werr* 2C **36**
Capewell St. *Stoke* 2H **41**
Capewell St. *Stoke* 7B **28** (1E **5**)
Capitol Wlk. *Cong* 5F **9**
(off High St.)
Capper Clo. *Kid* 1D **20**
Cappers La. *B'ton* 1D **10**
Capper St. *Stoke* 1H **27**
Capricorn Way. *Stoke* 5J **21**
Caraway Pl. *Stoke* 1B **48**
Carberry Way. *Stoke* 2A **42**
Cardiff Gro. *Stoke* 2B **34** (5E **5**)
Cardigan Gro. *Stoke* 1B **46**
Cardington Clo. *New* 2D **38**
Card St. *Stoke* 5J **27**
Cardway, The. *New* 5E **26**
Cardwell St. *Stoke* 7D **28**
Carina Gdns. *Stoke* 3C **28**
Carisbrooke Way. *Stoke* 2B **46**
Carling Gro. *Stoke* 1F **41**
Carlisle St. *Stoke* 5G **41**
Carlos Pl. *New* 3E **26**
Carlton Av. *Brn E* 5G **23**
Carlton Av. *New* 3E **38**
Carlton Av. *Stoke* 6K **21**
Carlton Clo. *Brn E* 5G **23**
Carlton Clo. *C'dle* 5G **45**
Carlton Ho. *Stoke* 5A **34**
Carlton Rd. *Stoke* 5B **34**
Carlton Ter. *Leek* 3H **17**
Carlyle Clo. *Rode H* 2F **11**
Carlyon Pl. *Stoke* 4C **28**
Carmounthead. 3H **29**
Carmount Rd. *Stoke* 5G **29**
Carmountside. 5G **29**
Carmountside Crematorium.
Stoke 4G **29**
Carnation Clo. *Stoke* 7C **36**

Carnforth Gro. *Stoke* 3H 21
Caroline Clo. *Werr* 1C 36
Caroline Cres. *Brn E* 5G 23
Caroline St. *Stoke* 2H 41
Carpenter Rd. *Stoke* 2F 41
Carriage Dri. *Bid* 1D 14
Carrick Pl. *Stoke* 5K 39
Carr La. *A'ly* 3B 24
Carroll Dri. *Stoke* 2J 41
Carron St. *Stoke* 1G 41
Carr St. *Pac* 2J 21
Carryer Pl. *New* 5C 32
Carson Rd. *Stoke* 1J 27
Cartlich St. *Stoke* 6G 21
Cartlidge St. *Stoke* 4G 33 (3G 7)
Cartmel Pl. *Stoke* 1A 28
Cartwright Ind. Est., The.
. . . . *Stoke* 4G 41
Cartwright St. *Stoke* 4G 41
Casewell Rd. *Stoke* 5B 28
Caspian Gro. *Stoke* 7A 40
Castel Clo. *New* 3B 38
Castledine Gro. *Stoke* 2J 41
Castlefield St. *Stoke* 3K 33
Castle Gro. *Stoke* 7G 29
Castle Hill Rd. *New* 4D 32 (3B 6)
Castle Keep Ct. *New* . . .5D 32 (4B 6)
Castle Keep Gdns.
. . . . *New* 4D 32 (3B 6)
Castle Keep M. *New* . . .5D 32 (3B 6)
Castle La. *Mad* 3B 30
Castle Mt. *New* 6B 26
Castle Ridge. *New* 5C 32 (5A 6)
Castle Rd. *Mow C* 3G 13
Castle St. *Ches* 5B 26
Castle St. *New* 4F 33 (3F 7)
Castleton Rd. *Stoke* 7K 41
Castletown Grange.
. . . . *New* 3D 32
Castle Vw. *Bid* 4B 14
Castleview Gro. *Stoke* 4J 21
Castleview Rd. *Kid* 7E 12
Castle Wlk. *New* 3D 6
Catalina Pl. *Stoke* 1D 48
Caterham Pl. *Stoke* 1C 48
Catharine Rd. *Stoke* 5A 22
Catherine St. *New* 1G 33
Caton Cres. *Stoke* 2E 28
Cauldon Av. *New* 5D 26
Cauldon Clo. *Leek* 5G 17
Cauldon Pl. *Stoke* 4A 34
Cauldon Rd. *Stoke* 4A 34
Caulton St. *Stoke* 3J 27
Causeley Gdns. *Stoke* 2G 35
Causeley Rd. *Stoke* 2G 35
Cavendish Cres. *Als* 5D 10
Cavendish Gro. *New* 3E 38
Cavendish St. *Stoke* . . .2K 33 (4B 4)
Caverswall. 4F 43
Caverswall Common. 1E 42
Caverswall Comn. *Cav* 7D 36
Caverswall La. *Stoke* 6D 42
Caverswall Old Rd. *For* 6G 43
Caverswall Rd. *B Bri* 7G 43
Caverswall Rd. *Dil* 3H 43
Caverswall Rd.
. . . . *Stoke & Cav* 2C 42
Caverswall Road Station. . . .5G 43
Cavour St. *Stoke* 3J 33
Cawdry Bldgs. *Leek* 3G 17
. . . . (off Fountain St.)
Cayley Pl. *Stoke* 1D 48
Cecil Av. *Stoke* 7A 28 (1D 4)
Cecilly St. *C'dle* 2H 45
Cecilly Ter. *C'dle* 2H 45
. . . . (off King Edward St.)
Cecil Rd. *Gil H* 2H 15
Cedar Av. *Als* 7D 10
Cedar Av. *B Bri* 1H 49
Cedar Av. *Tal* 2A 20
Cedar Clo. *C'dle* 4J 45
Cedar Ct. *Als* 6F 11
Cedar Ct. *Cong* 7H 9
Cedar Cres. *Big E* 3G 25
Cedar Cres. *End* 5K 23
Cedar Gro. *Bid M* 1F 15
Cedar Gro. *Stoke* 3D 40

Cedar Rd. *New* 3A 26
. . . . (in two parts)
Cedars, The. *Als* 7E 10
Cedartree Gro. *Stoke* 3C 28
Celandine Clo. *Stoke* 3G 29
Celebration Ct. *Stoke* 1B 28
Cellarhead. 1G 37
Cellarhead Rd. *Werr* 1E 36
Celtic Av. *Pac* 3J 21
Cemetery Av. *Stoke* 4G 41
Cemetery Rd. *Knut* 2B 32
Cemetery Rd. *Sil* 5A 32
Cemetery Rd. *Stoke* 3K 33
Cemetery Vw. *New* 2B 32
Cemetery Vw. *Stoke* 4G 41
Cemlyn Av. *Stoke* 3D 40
Centenary Pl. *Cong* 4G 9
Central Av. *Rad G* 2A 18
Central Av. *Stoke* 1F 35
Central Dri. *Stoke* 3D 40
Central St. *Mow C* 4E 12
Centre Ct. *Als* 6F 11
Centre 500. *Wol* 6H 27
Century Retail Pk.
. . . . *Stoke* 1A 34 (3C 4)
Century Rd. *High B* 2C 26
Century St. *Stoke* 7K 27 (1B 4)
. . . . (in two parts)
Ceramica. 4J 27
Chadwell Way. *Stoke* 4J 35
Chadwick St. *Stoke* 3H 41
Chadwyn Dri. *Stoke* 2G 29
Chaffinch Clo. *Cong* 6G 9
Chaffinch Dri. *Bid* 2D 14
Chain St. *Stoke* 2B 28
Chalfont Grn. *Stoke* 3G 35
Challenge Clo. *Stoke* 1B 28
. . . . (off Unwin St.)
Challinor Av. *Leek* 5F 17
Challinor St. *Stoke* 1H 27
Chamberlain Av. *Stoke* 7K 33
Chamberlain St. *Stoke* 3B 34
Chamberlain Way. *Bid* 2D 14
Chance Hall La. *Sch G* 2J 11
Chancery La. *Als* 7C 10
Chancery La. *Stoke* 3H 41
Chantree Row. *Mow C* 3G 13
Chantry Rd. *New* 7E 32
Chapel Bank. *Mow C* 4G 13
Chapel Clo. *Mow C* 4E 12
Chapel Cotts. *Stoke* 1G 23
Chapel Ct. *New* 3K 31
Chapel La. *A'ly* 2E 24
Chapel La. *Bid M* 2F 15
Chapel La. *Brn E* 2G 23
Chapel La. *Har* 6H 13
Chapel La. *Rode H* 3G 11
Chapel La. *Stoke* 4K 27
Chapel St. *Big E* 1F 25
Chapel St. *C'dle* 3G 45
Chapel St. *Cong* 5F 9
Chapel St. *For* 6H 43
Chapel St. *Knut* 2B 32
Chapel St. *Mow C* 4E 12
Chapel St. *New* 2F 33
Chapel St. *Sil* 3K 31
Chapel St. *Stoke* 1G 35
Chapel St. *Tal* 1A 20
Chaplin Rd. *Stoke* 6H 41
Chapter Wlk. *Stoke* 7F 29
Charles Cotton Dri. *Mad* 2A 30
Charles Sq. *Has G* 1A 10
Charles St. *Bid* 3B 14
Charles St. *C'dle* 3G 45
Charles St. *New* 2G 33
Charles St. *Stoke* 2C 34 (3F 5)
Charlestown Gro. *Stoke* 7B 42
Charlesworth Pl. *Cong* 3H 9
Charlotte St. *Stoke* 4F 21
Charlton St. *Stoke* 5A 34
Charminster Rd. *Stoke* 7B 42
Charmouth Clo. *Stoke* 6F 29
Charnock Pl. *Stoke* 4K 21
Charnwood. *Kid* 2E 20
Charnwood Clo. *Leek* 5D 16
Charnwood Rd. *Stoke* 5A 42
Charolais Cres. *Stoke* 6J 41

Charsley Pl. *Stoke* 5E 40
Charter Rd. *New* 2D 32
Chartley Clo. *B Bri* 1F 49
Chartwell Clo. *Werr* 2B 36
Chase La. *T'sor* 7A 46
Chase Wlk. *Stoke* 7A 42
Chatfield Pl. *Stoke* 4J 41
Chatham St. *Stoke* 3A 34
Chatsworth Av. Pk. *Stoke* . . .5K 39
Chatsworth Dri. *Cong* 4B 8
Chatsworth Dri. *Stoke* 7D 22
Chatsworth Dri. *Werr* 3B 36
Chatsworth Pl. *New* 5C 26
Chatsworth Pl. *Stoke* 5A 42
Chatteris Clo. *Stoke* 1C 48
Chaucer Courts. *Stoke* 5G 41
Cheadle. 3G 45
CHEADLE HOSPITAL. 4G 45
Cheadle Rd.
. . . . *B Bri, For & C'dle* 7H 43
Cheadle Rd. *C'dle* 7C 44
Cheadle Shop. Cen. *C'dle* 3G 45
Cheapside. *New* 5E 32 (3D 6)
Cheapside. *Stoke* 1B 34 (3F 5)
Chebsey Clo. *Stoke* 1H 35
Checkley Dri. *Bid* 1C 14
Checkley Rd. *New* 3K 25
Checkly Gro. *Stoke* 7J 35
Cheddar Dri. *New* 3G 31
Cheddleton Rd. *Leek* 5F 17
Chelford Rd. *Som* 3A 8
Chell Grn. Av. *Stoke* 5K 21
Chell Grn. Ct. *Stoke* 5K 21
Chell Gro. *New* 5D 26
Chell Heath. 7A 22
Chell Heath Rd. *Stoke* 5A 22
Chells Hill. *B'ton* 2E 10
Chell St. *Stoke* 7C 28
Chelmorton Dri. *Stoke* 5K 41
Chelmsford Dri. *Stoke* 3H 35
Chelmsford Rd. *New* 7E 26
Chelsea Clo. *Bid* 1B 14
Chelson St. *Stoke* 3H 41
Cheltenham Av. *C'dle* 1H 45
Cheltenham Gro. *New* 3G 31
Cheltenham Gro. *Stoke* 7E 28
Chelwood St. *Stoke* . .7A 28 (1D 4)
Chemical La. *Stoke* 2E 26
Chemical La. Ind. Est.
. . . . *Stoke* 3F 27
Chepstow Clo. *Bid* 1B 14
Chepstow Pl. *Stoke* 7H 35
Cheriton Grn. *Stoke* 4J 35
Cherry Clo. *Ful* 7F 49
Cherry Clo. *New* 3A 26
Cherry Gro. *Stoke* 3D 40
Cherry Hill. *Mad* 2B 30
Cherry Hill Av. *Stoke* 3B 42
Cherry Hill La. *New* 3B 32
. . . . (in two parts)
Cherry La. *C'dle* 1K 45
Cherry La. *Chu L & Rode H* . . .4E 10
Cherry Orchard. *New*
. . . . .4E 32 (2D 6)
Cherry Tree Av. *Chu L* 5H 11
Cherry Tree Clo. *Stoke* 7K 39
Cherry Tree La. *Bid M* 1F 15
Cherry Tree Rd. *Big E* 3G 25
Cherry Tree Rd. *New* 3B 26
Cherrywood Gro. *Stoke* 1A 48
Chertsey Pl. *Stoke* 4C 28
Chervil Clo. *Stoke* 1B 48
Chesham Gro. *Stoke* 1B 48
Chessington Cres. *Stoke* 7B 40
Chester Clo. *Tal* 4B 20
Chester Cres. *New* 1D 38
Chester Rd. *A'ly* 2E 24
Chester Rd. *Tal* 4A 20
Chesterton. 5B 26

Chesterton Speedway Stadium.
. . . . .7A 26
Chesterwood Rd. *Stoke* 1A 28
Chestnut Av. *Rode H* 3G 11
Chestnut Cres. *B Bri* 1H 49
Chestnut Dri. *Als* 1F 19
Chestnut Dri. *Cong* 3B 8
Chestnut Gro. *New* 3B 26
Chestnut Rd. *Brn E* 4H 23
Cheswardine Rd. *New* 4E 26
Chetwynd Av. *Ash B* 2B 36
Chetwynd Av. *Stoke* 6D 22
Chetwynd Rd. *New* 6E 26
Chetwynd St. *New* 7G 27
Chetwynd St. *Stoke* 2C 28
Cheviot Clo. *New* 2B 32
Cheviot Dri. *Stoke* 1B 28
Chichester Wlk. *Stoke* 1H 5
Childerplay Rd. *Bid* 7B 14
Chilgrove Clo. *Stoke* 7E 28
Chiltern Pl. *New* 2B 32
Chilton St. *Stoke* 1D 40
Chilworth Gro. *Stoke* 5E 40
China St. *Stoke* 1E 40
Chivelstone Gro. *Stoke* 1B 46
Cholerton Clo. *Stoke* 1D 40
Chorley Av. *Stoke* 5K 21
Chorley St. *Leek* 4F 17
Chorlton Rd. *Stoke* 6C 28
Christchurch St. *Stoke* 7D 34
Christie Pl. *Stoke* 1A 42
Christine St. *Stoke* 2F 35
Chubb Way. *Stoke* 2H 39
Chumleigh Gro. *Stoke* 2K 27
Church Av. *Stoke* 2G 29
Church Bank. *A'ly* 2E 24
Church Bank. *K'le* 6G 31
Church Clo. *Bid* 4C 14
Church Clo. *Stoke* 2A 48
Church Dri. *B'stn* 5D 46
Churchfield Av. *Stoke* 5H 41
Church Fields. 6D 26
Church Fields. *K'le* 6G 31
Church Gdns. *Stoke* 2H 41
Churchill Av. *Stoke* 7J 39
Churchill Clo. *B Bri* 1F 49
Churchill Clo. *Cong* 4C 8
Churchill Ho. *Stoke* . . .3B 34 (6F 5)
Churchill Rd. *C'dle* 1H 45
Churchill Way. *Stoke* 7J 39
Church La. *Bid M* 1G 15
Church La. *Chu L* 6K 11
Church La. *End* 1K 23
Church La. *Knut* 4B 32
Church La. *Leek* 3F 17
Church La. *Mow C* 3H 13
Church La. *New* 1G 33
Church La. *Sch G* 2J 11
Church La. *Stoke* 4J 39
Church Lawton. 5H 11
Church Plantation. *K'le* 6H 31
Church Rd. *Als* 6C 10
Church Rd. *Bid* 3C 14
Church Rd. *Brn E* 2F 23
Church Rd. *Stoke* 5E 40
Church Sq. *Stoke* 4H 27
Church St. *A'ly* 2E 24
Church St. *Big E* 3H 25
Church St. *C'dle* 3G 45
Church St. *Ches* 5B 26
Church St. *Kid* 6E 12
Church St. *Leek* 3F 17
Church St. *Mow C* 4F 13
Church St. *New* 4E 32 (3C 6)
Church St. *Sil* 3J 31
Church St. *Stoke* 6A 34
Church St. *Tal* 1A 20
Church Ter. *Stoke* 6A 28
Church Vw. *New* 3B 32
Church Vw. *S Hay* 2F 31
Church Wlk. *New* 5B 26
Churnet Gro. *C'dle* 5H 45
Churnet Rd. *For* 7H 43
Churnet Vw. *Leek* 1H 17
Churnet Works Ind. Est.
. . . . *Leek* 2D 16
Churston Clo. *New* 4E 38

Churston Pl.—Crescent, The

Churston Pl. *Stoke* . . . 4C **28**
Cinderhill Ind. Est. *Stoke* . . . 2A **42**
Cinder-Hill La. *Sch G* . . . 4B **12**
Cinderhill La. *Stoke* . . . 3J **41**
City Bank. *Gil H* . . . 2H **15**
CITY GENERAL HOSPITAL (STOKE) . . . 6G 33 (6G 7)
City La. *Long* . . . 5A **16**
City Rd. *Stoke* . . . 6B **34**
Clandon Av. *Stoke* . . . 7H **21**
Clanway La. *Stoke* . . . 6G **21**
Clanway St. *Stoke* . . . 6G **21**
Clare Av. *New* . . . 6E **26**
Claremont Clo. *New* . . . 5F **27**
Clarence Rd. *Stoke* . . . 2G **41**
Clarence St. *New* . . . 5G **33** (4G **7**) (Mount Pleasant)
Clarence St. *New* . . . 7E **26** (Watlands Vw.)
Clarence St. *Stoke* . . . 6D **34**
Clarendon St. *Stoke* . . . 7B **34**
Clare St. *Har* . . . 6H **13**
Clare St. *Mow C* . . . 4F **13**
Clare St. *Stoke* . . . 4G **33** (2H **7**)
Clarice Cliff Ct. *Stoke* . . . 6B **34**
Claridge Rd. *Stoke* . . . 4H **33** (3H **7**)
Clark Clo. *Rode H* . . . 2F **11**
Clarke St. *Stoke* . . . 3A **34** (6C **4**)
Claud St. *Stoke* . . . 2C **40**
Claydon Cres. *New* . . . 4E **38**
Clayfield Gro. *Stoke* . . . 7H **35**
Clayfield Gro. W. *Stoke* . . . 7G **35**
Clayhanger Clo. *New* . . . 4D **26**
Clayhanger St. *Stoke* . . . 4J **27**
Clay Hills. *Stoke* . . . 1F **27**
Clay Lake. *End* . . . 4J **23**
Clayton. . . . **1F** 39
Clayton Av. *Cong* . . . 2H **9**
Clayton By-Pass. *Cong* . . . 4E **8**
Clayton La. *New & Stoke* . . . 2F **39**
Clayton Rd. *New* . . . 6E **32** (6D **6**)
Clayton Sports Cen. . . . 1G 39
Clayton St. *Stoke* . . . 3G **41**
Claytonwood Rd. *Stoke* . . . 3H **39**
Cleadon Pl. *Stoke* . . . 6G **29**
Clematis Av. *B Bri* . . . 1G **49**
Clement Pl. *Stoke* . . . 1D **28**
Clement Rd. *Stoke* . . . 6K **21**
Clerk Bank. *Leek* . . . 3F **17**
Clermont Av. *Stoke* . . . 4K **39**
Cleveland Rd. *New* . . . 2B **32**
Cleveland Rd. *Stoke* . . . 3B **34** (6E **5**)
Cleveland St. *Stoke* . . . 4J **27**
Clewlow Pl. *Stoke* . . . 1J **41**
Clewlows Bank. *Bag* . . . 7K **23**
Clews St. *Stoke* . . . 5H **27**
Clews Wlk. *New* . . . 7F **27**
Cley Gro. *New* . . . 4E **38**
Cliffe Pl. *Stoke* . . . 1K **27**
Clifford Av. *Stoke* . . . 6E **22**
Clifford St. *Stoke* . . . 3C **34** (6G **5**)
Cliff St. *Smal* . . . 3B **28**
Cliff Vale. . . . **4J** 33
Cliff Va. Pl. *Stoke* . . . 4J **33**
Clifton Clo. *Stoke* . . . 1D **40**
Clifton St. *New* . . . 1G **33**
Clifton St. *Stoke* . . . 1D **40**
Clinton Sq. *Stoke* . . . 2B **34** (5D **4**)
Clive Av. *Stoke* . . . 1G **29**
Cliveden Pl. *Stoke* . . . 4H **41**
Cliveden Rd. *Stoke* . . . 7G **29**
Clive Rd. *New* . . . 6G **27**
Clive St. *Stoke* . . . 7H **21**
Cloister Wlk. *Stoke* . . . 7F **29**
Close La. *Als* . . . 6A **10**
Close La. *Mow C* . . . 3G **13**
Close, The. *Als* . . . 7B **10**
Close, The. *End* . . . 2K **23**
Close, The. *Mad* . . . 1B **30**
Close, The. *W Coy* . . . 1C **42**
Cloud Vw. *Cong* . . . 5J **9**
Clough Hall. . . . **3C** 20
Clough Hall Dri. *Kid & Tal* . . . 4B **20**
Clough Hall Rd. *Kid* . . . 3C **20**
Clough La. *Werr* . . . 2B **36**
Clough St. *Stoke* . . . 2K **33** (5B **4**)
Cloughwood Way. *Stoke* . . . 3G **27**
Clovelly Wlk. *Stoke* . . . 5H **27**
Cloverdale Pl. *Stoke* . . . 3A **42**
Cloverdale Rd. *New* . . . 2E **32**
Clover Rd. *New* . . . 6G **27**
Clowes Av. *Als* . . . 7G **11**
Clowes Rd. *Stoke* . . . 2F **35**
Club St. *Stoke* . . . 7A **34**
Clumber Av. *New* . . . 7F **33**
Clumber Gro. *New* . . . 1F **39**
Cluny Pl. *Stoke* . . . 7F **29**
Clyde Av. *Bid* . . . 1D **14**
Clyde Pl. *New* . . . 2D **38**
Clyde Rd. *Stoke* . . . 5K **27**
Clyde St. *Stoke* . . . 2A **34** (5C **4**)
Clyde Wlk. *Stoke* . . . 2A **34** (5C **4**)
Clynes Way. *Stoke* . . . 3C **42**
Coalpit Hill. . . . **3J** 19
Coalpit Hill. *Tal* . . . 4A **20**
Coalport Clo. *C'dle* . . . 5F **45**
Coalville Pl. *Stoke* . . . 1C **42**
Coates Pl. *Stoke* . . . 3A **22**
Cobden St. *New* . . . 6G **27**
Cobden St. *Stoke* . . . 5G **41**
Cobham Pl. *Stoke* . . . 6B **42**
Cob Moor Rd. *Kid* . . . 5D **12**
Cobridge. . . . **6A** 28
Cobridge Ind. Est. *Stoke* . . . 5A **28**
Cobridge Rd. *Stoke* . . . 1K **33** (3B **4**)
Cocklesall La. *Ful* . . . 7F **49**
Cocknage. . . . **2H** 47
Cocknage Rd. *Stoke* . . . 5G **41**
Cockshuts. *Cong* . . . 5F **9**
Cocks La. *Stoc B* . . . 1H **29**
Cockster Brook La. *Stoke* . . . 3E **40**
Cockster Rd. *Stoke* . . . 3E **40**
Colclough Av. *New* . . . 4D **26**
Colclough La. *Stoke* . . . 4G **21**
Colclough Rd. *Stoke* . . . 5B **42**
Colehill Bank. *Cong* . . . 5G **9**
Colenso Way. *New* . . . 4E **26**
Coleridge Dri. *C'dle* . . . 4F **45**
Coleridge Rd. *Stoke* . . . 4E **40**
Cole St. *Bid* . . . 3B **14**
Colin Cres. *Stoke* . . . 2C **42**
Colindene Gro. *Stoke* . . . 7J **33**
Collard Av. *New* . . . 2E **32**
College Clo. *Mad* . . . 1B **30**
College Rd. *Als* . . . 5C **10**
College Rd. *Stoke* . . . 3A **34** (6D **4**)
Colley Rd. *Stoke* . . . 5J **21**
Collinbourne Clo. *Stoke* . . . 1A **46**
Collingwood Gro. *Stoke* . . . 5H **33**
Collin Rd. *Stoke* . . . 2H **39**
Collinson Rd. *Stoke* . . . 4G **21**
Collis Av. *Stoke* . . . 4G **33** (3H **7**)
Columbine Wlk. Stoke . . . 1G 27 (off Ladywell Rd.)
Colville St. *Stoke* . . . 7E **34**
Colwyn Dri. *Knyp* . . . 5C **14**
Combe Dri. *Stoke* . . . 2B **48**
Comfrey Clo. *Stoke* . . . 1B **48**
Commerce St. *Stoke* . . . 3H **41**
Commercial Rd. *Stoke* . . . 2C **34** (5H **5**)
Commercial St. *Stoke* . . . 5K **27**
Common La. *R'gh C* . . . 3K **47**
Commonside. . . . **5C** 44
Common, The. *Dil* . . . 2K **43**
Community Dri. *Stoke* . . . 3C **28**
Como Pl. *New* . . . 7B **32**
Compton. *Leek* . . . 4F **17**
Compton St. *Stoke* . . . 2A **34** (5C **4**)
Condlyffe Rd. *Leek* . . . 5F **17**
Conewood Pl. *Stoke* . . . 5D **40**
Coneygreave. . . . **7D** 44
Coneygreave Clo. *C'dle* . . . 5G **45**
Conford Clo. *Stoke* . . . 3E **34**
Congleton. . . . **5F** 9
Congleton Bus. Cen. *Cong* . . . 4G **9**
Congleton Bus. Pk. *Cong* . . . 3D **8**
Congleton Edge Rd. *Cong* . . . 7K **9**
Congleton Leisure Cen. . . . 4G 9
Congleton Rd. *Bid* . . . 1C **14**
Congleton Rd. *Ker & Sch G* . . . 1B **12**
Congleton Rd. *Mow C* . . . 2H **13**
Congleton Rd. *Tal* . . . 3A **20**
Congleton Rd. N. *Chu L & Sch G* . . . 7A **12**
Congleton Rd. S. *Chu L* . . . 7A **12**
CONGLETON STATION. RAIL . . . **6J 9**
CONGLETON WAR MEMORIAL HOSPITAL. . . . 6H 9
Congreve Rd. *Stoke* . . . 4E **40**
Conifer Gro. *Stoke* . . . 4E **40**
Conifers, The. *Als* . . . 7C **10**
Coniston Av. *Cong* . . . 5B **8**
Coniston Dri. *C'dle* . . . 2J **45**
Coniston Gro. *New* . . . 2E **38**
Coniston Pl. *Stoke* . . . 7J **39**
Connaught St. *Stoke* . . . 2G **27**
Conrad Clo. *Stoke* . . . 3J **41**
Consall Gro. *Stoke* . . . 1B **46**
Consall La. *Wet R* . . . 1K **37**
Consett Rd. *Stoke* . . . 6E **40**
Consort St. *Stoke* . . . 6A **34**
Constable Av. *New* . . . 6B **26**
Constable Clo. *Stoke* . . . 7C **42**
Constance Av. *Stoke* . . . 6A **40**
Convent Clo. *Stoke* . . . 5K **33**
Convent Ct. *Stoke* . . . 5K **33**
Conway Gro. *C'dle* . . . 5H **45**
Conway Rd. *Knyp* . . . 4B **14**
Conway St. *Stoke* . . . 5B **34**
Cookshill. . . . **3E** 42
Cookson Av. *Stoke* . . . 5H **41**
Coolidge St. *Stoke* . . . 1G **27**
Co-operative La. *Halm* . . . 5E **24**
Cooper Av. *New* . . . 3H **33**
Coopers Clo. *Leek* . . . 4D **16**
Cooper St. *Cong* . . . 4G **9**
Cooper St. *New* . . . 6B **26**
Cooper St. *Stoke* . . . 3A **34** (6D **4**)
Coopers Way. *Bid* . . . 2A **14**
Copeland Av. *New* . . . 3E **38**
Copeland Av. *T'sor* . . . 6A **46**
Copeland Clo. *C'dle* . . . 5G **45**
Copeland St. *Stoke* . . . 5A **34**
Copes Av. *Stoke* . . . 7H **21**
Cope St. *Stoke* . . . 3F **29**
Copperhill Rd. *Cong* . . . 7K **9**
Coppice Av. *New* . . . 4H **31**
Coppice Clo. *Bid* . . . 3C **14**
Coppice Gro. *Stoke* . . . 3A **42**
Coppice La. *C'dle* . . . 6J **37**
Coppice Rd. *Tal* . . . 3K **19**
Coppice, The. *Stoke* . . . 5B **28**
Coppice Vw. *New* . . . 1D **32**
Copp La. *Stoke* . . . 2F **27**
Copplestone Gro. *Stoke* . . . 3K **41**
Coppull Pl. *Stoke* . . . 4K **21**
Copthall Ho. *New* . . . 3E **7**
Copthorne Clo. *Cong* . . . 5H **9**
Coracle Gro. *Knyp* . . . 4D **14**
Coral Gro. *Stoke* . . . 7A **40**
Corbett Wlk. Stoke . . . 1G 27 (off Ladywell Rd.)
Corby Pl. *Stoke* . . . 3F **41**
Corfe Grn. *Stoke* . . . 1H **41**
Corfield Pl. *Stoke* . . . 6C **22**
Corina Ct. *Stoke* . . . 2J **41**
Corina Way. *Stoke* . . . 2J **41**
Corinth Way. *Stoke* . . . 1G **27**
Cormie Clo. *Stoke* . . . 6A **22**
Cornelious St. *Stoke* . . . 5B **42**
Cornes St. *Stoke* . . . 4C **34**
Corneville Rd. *Stoke* . . . 2G **35**
Cornfield Rd. *Bid* . . . 3C **14**
Cornhill. . . . **6D** 22
Cornhill. *Leek* . . . 5F **17**
Cornhill Clo. *New* . . . 3A **26**
Cornhill Gdns. *Leek* . . . 5F **17**
Cornhill Rd. *Stoke* . . . 6B **22**
Cornhill St. *Leek* . . . 4F **17**
Cornwall Av. *New* . . . 2F **39**
Cornwall Clo. *Cong* . . . 7J **9**
Cornwallis St. *Stoke* . . . 7A **34**
Cornwall St. *Stoke* . . . 2H **41**
Cornwood Gro. *Stoke* . . . 6K **41**
Corona Pk. *New* . . . 4B **26**
Coronation Av. *Als* . . . 7B **10**
Coronation Av. *Knyp* . . . 5A **14**
Coronation Av. *Stoke* . . . 3G **41**
Coronation Cres. *Kid* . . . 2B **20**
Coronation Gdns. *Als* . . . 6D **10**
Coronation Rd. *Cong* . . . 4H **9**
Coronation Rd. *New* . . . 5F **33** (4E **7**)
Coronation Rd. *Stoke* . . . 5H **33** (5H **7**)
Coronation St. *C'dle* . . . 3G **45**
Coronation St. *Stoke* . . . 7H **21**
Corporation St. *New* . . . 4E **32** (3C **6**)
Corporation St. *Stoke* . . . 7K **33**
Coseley St. *Stoke* . . . 3B **28**
Cotehill Rd. *Werr* . . . 2C **36**
Cotesheath St. *Stoke* . . . 4C **34**
Coton Ri. *B'stn* . . . 6D **46**
Cotswold Av. *New* . . . 2B **32**
Cotswold Cres. *Stoke* . . . 3F **29**
Cottage Clo. *Stoke* . . . 5K **41**
Cottage La. *Bid M* . . . 2F **15**
Cottages, The. *Stoke* . . . 5B **36**
Cotterill Dri. *New* . . . 4E **26**
Cotterill Gro. *Stoke* . . . 5J **27**
Cotton Rd. *Stoke* . . . 5F **21**
Cottons Row. *Stoke* . . . 4G **33** (4H **7**)
Cottonwood Gro. *Har* . . . 7H **13**
Cottonwood Gro. *Stoke* . . . 2H **41**
Country Pk. Vw. *Big E* . . . 4H **25**
Coupe Dri. *Stoke* . . . 1B **42**
Court La. *New* . . . 1E **32**
Courtney Pl. *Stoke* . . . 6K **41**
Court Number 1. *Stoke* . . . 4K **41**
Courtway Dri. *Stoke* . . . 4C **28**
Court Yd., The. *Cong* . . . 4D **8**
Coverdale Clo. *Stoke* . . . 7B **42**
Coverley Pl. *Stoke* . . . 7J **33**
Covert Gdns. *Tal* . . . 3A **20**
Covert, The. *K'le* . . . 6J **31**
Covert, The. *New* . . . 4F **39**
Cowall Moor. . . . **6G** 15
Cowallmoor La. *Lask E* . . . 6G **15**
Cowen St. *Stoke* . . . 5D **22**
Cowley Way. *Stoke* . . . 6K **35**
Cowlishaw Clo. *Brn L* . . . 5K **13**
Cowlishaw Rd. *Stoke* . . . 5A **22**
Cowper St. *Stoke* . . . 7E **34**
Coyney Gro. *Stoke* . . . 3B **42**
Crabtree Av. *Bid* . . . 2B **14**
Crabtree Clo. *Fen I* . . . 5E **34**
Crackley. . . . **4B** 26
Crackley Bank. *New* . . . 2B **26**
Crackley Gates. . . . **2F** 31
Crackley La. *S Hay* . . . 2F **31**
Craig Rd. *Cong* . . . 3H **9**
Craigside. *Bid* . . . 2B **14** (in two parts)
Craig Wlk. *Als* . . . 1G **19**
Cranage Ct. Cong . . . 4H 9 (off Brunswick St.)
Cranberry Dri. *New* . . . 3A **26**
Cranberry La. *Als* . . . 6A **10**
Cranberry Moss. . . . **7B** 10
Cranberry Moss La. *Als* . . . 7B **10**
Cranbourne Av. *Stoke* . . . 2G **29**
Cranbrook Clo. *Stoke* . . . 7K **39**
Crane St. *Stoke* . . . 6A **28**
Cranfield Dri. *Als* . . . 7B **10**
Cranfield Pl. *Stoke* . . . 3G **35**
Cranford M. *Als* . . . 7B **10**
Cranford Way. *Stoke* . . . 2J **35**
Cranleigh Av. *Stoke* . . . 4C **28**
Cranmer St. *Stoke* . . . 6A **34**
Cranswick Gro. *Stoke* . . . 4J **35**
Cranwell Pl. *Stoke* . . . 6A **42**
Cranworth Gro. *Stoke* . . . 6K **41**
Craven Clo. *Stoke* . . . 6K **39**
Crawfurd St. *Stoke* . . . 1C **40**
Crayford Av. *Cong* . . . 2J **9**
Crediton Av. *Stoke* . . . 7B **22**
Crescent Gro. *Stoke* . . . 4H **33**
Crescent Rd. *Cong* . . . 5E **8**
Crescent, The. *Cong* . . . 5E **8**
Crescent, The. *Leek* . . . 3H **17**
Crescent, The. *New* . . . 7D **32**
Crescent, The. *Sil* . . . 3J **31**
Crescent, The. *Stoke* . . . 2H **39** (Springfields)
Crescent, The. *Stoke* . . . 2C **42** (Weston Coyney)

56 A-Z Stoke

Cresswell. 4K 49
Cresswell Av. *New* 3A 26
Cresswell La. *C'wll* 4K 49
Cresswell Old La. *C'wll* 4K 49
Cresswell Rd. *Stoke* 2D 34
Cresswellshawe Rd. *Als* 6E 10
Crestbrook Rd. *Stoke* 5G 29
Crestfield Rd. *Stoke* 6A 42
Crestway Rd. *Stoke* 2H 29
Crewe Rd. *Als* 1A 18
Crewe Rd. *Chu L* 6G 11
Crewe Rd. *Mad H* 5B 30
Crick Rd. *Stoke* 3D 34 (6H 5)
Critchlow Gro. *Stoke* 5F 41
Croft Av. *New* 6E 26
Croft Clo. *Cong* 5H 9
Croft Ct. *Stoke* 3B 28
Croft Cres. *Stoke* 7K 33
Crofter Clo. *Bid* 2A 14
Crofters Ct. *Red S* 1A 26
Croftfield St. *Stoke* 5J 35
Croft Rd. *C'dle* 3G 45
Croft Rd. *New* 3E 32 (1D 6)
Croft Rd. Ind. Est.
    New 3E 32 (1D 6)
Croft St. *Stoke* 5J 27
Croft, The. *C'dle* 1H 45
Croft, The. *Stoke* 1J 39
Cromartie St. *Stoke* 4H 41
    (in two parts)
Cromer Cres. *Stoke* 1D 34
Cromer Rd. *Stoke* 1D 34
Cromer St. *New* 1G 33
Crompton Gro. *Stoke* 2B 46
Cromwell St. *Bid* 1B 14
Cromwell St. *Stoke* 6C 28
Cromwell Ter. Leek 4G 17
    (off Livingstone St.)
Crosby Rd. *Stoke* 3H 39
Crossdale Av. *Stoke* 2F 29
Cross Edge. *Brn E* 4G 23
Crossfield Av. *B Bri* 1G 49
Crossfield Av. *Knyp* 4B 14
Crossfields La. *Cong* 7H 9
Crossgate. 7E 48
Cross Heath. 2D 32
Cross Hill. *Stoke* 5J 27
Crossland Pl. E. *Stoke* 6B 42
Crossland Pl. W. *Stoke* 5B 42
Crosslands. *Cong* 6J 9
Cross La. *Big E* 7E 18
Cross La. *Cong* 7H 9
Crossledge. *Cong* 4D 8
Crossley Rd. *Stoke* 1K 27
Cross May St. *New* 5D 32 (5B 6)
Crossmead Gro. *Stoke* 6E 28
Cross St. *Als* 7D 10
Cross St. *Bid* 2B 14
Cross St. *C'dle* 3G 45
Cross St. *Ches* 4A 26
Cross St. *Cong* 4F 9
Cross St. *Leek* 4G 17
Cross St. *Long H* 4F 27
Cross St. *W Coy* 1C 42
Crossway Rd. *Chu L* 6H 11
Crossway Rd. *Stoke* 5B 28
Crossways. *Bid* 1D 14
Crossway, The. *New* 2F 33
Croston St. *Stoke* 3A 34
Crouch Av. *Stoke* 1K 27
Crowborough. 4F 15
Crowborough Rd.
    Bid M & Lask E 4E 14
Crowcrofts Rd. *Stoke* 7D 40
Crown Bank. *Stoke* 3F 5
Crown Bank. *Tal* 4A 20
Crown Bank Cres. *Tal P* 5A 20
Crowndale Pl. *Stoke* 3H 21
Crown Gdns. *Tal* 5A 20
Crown St. *New* 4K 31
Crown St. *Stoke* 2B 34 (4E 5)
Crowther St. *Stoke* 5B 34
Croxden Clo. *C'dle* 6G 45
Croxden Rd. *Stoke* 6G 29
Croyde Pl. *Stoke* 1C 48
Cruso St. *Leek* 4E 16
Crystal St. *Stoke* 6A 28

Cumberbatch Av. *Stoke* 4A 22
Cumberland Clo. *Kid* 4B 20
Cumberland Rd. *Cong* 4C 8
Cumberland St. *New* . .4G 33 (3G 7)
Cumberland St. *Stoke* 6D 34
Cumbria Ho. *New* 1F 39
Cumming St. *Stoke* 4H 33
Curland Pl. *Stoke* 4A 42
Curlew Rd. *Pac* 2H 21
Curtiss Pl. *Stoke* 1D 48
Curzon Av. *Als* 5E 10
Curzon Ri. *Leek* 4C 16
Curzon Rd. *Stoke* 2K 27
Curzon St. *New* 3G 33 (1H 7)
Cutts St. *Stoke* 3A 34 (6D 4)
Cygnet Clo. *Mad H* 5B 30
Cynthia Gro. *Stoke* 2K 27
Cypress Gro. *B Bri* 1H 49
Cypress Gro. *New* 4A 26

D

Dace Gro. *Stoke* 1A 28
Dahlia Clo. *Stoke* 7C 36
Dain Pl. *New* 6E 26
Dain St. *Stoke* 5H 27
Daintry Clo. *Leek* 5F 17
Daintry St. *Leek* 4F 17
Daintry St. *Stoke* 2J 39
Dairy Clo. *Leek* 3H 17
Dairyfields Way. *Stoke* 5B 28
Dairyhouse La. *Dil* 3K 37
Dairylands Rd. *Chu L* 6G 11
Daisy Bank. *Als* 6B 10
Daisy Bank. *Leek* 3F 17
Daisybank Dri. *Cong* 2F 9
Daisy Pl. *Stoke* 2D 40
Dakota Gro. *Stoke* 7G 21
Dale Av. *Stoke* 5C 22
Dale Clo. *C'dle* 4H 45
Dalecot Grn. *Stoke* 5J 35
Dale Cres. *Cong* 5H 9
Dalegarth Gro. *Stoke* 6K 41
Dale Gro. *Cong* 5J 9
Dalehall Gdns. *Stoke* 4H 27
Dalehead Ct. *Stoke* 6A 42
Daleian Ct. New 4K 31
    (off Bridge St.)
Dale Pl. *Cong* 5H 9
Dales Clo. *Bid M* 2G 15
Dales Green. 5F 13
Dales Grn. Rd. *Mow C* 4F 13
Dale St. *Stoke* 4H 27
Dale, The. *Ful* 6F 49
Dale Vw. *Mow C* 5F 13
Dale Vw. *Stoke* 3C 42
Dale Vw. Ct. *Ful* 6F 49
Daleview Dri. *New* 4K 31
Dalewood Rd. *Lyme B* 7B 26
Dalton Gro. *Stoke* 4J 35
Daltry Way. *Mad* 6A 30
Daly Cres. *New* 4J 31
Dam La. *Bid M* 1F 15
Dampier St. *Leek* 4F 17
Dams, The. *Cav* 4E 42
Dandillion Av. *C'dle* 6G 45
Dane Bank Av. *Cong* 3G 9
Danebower Rd. *Stoke* 1B 46
Danebridge Gro. *Stoke* 7D 28
Dane Clo. *Als* 7B 10
Dane Dri. *Bid* 1D 14
Dane Gdns. *Kid* 1F 21
Dane Gro. *C'dle* 5H 45
Danehill Gro. *Stoke* 5J 39
Dane-in-Shaw. 7K 9
Danemead Clo. *Stoke* 7B 42
Danes Cft. *Stoke* 7A 40
Danesgate. *Leek* 3G 17
Dane Side. *Cong* 4E 8
Daneside Bus. Pk. *Cong* 3G 9
Daneside Theatre. 4G 9
Dane St. *Cong* 4E 8
Dane Wlk. *Stoke* 1C 34 (3H 5)
Darius Clo. *New* 4E 26
Darley Gro. *C'dle* 5H 45
Darnley St. *Stoke* 5B 34

Darrall Gdns. *Stoke* 3H 39
Darsham Gdns. *New* 4F 39
Dart Av. *Stoke* 7K 21
Dart Clo. *Als* 6B 10
Dart Clo. *Bid* 1C 14
Dartford Pl. *Stoke* 7B 22
Dart Gro. *C'dle* 5H 45
Dartmouth Av. *New* 7D 32
Dartmouth Pl. *Stoke* 4H 42
Dartmouth St. *Stoke* 3A 28
Dart Pl. *New* 2D 38
Dash Gro. *Stoke* 3B 28
Davenport Clo. *Leek* 5C 16
Davenport St. *Cong* 5E 8
Davenport St. *Stoke* 4G 27
Davenport Way. *New* 3C 38
Daven Rd. *Cong* 6H 9
Daventry Clo. *Stoke* 3E 34
David Rd. *Stoke* 5A 42
Davidson Av. *Cong* 2J 9
Davis Clo. *Als* 6F 11
Davison St. *Stoke* 5K 27
Davis St. *Stoke* 3K 33 (6B 4)
Davy Clo. *Stoke* 2F 35
Dawlish Dri. *Stoke* 3G 35
Dawn Av. *Stoke* 7K 21
Dawn Vw. *Stoke* 3C 42
Dayson Pl. *New* 5D 26
Deakin Gro. *New* 1F 39
Deakin Rd. *Stoke* 6A 22
Dean Hollow. *A'ly* 2E 24
Dean Pl. *Stoke* 3C 34
Deansberry Clo. *Stoke* 6K 39
Deanscroft Way. *Stoke* 2K 41
Deansgate. *New* 5D 32 (5A 6)
Dean's La. *New* 2K 25
Dean St. *Stoke* 1H 35
Deans Way. *Stoke* 1A 46
Deaville Rd. *Stoke* 2H 35
Debenham Cres. *Stoke* 3E 34
Decade Clo. *High B* 2C 26
Deebank Av. *Leek* 3J 17
Dee Clo. *Bid* 1D 14
Dee Clo. *Tal* 4B 20
Dee La. *New* 6A 10
Deepdale Clo. *Stoke* 2E 28
Defoe Dri. *Stoke* 2K 41
Delamere Ct. *Als* 6A 10
Delamere Gro. *New* . . .3F 33 (1D 6)
Delamere Gro. *Stoke* 7K 39
Delamere Rd. *Cong* 4B 8
Delaney Dri. *Stoke* 2A 42
Delius Gro. *Stoke* 7E 28
Dell, The. *New* 4K 31
Dellwood Gro. *Stoke* 7J 35
Delphouse Rd. *C'dle* 4B 44
Delph Side. *Big E* 2G 25
Delph Wlk. *Stoke* 7E 34
Delves Pl. *New* 1E 38
Denbigh Clo. *Knyp* 4B 14
Denbigh Clo. *New* 2G 39
Denbigh St. *Stoke* . . .7A 28 (1C 4)
Denby Av. *Stoke* 1H 41
Dency Gro. *Stoke* 1K 27
Denehurst Clo. *Stoke* 4B 42
Dene Side. *New* 5D 32 (5A 6)
Denewood Pl. *Stoke* 5C 42
Denford Pl. *Chu L* 4E 10
Denham Sq. *Stoke* 5D 40
Denmark Ho. *Stoke* 1E 40
Dennington Cres. *Stoke* 5D 40
Dennis Round Ct. *Als* 7D 10
Dennis St. *Stoke* 1E 40
Dennis Viollet Av. *Stoke* 3B 40
Denry Cres. *New* 5D 26
Denshaw Wlk. Stoke 2H 41
    (off Forrister St.)
Denstone Cres. *Stoke* 4E 40
Dentdale Clo. *Stoke* 7B 42
Denton Clo. *New* 3E 38
Denton Gro. *Stoke* 3K 41
Derby Pl. *New* 2F 39
Derby Rd. *Tal* 4A 20
Derby St. *Cong* 4F 9
Derby St. *Leek* 4F 17
Derby St. *Stoke* 2C 34 (5G 5)

Dereham Way. *Stoke* 4J 35
Derek Dri. *Stoke* 6D 28
Derry St. *Stoke* 2D 40
Derwent Clo. *Als* 6B 10
Derwent Cres. *Kid* 1F 21
Derwent Dri. *Bid* 1D 14
Derwent Dri. *C'dle* 5H 45
Derwent Dri. *Cong* 6H 9
Derwent Pl. *New* 2D 32
Derwent St. *Stoke* 7A 28
Devana Wlk. *Stoke* 4D 42
Devil's La. *Long* 5A 16
Devon Clo. *New* 2F 39
Devon Gro. *Bid* 1B 14
Devon Pl. *Cong* 3G 9
Devonshire Sq. *Stoke* 4H 35
Devon Way. *Stoke* 5J 41
Dewsbury Rd. *Fen I* 6D 34
Diamond Av. *Kid* 1E 20
Diamond Clo. *B'stn* 7B 46
Diamond Clo. *Bid* 2B 14
Diamond Clo. *Stoke* 3B 48
Diamond Ridge. *B'stn* 6B 46
Diana Rd. *Stoke* 6E 28
Diarmid Rd. *Stoke* 5J 39
Dibden Ct. *Stoke* 6K 33
Dickenson Rd. E. *Stoke* 5B 28
Dickenson Rd. W. *Stoke* 5B 28
Dickens St. *Stoke* 1H 35
Dickinson Way. *Als* 7B 10
Dickson Ho. *Stoke* 4C 34
Diglake. 1H 25
Diglake Clo. *Tal P* 5K 19
Diglake St. *Big E* 1G 25
Dilhorne. 2K 43
Dilhorne Gro. *Stoke* 5H 41
Dilhorne La. *Cav* 3F 43
Dilhorne Rd. *C'dle* 3E 44
Dilhorne Rd. *Dil* 3J 37
Dilhorne Rd. *For & Dil* 6J 43
Dilke St. *Stoke* 7C 28 (1G 5)
Dill Gro. *Stoke* 1C 48
Dimensions Leisure Cen. 2J 27
Dimmelow St. *Stoke* 1C 42
Dimsdale. 7E 26
Dimsdale Pde. E. *New* 7E 26
Dimsdale Pde. W. *New* 6D 26
Dimsdale St. *Stoke* 5H 27
Dimsdale Vw. *New* 6C 26
Dimsdale Vw. E. *New* 6E 26
Dimsdale Vw. W. *New* 6E 26
Dingle, The. *Brn E* 4G 23
Dividy Rd. *Stoke* 2E 34
Dixon Rd. *Cong* 2J 9
Dobell Gro. *Stoke* 2J 41
Doctors Clo. *Bid* 2B 14
Doddington Pl. *New* 7E 32
Dodd's La. *A'bry* 7E 8
Doddswood Dri. *Cong* 3H 9
Dodson St. *Stoke* 5B 28
Dogcroft Rd. *Stoke* 6B 22
Dog La. *Leek* 3F 17
Dolespring Clo. *For* 6H 43
Dolly's La. *Stoke* 2K 27
Dominic St. *Stoke* 5K 33
Donald Bates Ho. *Stoke* 7J 33
Donald Rd. *Stoke* 6D 28
Doncaster La. *Stoke* 6J 33
Donkey La. *C'dle* 1H 45
Dorcas Dri. *Stoke* 2E 40
Dorchester Clo. *Kid* 7D 12
Dorchester Wlk. *Stoke* 3H 35
Doreen Av. *Cong* 7K 9
Dorian Way. *End* 2K 23
Doris Robinson Ct. *Stoke* 7A 42
Dorking Clo. *Stoke* 3E 34
Dorlan Clo. *Stoc B* 1H 29
Dorridge Gro. *New* 1H 33
Dorrington Clo. *Stoke* 2F 29
Dorrington Gro. *New* 6F 27
Dorset Clo. *Cong* 3G 9
Dorset Clo. *Stoke* 2H 35
Dorset Dri. *Bid* 2B 14
Dorset Pl. *Kid* 7D 12
Dorset Pl. *New* 2G 39
Douglas Av. *Bid* 3B 14
Douglas Av. *Stoke* 1J 39

DOUGLAS MACMILLAN HOSPICE.
. . . . .7F 41
Douglas Pl. *Stoke* 3D 34 (6H 5)
Douglas Rd. *New* 2D 32 (1B 6)
Douglas St. *Stoke* 6A 28
Doulton Clo. *C'dle* 5G 45
Doulton Dri. *New* 5E 26
Doulton St. *Stoke* 4K 27
Dove Bank. 1D 20
Dovebank Gro. *Stoke* 1B 48
Dovecote Pl. *Stoke* 6K 41
Dovedale Clo. *Cong* 3J 9
Dovedale Clo. *Stoke* 4E 20
Dovedale Pl. *New* 4H 31
Dove Gro. *Bid* 1C 14
Dove Pl. *New* 2D 38
Doveridge St. *Stoke* 1C 40
Dover St. *Stoke* 7C 28 (1H 5)
Downey St. *Stoke* 2B 34 (5F 5)
Downfield Pl. *Stoke* 3E 28
Downham Rd. *New* 3B 32
Downing Av. *New* 2G 33
Downsview Gro. *Stoke* 3E 40
Dragon Sq. *New* 4B 26
Drake Clo. *Stoke* 4E 34
Drakeford Ct. *Stoke* 7D 22
Drakeford Gro. *Stoke* 7D 22
Draw-well La. *Werr* 1C 36
(in three parts)
Draycott Cross. 6C 44
Draycott Cross Rd. *C'dle* 6C 44
Draycott Dri. *C'dle* 5G 45
Draycott Dri. *New* 2A 26
Draycott Old Rd. *For & Dray*
. . . . .7J 43
Drayton Grn. *Stoke* 3F 35
Drayton Rd. *Stoke* 2G 41
Drayton St. *New* 5D 32 (4B 6)
Drenfell Rd. *Sch G* 3C 12
Dresden. 5G 41
Dresden St. *Stoke* . . .2C 34 (4H 5)
Dreys, The. *Stoke* 7A 40
Driffield Clo. *Stoke* 4K 35
Drive, The. *Als B & New* 6G 25
Droitwich Clo. *New* 3G 31
Drubbery La. *Stoke* 5E 40
Drumber La. *Sch G* 2D 12
Drumburn Clo. *Stoke* 4J 21
Drummond St. *Stoke* 4F 21
Dryberg Wlk. *Stoke* 1F 35
Dryden Rd. *Stoke* 6K 27
Dryden Way. *C'dle* 4F 45
Duddell Rd. *Stoke* 2B 28
Dudley St. *Stoke* 6B 42
Dudson Cen., The. (Mus.)
. . . . .1B 34 (2E 5)
Duesbury Grn. *Stoke* 3F 41
Duke Bank. 7E 22
Duke Bank Ter. *Stoke* 7E 22
Duke Pl. *New* 4K 31
Duke St. *Bid* 3C 14
Duke St. *Cong* 5F 9
Duke St. *Leek* 4F 17
Duke St. *New* 6F 33 (6F 7)
Duke St. *Stoke* 2D 40
(in two parts)
Dulverton Av. *New* 1D 38
Duncalf Gro. *New* 5E 26
Duncalf St. *Stoke* 4J 27
Duncan St. *Stoke* 7D 34
Dundas St. *Stoke* 7C 28 (1G 5)
Dundee Rd. *Stoke* 2K 33 (5A 4)
Dundee St. *Stoke* 4G 41
Dunham Clo. *Als* 7D 10
Dunkirk. 5H 19
Dunkirk. *New* 4D 32 (2B 6)
Dunkirk Ct. *New* 4D 32 (2B 6)
Dunning St. *Stoke* 7G 21
Dunnocksfold Rd. *Als* 6A 10
Dunnock Way. *Bid* 2D 14
Dunrobin St. *Stoke* 5H 41
Dunsany Gro. *Stoke* 6D 28
Dunsford Av. *Stoke* 4G 41
Dunster Rd. *Stoke* 1G 41
Dunwood Dri. *Chu L* 4E 10

Dunwood Dri. *Stoke* 1K 27
Durber Clo. *A'ly* 3E 24
Durber Clo. *Stoke* 2H 39
Durham Dri. *Stoke* 6H 41
Durham Gro. *New* 2G 39
Durston Pl. *Stoke* 3K 41
Dyke St. *Stoke* 1C 34 (2G 5)
Dylan Rd. *Knyp* 4D 14
Dylan Rd. *Stoke* 3J 41

E

Eagland Pl. *Cong* 3G 9
Eagle St. *Stoke* 1D 34 (3H 5)
Eamont Av. *Stoke* 7K 21
Eardley Cres. *Cong* 3G 9
Eardleyend Rd. *A'ly & Big E* 5E 18
Eardley St. *Stoke* 7J 33
Earlsbrook Dri. *Stoke* 7B 40
Earls Ct. *New* 4F 33 (2G 7)
Earl's Dri. *New* 7E 32
Earls Rd. *Stoke* 7A 40
Earl St. *Leek* 3G 17
Earl St. *New* 4G 33 (2G 7)
Earl St. *Sil* 4K 31
Earlswood Rd. *Stoke* 6F 29
Easdale Pl. *New* 1E 38
Easedale Clo. *Stoke* 2F 29
E. Bank Ride. *For* 6H 43
Eastbank Rd. *Stoke* . . .7A 28 (1C 4)
Eastbourne Clo. *Leek* 3E 16
Eastbourne Rd. *Stoke*
. . . . .1C 34 (2H 5)
Eastbridge Av. *Stoke* 4C 28
Eastcott Clo. *Cong* 3B 8
East Ct. *Als* 5F 11
East Cres. *New* 2G 33
East Cres. *Stoke* 4D 28
Eastdean Av. *Stoke* 3F 35
East Dri. *Bid* 2C 14
Easters Gro. *Stoke* 3G 29
Eastfield Clo. *Stoke* 6D 40
East Gro. *Stoke* 4B 42
Easthead Wlk. *Stoke* . .2A 34 (5C 4)
E. Precinct. *Stoke* 1C 34 (3G 5)
East St. *Leek* 3H 17
East St. *Stoke* 1C 42
East Ter. *Stoke* 5A 22
East Vw. *Stoke* 5J 27
Eastwick Cres. *Stoke* 6K 39
Eastwood Av. *Stoke* 7K 21
Eastwood Pl. *Stoke* . . .2B 34 (5F 5)
Eastwood Rd. *Stoke* . . .2C 34 (5G 5)
Eaton Bank. *Cong* 2G 9
Eaton Bank Ind. Est. *Cong* 3H 9
Eaton Rd. *Als* 6D 10
Eaton St. *Stoke* 1C 34 (2G 5)
Eaves La. *C'dle* 6G 45
Eaves La. *Stoke* 7H 29
Eaveswood Rd. *Stoke* 6H 29
Ebenezer Ho. *New* 2E 7
Ebury Gro. *Stoke* 5A 42
Ecclestone Pl. *Stoke* 5K 21
Edale Clo. *Stoke* 4J 31
Edale Clo. *Stoke* 4E 20
Eddisbury Dri. *New* 2A 26
Eden Clo. *Bid* 1D 14
Eden Clo. *Kid* 1E 20
Eden Gro. *C'dle* 5H 45
Eden Gro. *Stoke* 5A 42
Edenhurst Av. *Stoke* 5C 42
Edensor Ct. *New* 5B 26
Edensor Rd. *Stoke*
. . . . (in two parts)
Edensor St. *New* 5B 26
Edensor Ter. *Stoke* 4G 41
Edgar Pl. *Stoke* 7H 35
Edgbaston Dri. *Stoke* 6C 40
Edge Av. *Stoke* 5K 21
Edgefield La. *Stoc B* 5H 23
Edgefield Rd. *Stoke* 1H 41
Edgehill Rd. *Leek* 4D 16
Edge La. *End* 4J 23
Edgeley Rd. *Bid* 3C 14
Edge Vw. Clo. *Stoke* 2H 29

Edge Vw. Ct. *Bid* 3B 14
Edgeview Rd. *Cong* 7K 9
Edge Vw. Rd. *Stoke* 1H 29
Edgeware St. *Stoke* 7A 28
Edinburgh Pl. *Cong* 5H 9
Edinburgh Rd. *Cong* 5H 9
Edison St. *Stoke* 7C 34
Edmonton Gro. *Stoke* 3E 28
Edman Pl. *Stoke* 5B 42
Edwal Rd. *Stoke* 2B 42
Edward Av. *New* 7E 32
Edward Av. *Stoke* 7A 40
Edward Davies Rd. *Stoke* 2B 28
Edward St. *Big E* 1G 25
Edward St. *New* 1G 33
Edward St. *Stoke* 6D 34
Edwards Way. *Als* 6F 11
Egerton Rd. *Stoke* 5H 33 (4H 7)
Egerton St. *Cong* 5E 8
Egerton St. *Stoke* 4C 34
Elaine Av. *Stoke* 3A 28
Elburton Rd. *Stoke* 7F 35
Elder Pl. *Stoke* 6A 28
Elder Rd. *Stoke* 6A 28
Eldon St. *Stoke* 6C 28
Eleanor Cres. *New* 7D 32
Eleanor Pl. *New* 7D 32
Eleanor Vw. *New* 7E 32
Elenora St. *Stoke* 6A 34
Elers Gro. *Stoke* 5H 27
Elgar Cres. *Stoke* 7F 29
Elgin St. *Stoke* 4A 34
Elgood La. *Stoke* 4F 21
Elizabeth Ct. *Stoke* 5J 33
Elizabeth Ct. *Tal P* 6A 20
Elizabeth Dri. *New* 5B 26
Elizabeth St. *Cong* 5E 8
Elizabeth St. *Stoke* 1D 34 (3H 5)
Elkington Ri. *Mad* 6A 30
Elkstone Clo. *Stoke* 7H 21
Ellam's Pl. *New* 4B 32
Ellastone Gro. *Stoke* 7J 33
Elldawn Av. *Stoke* 2E 28
Ellerby Rd. *Stoke* 6D 40
Ellgreave St. *Stoke* 4H 27
Ellington Clo. *Stoke* 3F 35
Elliot Dri. *Werr* 1C 36
Elliot Rd. *Stoke* 7E 34
Elliott St. *New* 4G 33 (2G 7)
Ellison St. *New* 7G 27
Ellis St. *Stoke* 5B 28
Elmbrook Clo. *Stoke* 6A 42
Elm Clo. *Kid* 3E 20
Elm Clo. *Leek* 4D 16
Elmcroft Rd. *Stoke* 6G 29
Elmdon Pl. *Stoke* 7C 42
Elm Dri. *C'dle* 4J 45
Elm Gro. *Als* 6F 11
Elmhurst. *New* 2C 38
Elmhurst Clo. *Stoke* 3E 34
Elm Pl. *Stoke* 5E 40
Elm Rd. *Cong* 4D 8
Elmsmere Av. *Stoke* 5F 41
Elmsmere Rd. *Stoke* 6G 29
Elmstead Clo. *Stoke* 5J 39
Elms, The. *New* 5F 27
Elm St. *New* 5H 27
Elm St. *Stoke* 5K 27
Elms Way. *Stoke* 4B 42
Elm Tree Dri. *Big E* 3G 25
Elmwood Clo. *B Bri* 1H 49
Elmwood Clo. *Chu L* 6H 11
Elmwood Dri. *B Bri* 1H 49
Elphinstone Rd. *Stoke* 3J 39
Elsby Pl. *Stoke* 5K 21
Elsby Rd. *Als* 1G 19
Elstree Clo. *Stoke* 4A 42
Elstree Gro. *Stoke* 6F 29
Elswick Rd. *Fen I* 5D 34
Eltham Gdns. *New* 2G 33
Elton Ter. *Stoke* 4G 21
Elvington Clo. *Cong* 5G 9
Elworth Ct. *Cong* 4H 9
(off Herbert St.)
Ely Wlk. *Stoke* 2H 41
Embers Way. *End* 1K 23

Emberton St. *Ches* 5B 26
Emberton St. *New* 7F 27
Embleton Wlk. *Stoke* 5H 27
Emerson Rd. *Stoke* 6K 27
Emery Av. *New* 6C 32 (6A 6)
Emery Av. *Stoke* 4D 28
Emery St. *Stoke* 6A 28
Empire Pas. *Stoke* 7K 33
Empire St. *Stoke* 7K 33
Emsworth Rd. *Stoke* 6D 40
Encounter Pl. *Stoke* 7D 28
Enderley St. *New* 4E 32 (2C 6)
Endon. .3K 23
Endon Bank. 1K 23
Endon Dri. *Brn L* 5A 14
Endon Edge. 5J 23
Endon Rd. *Stoke* 7D 22
Englesea Av. *Stoke* 1B 42
Ennerdale Clo. *Stoke* 4H 27
Ennerdale Dri. *Cong* 5D 8
Enoch St. *Stoke* 5J 27
Enstone Clo. *Stoke* 6E 40
Enstone Ct. *New* 3E 38
Enterprise Cen. *Stoke* 3K 33
Ephraim St. *Stoke* 3C 34 (6G 5)
Epping Rd. *Stoke* 3H 39
Epsom Clo. *C'dle* 1H 45
Epworth St. *Stoke* 6K 33
Ernest Egerrton Clo. *Stoke* 6F 21
Ernest Pl. *Stoke* 6D 34
Eros Cres. *Stoke* 6D 28
Errill Clo. *Stoke* 7B 34
Erskine St. *Stoke* 5H 41
Eskdale Pl. *New* 1E 38
Eskdale Rd. *Stoke* 7J 39
Esk Way. *New* 2E 38
Esperanto Way. *Smal* 4B 28
Esporta Health & Fitness.
. . . . .7K 27 (1B 4)
Essex Clo. *Cong* 2G 9
Essex Dri. *Gil H* 2J 15
Essex Dri. *Kid* 1C 20
Essex Pl. *New* 7D 32
Eton Av. *New* 2C 38
Etruria. 2K 33 (4A 4)
Etruria Industrial Mus.
. . . . .3K 33 (6B 4)
Etruria Old Rd. *Stoke* 2J 33
Etruria Rd. *Stoke & New*
. . . . .4G 33 (1G 7 & 4A 4)
ETRURIA STATION. RAIL 2C 20
Etruria Trad. Est. *Stoke* 2H 33
Etruria Va. Rd. *Stoke*
. . . . .2K 33 (4A 4)
Etruria Way. *Stoke* 2H 33
Etruscan Ho. *Stoke* . . .3K 33 (6B 4)
Etruscan St. *Stoke* 3J 33 (6A 4)
Etruscan Wlk. *B'stn* 3E 46
Eva Gro. *New* 6G 39
Evans St. *Stoke* 3J 27
Evelyn St. *Stoke* 1D 40
Everest Rd. *Kid* 7E 12
Eversley Av. *Leek* 4F 17
Eversley Rd. *Stoke* 4K 41
Evesham Way. *Stoke* 3K 41
Excalibur Ind. Est. *Als* 7F 11
Exeter Grn. *Stoke* 3H 35
Exmouth Gro. *Stoke* 5K 27
Eyre St. *Stoke* 5H 27

F

Faceby Gro. *Stoke* 7D 42
Fairbank Av. *Stoke* 1J 39
Fairclough Pl. *Stoke* 1K 27
Fairfax St. *Stoke* 6C 28
Fairfield Av. *Brn E* 4G 23
Fairfield Av. *New* 1F 33
Fairfield Av. *Stoke* 6H 41
Fairfields. *Big E* 2G 25
Fairfields Rd. *Bid M* 1G 15
Fairhaven Gro. *Stoke* 6D 28
Fairlawn Clo. *Stoke* 6K 41
Fairlawns. *New* 3E 32
Fairlight Gro. *Stoke* 7B 42
Fairoak. *New* 2C 38

Fair Oak Rd. *New* 3A **26**
Fairview Av. *Als* 6E **10**
Fair Vw. Rd. *Leek* 4H **17**
Fairway. *Stoke* 6H **39**
Fairway Rd. *Stoke* 1K **27**
Fairway, The. *Als* 6D **10**
Falcon Rd. *Stoke* 1B **48**
Falkirk Grange. *New* 6C **32**
Fallowfield. *Stoke* 6E **40**
Falmouth Rd. *Cong* 7G **9**
Fanny's Cft. *Als* 1F **19**
Faraday Pl. *Stoke* 6H **33**
Farams Rd. *Rode H* 3F **11**
Farcroft Av. *New* 6C **26**
Fareham Gro. *Stoke* 7K **41**
Far Grn. Ind. Est. *Stoke* 7C **28**
Farington Pl. *Stoke* 5K **21**
Farland Gro. *Stoke* 5K **21**
Farleigh Gro. *Stoke* 4H **35**
Farmadine. *Stoke* 7A **40**
Farman Clo. *Stoke* 7D **42**
Farmers Bank. *New* 4K **31**
Farmer St. *Stoke* 4H **41**
Farm Hollow. *Big E* 2H **25**
Farm Lea. *Stoke* 5D **22**
Farmside La. *Bid M* 1G **15**
Farmwood Clo. *Stoke* 5C **42**
Farnborough Dri. *Stoke* 7D **42**
Farndale St. *Stoke* 1G **27**
Farne Gro. *Stoke* 3F **41**
Farnham Dri. *Brn L* 5A **14**
Farnham Rd. *Stoke* 6K **33**
Farnworth Clo. *Knyp* 4A **14**
Farnworth Rd. *Stoke* 2K **41**
Farrington Clo. *Stoke* 1D **28**
Faulkner Pl. *Stoke* 2A **42**
Fawcett Way. *Stoke* 1G **5**
Fawfield Dri. *Stoke* 5F **21**
Fawn Clo. *Stoke* 6B **42**
Fearns Av. *New* 3D **26**
Fearon Grn. *Stoke* 1D **28**
Featherstone Gro. *Stoke* 6K **33**
Federation Rd. *Stoke* 3H **27**
Fegg Hayes. 5A **22**
Fegg Hayes Rd. *Stoke* 5K **21**
Felcourt Gdns. *Stoke* 7D **28**
Fellbrook Ct. *Stoke* 1F **35**
Fellbrook La. *Stoke* 1F **35**
Fellgate Ct. *New* 4E **32** (3C **6**)
Fell St. *Stoke* 3B **28**
Felstead St. *Stoke* 1G **29**
Fenlow Av. *Stoke* 3E **34**
Fennel Gro. *Stoke* 1C **48**
Fenners Gro. *Stoke* 6C **40**
Fen Pk. Ind. Est. *Stoke* 1F **41**
Fenpark Rd. *Stoke* 7E **34**
Fenton. 7D **34**
Fenton Clo. *Cong* 6J **9**
Fenton Ind. Est. *Fen I* 5D **34**
Fenton Ind. Est. *Stoke* 5D **34**
Fenton Low. 6D **34**
Fenton Manor Leisure Cen.
. . . . .6C **34**
Fenton Pk. *Stoke* 6F **35**
Fenton Rd. *Stoke* 4E **34**
Fermain Clo. *New* 3C **38**
Fern Cres. *Cong* 4J **9**
Ferncroft Clo. *Stoke* 7A **40**
Ferndale Clo. *B Bri* 1G **49**
Ferndale Clo. *Werr* 1B **36**
Ferndale Gdns. *Har* 7H **13**
Fern Dene. *Mad* 1A **30**
Ferndown Clo. *Stoke* 5J **41**
Ferndown Dri. S. *New* 5G **39**
Ferney Pl. *Stoke* 5F **21**
Fernhurst Gro. *Stoke* 6K **41**
Fernlea Cres. *End* 1K **23**
Fernleaf Clo. *Rode H* 2G **11**
Fernlea Gro. *Meir H* 3B **48**
Fernlea Gro. *W Coy* 1C **42**
Fern Pl. *Stoke* 4H **41**
Fernwood Cft. *Stoke* 5D **16**
Fernwood Dri. *Leek* 5D **16**
Fernwood Grn. *Stoke* 7B **40**
Ferrand Rd. *Stoke* 4K **39**
Festing St. *Stoke* 7C **28** (1G **5**)
Festival Clo. *Stoke* 7K **27**

Festival Heights Retail Pk.
Stoke 7K **27** (1B **4**)
Festival Hill. *Cong* 5H **9**
Festival Park. 7K **27** (1B **4**)
Festival Way. *Stoke* . . .7J **27** (2A **4**)
Fiddlers Bank. *Brn E* 3G **23**
Field Av. *Stoke* 2G **29**
Field Clo. *Als* 6F **11**
Field Clo. *B Bri* 1F **49**
Fielden Clo. *Stoke* 2E **28**
Field End Clo. *Stoke* 7A **40**
Fielding St. *Stoke* 1A **40**
Field Pl. *Stoke* 1H **41**
Fields Rd. *Als* 6E **10**
Fields Rd. *Cong* 7G **9**
Field St. *Leek* 4F **17**
Field Vw. *Bid* 1C **14**
Field Vw. *Stoke* 2C **42**
Field Way. *Als* 6F **11**
Fieldway. *Ash B* 2A **36**
Fieldway. *B Bri* 7E **42**
Fieldway. *L'tn* 3D **40**
Fieldway. *Stoke* 7H **39**
Fife St. *Stoke* 2F **41**
Filey Clo. *Stoke* 3J **35**
Finchdean Clo. *Stoke* 7B **42**
Finch Pl. *B Frd* 1A **22**
Finchsmith Pl. *Stoke* 4G **41**
Finch St. *B Frd* 2B **22**
Finney Green. 4E **30**
Finney Grn. *Stoke* 1F **35**
Finstock Av. *Stoke* 6D **40**
Firbank Pl. *Stoke* 2A **42**
Firbeck Clo. *Cong* 4B **8**
First Av. *Kid* 2B **20**
First Av. *New* 5F **27**
First Av. *Stoke* 1J **35**
Firs, The. 3F **33** (1F **7**)
(Mus. & Art Gallery)
Fir Tree Pl. *New* 4B **26**
Fir Tree Rd. *Stoke* 6K **41**
Firwood Rd. *Bid* 1E **14**
Fisher St. *B Frd* 1A **22**
Fishpond Way. *Stoke* 6F **29**
Fistral Clo. *Stoke* 2J **41**
Fitness First Health Club. . . .5C **34**
Fitzgerald Clo. *Stoke* 2C **42**
Fitzherbert Rd. *Stoke* 4D **28**
Five Oaks Clo. *New* 3B **38**
Flackett St. *Stoke* 1H **41**
Flamborough Gro. *Stoke* 5H **27**
Flash La. *L Oaks* 2H **29**
Flash La. *Stoke* 3H **39**
Flatts Rd. *Stoke* 6D **22**
Flaxman Clo. *B'stn* 3D **46**
Flax St. *Stoke* 7A **34**
Fleckney Av. *Stoke* 3K **41**
Fleming Rd. *Stoke* 6A **34**
Fletcher Bank. *New* 4D **32** (2B **6**)
Fletcher Cres. *Stoke* 2G **29**
Fletcher Rd. *Stoke* 1K **39**
Fletcher St. *Stoke* 3A **34** (6D **4**)
Fleur Gro. *Stoke* 7G **35**
Flintsham Gro. *Stoke*
. . . . .7B **28** (1E **5**)
Flint St. *Stoke* 1C **42**
Florence. 6J **41**
Florence Rd. *Stoke* 5J **39**
Florence St. *New* 4E **32** (2D **6**)
Florida Clo. *Hot I* 4A **28**
Floyd St. *Stoke* 5A **34**
Flynn Row. *Fen I* 5D **34**
Foden Av. *Als* 7G **11**
Foden St. *Stoke* 1K **39**
Fogg St. *New* 4E **32** (3D **6**)
Fogg St. E. *New* 4E **32** (3D **6**)
Fogg St. W. *New* 4E **32** (3D **6**)
Fold La. *Bid* 1J **15**
Foley Pl. *Stoke* 2F **41**
Foley Rd. *Stoke* 3F **41**
(in two parts)
Foley St. *Stoke* 2G **41**
Fol Hollow. *A'bry* 6D **8**
Fontaine Pl. *Stoke* 1K **39**
Fonthill Wlk. *Stoke* 1G **35**
Forber Rd. *Stoke* 2J **39**

Ford Av. *Stoke* 6A **22**
Ford Green. 2C **28**
Ford Green Hall. (Mus.) 2C **28**
Ford Green Nature Reserve.
. . . . .1C **28**
Ford Grn. Rd. *Stoke* 3B **28**
Ford Hayes La. *Stoke & Hul* . .5J **35**
Fords La. *Mow C* 4G **13**
Ford St. *Leek* 3G **17**
Ford St. *Sil* 3J **31**
Ford St. *Stoke* 4H **33** (2H **7**)
Forest Clo. *New* 2B **38**
Forest Ct. *Stoke* 1F **5**
Forest Edge. *Stoke* 6B **28**
Forest Rd. *Stoke* 7A **42**
Forestside Gro. *Stoke* 4J **39**
Forge La. *Cong* 4D **8**
Forge La. *Stoke* 1J **33**
Forge Way. *Knyp* 6A **14**
Forrester Clo. *Bid* 2B **14**
Forresters Bank. *L Oaks* 1H **29**
Forrister St. *Stoke* 2H **41**
Forsbrook. 7J **43**
Forster St. *Stoke* 1G **27**
Forsyte Rd. *Stoke* 7G **35**
Forum Rd. *Stoke* 7A **26**
Fosbrook Pl. *Stoke* 5G **33** (5H **7**)
Foster Ct. *Stoke* 4E **40**
Foster Rd. *Cong* 2J **9**
Foundry Bank. *Cong* 4G **9**
Foundry La. *Sch G* 3C **12**
Foundry La. *Stoke* 2F **35**
Foundry Sq. *Stoke* 6E **22**
Foundry St. *Stoke* 1B **34** (2E **5**)
Fountain Ct. *Bid* 1C **14**
Fountain Ct. *Stoke* 4J **27**
(off Westport Rd.)
Fountain Pl. *Stoke* 4J **27**
Fountains Av. *New* 2E **38**
Fountain Sq. *Stoke* 1B **34** (3F **5**)
Fountain St. *Cong* 5F **9**
Fountain St. *Leek* 3G **17**
Fountain St. *Stoke* 7D **34**
Fourth Av. *Kid* 2C **20**
Fourth Av. *Stoke* 1J **35**
Fowlchurch Rd. *Leek* 2G **17**
Fowler's La. *L Oaks* 2J **29**
Foxfield Clo. *C'dle* 1H **45**
Foxfield Railway Mus. 5G **43**
Foxfield Steam Railway. 5G **43**
Foxfield Way. *Stoke* 6E **40**
Fox Gdns. *Tal* 3A **20**
Foxglove Clo. *Stoke* 1C **42**
Foxglove La. *New* 5F **39**
Fox Gro. *New* 4F **39**
Foxlands Clo. *Stoke* 2J **35**
Foxley. 4E **18**
Foxley La. *Stoke* 3E **28**
Fox St. *Cong* 4G **9**
Frampton Gro. *Stoke* 5H **21**
Francis St. *Stoke* 6J **21**
Franklin Rd. *Stoke* 6J **33**
Franklyn St. *Stoke* 3C **34** (6H **5**)
Frank St. *Stoke* 7K **33**
Fraser St. *Stoke* 5A **28**
Freckleton Pl. *Stoke* 7D **42**
Frederick Av. *Stoke* 6K **33**
Frederick St. *Stoke* 7D **34**
Freebridge Clo. *Stoke* 2K **41**
Freedom Dri. *Har* 7H **13**
Freedom Wlk. *Stoke* 1B **28**
(off Bradeley Village)
Freehay. 6J **45**
Freehold St. *New* 5F **33** (5F **7**)
Free Trade St. *Stoke* . . .7C **28** (1G **5**)
Fremantle Rd. *Stoke* 2J **39**
Frenchmore Gro. *Stoke* 5K **41**
Freshwater Gro. *Stoke* 2E **34**
Friars Clo. *C'dle* 3G **45**
Friars Ct. *C'dle* 3G **45**
(off Prince George St.)
Friars Pl. *Stoke* 5G **29**
Friars Rd. *Stoke* 5G **29**
Friars St. *New* 5E **32** (4D **6**)
Friar St. *Stoke* 2H **41**
Friars Wlk. *New* 7E **32**
Friarswood Rd. *New* 5E **32** (5C **6**)

Friendly Av. *New* 4E **26**
Friesian Gdns. *New* 2K **25**
Frith St. *Leek* 3E **16**
Frobisher St. *Stoke* 6F **23**
Frodingham Rd. *Stoke* 4J **35**
Froghall. 4E **32** (3C **6**)
Froghall Rd. *C'dle* 2G **45**
Frome Wlk. *Stoke* 6K **21**
Frozer Ho. *Stoke* 6A **42**
Fulford. 6F **49**
Fulford Dale. *Ful* 5C **48**
Fulford Rd. *Ful* 7E **48**
Fuller St. *Stoke* 7H **21**
Fullwood Wlk. *Stoke* 4H **35**
Fulmar Pl. *Stoke* 7C **42**
Furlong Ind. Est. *Stoke* 5H **27**
Furlong La. *Stoke* 5H **27**
Furlong Pde. *Stoke* 4J **27**
Furlong Pas. *Stoke* 4J **27**
Furlong Rd. *Stoke* 7H **21**
Furmston Pl. *Leek* 2H **17**
Furnace La. *Mad* 1A **30**
Furnace Pl. *Stoke* 4J **41**
Furnace Rd. *Stoke* 4J **41**
Furnival St. *Stoke* 6A **28**
Fynney St. *Leek* 4G **17**

G

Gables, The. *Als* 6D **10**
Gable St. *Stoke* 7A **34**
Gainsborough Rd. *New* 6B **26**
Gainsborough Rd. *Stoke* 6D **40**
Galbraith Clo. *Cong* 5E **8**
Galleys Bank. *Kid* 7E **12**
Gallimore Clo. *Stoke* 3H **27**
Galloway Rd. *Stoke* 5K **35**
Gallowstree La. *New* 6B **32**
Galsworthy Rd. *Stoke* 7G **35**
Galveston Gro. *Stoke* 1E **40**
Garbett St. *Stoke* 4F **21**
Gardeners Clo. *Brn L* 5A **14**
Gardenholm Clo. *Stoke* 6A **42**
Garden Pl. *Stoke* 5H **33** (5H **7**)
Garden Rd. *Leek* 3E **16**
Garden St. *Cong* 4C **8**
Garden St. *New* 5F **33** (4E **7**)
Garden St. *Stoke* 7J **33**
Gardiner Dri. *Stoke* 4F **41**
Garfield Av. *Stoke* 5J **39**
Garfield Clo. *Stoke* 5J **39**
Garfield Cres. *Stoke* 5J **39**
Garfield St. *Stoke* 3A **34** (6C **4**)
Garibaldi St. *Stoke* 2J **33** (5A **4**)
Garlick St. *Stoke* 3A **28**
Garner St. *Stoke* 2H **33**
(in two parts)
Garner's Wlk. *Mad* 1B **30**
Garnet St. *Stoke* 2K **33** (4B **4**)
Garnett Rd. E. *New* 7E **26**
Garnett Rd. W. *New* 6E **26**
Garsdale Cres. *Stoke* 6E **40**
Garth St. *Stoke* 1C **34** (2G **5**)
Gaskell Rd. *Stoke* 2J **35**
Gas Works Ind. Est. *Kid* 1B **20**
Gate St. *Stoke* 1C **42**
Gate Way. *New* 2A **26**
Gatley Gro. *Stoke* 1C **48**
Gaunt St. *Leek* 3E **16**
Gawsworth Clo. *Als* 7D **10**
Gawsworth Clo. *Stoke* 7H **35**
Gayton Av. *Stoke* 2G **29**
Gedney Gro. *New* 4E **38**
Geen St. *Stoke* 6A **34**
Gemini Gro. *Stoke* 5H **21**
Geneva Dri. *New* 7B **32**
Geneva Gro. *Stoke* 5E **28**
Geoffrey Av. *Leek* 4E **16**
Geoffrey Gro. *Stoke* 2B **42**
George Av. *Stoke* 5C **42**
George Bates Clo. *Als* 7D **10**
George Ct. *Stoke* 3G **41**
George Eardley Clo.
Stoke 6F **21**
George Eastham Av.
Stoke 3C **40**
George St. *A'ly* 3E **24**

George St.—Hallwater

George St. Ches 5B 26
George St. New . . . . . 6F 27 (Boulton St.)
George St. New . . . . . 4F 33 (3F 7) (Brunswick St.)
George St. Sil 4J 31
George St. Stoke 6D 34
Georges Way. Big E 2G 25
Gerrard St. Stoke 5K 33
Giantswood La. Hul W & Cong 1C 8
Gibbins St. Stoke 7C 28
Gibson Gro. New 4A 26
Gibson Pl. Stoke 4B 42
Gibson St. Stoke 2H 27
Gifford Pl. Stoke 7J 33
Gilbern Dri. Knyp 5A 14
Gilbert Clo. Kid 1D 20
Gilbert St. Stoke 4F 21
Gilchrist Ct. Stoke . . . . . 6A 28 (off Grange St.)
Giles Clo. C'dle 3G 45
Giles Wlk. Stoke 7D 28
Gill Bank Rd. Kid 3E 20
Gill Bank Rd. Stoke 4E 20
Gilliat Wlk. Stoke 5H 35
Gillow Heath. 2H 15
Gill Wlk. Stoke 5D 4
Gillyflower Clo. Stoke 2D 28
Gilman Av. Stoke 2G 29
Gilman Pl. Stoke 1C 34 (3G 5)
Gilman St. Stoke 2C 34 (4G 5)
Gimson St. Stoke 7D 34
Girsby Clo. Stoke 2B 46
Gitana St. Stoke 1B 34 (3E 5)
Glades, The. Stoke 7J 27
Glade, The. New 4D 38
Gladstone Gro. Bid 2C 14
Gladstone Pl. Stoke 1J 39
Gladstone Pottery Mus. 3H 41
Gladstone St. Leek 4F 17
Gladstone St. Stoke 3H 33 (1H 7)
Gladwyn St. Stoke 1H 35
Glaisher Dri. Stoke 7D 42
Glandore Rd. Stoke 2A 42
Glass St. Stoke 1B 34 (2F 5)
Glastonbury Clo. Stoc B 1J 29
Glebe Clo. B Bri 1H 49
Glebe Ct. C'dle 4E 44
Glebe Ct. Stoke 6B 34
Glebedale Ct. Stoke 1D 40
Glebedale Rd. Stoke 7D 34
Glebe Rd. King 4E 44
Glebe St. Stoke 6A 34
Glebe St. Tal 1A 20
Glebeville. Leek 5F 17
Glencastle Way. Stoke 2B 46
Glencoe St. Stoke 4G 41
Glendale Ct. New 4F 39
Glendale St. Stoke 5K 27
Glendue Gro. Stoke 1B 46
Gleneagles Cres. Stoke 6D 28
Glenfield Way. Stoke 5K 35
Glenroyd Av. Stoke 4F 35
Glenroyd Wlk. Stoke 4H 35
Glenwood Clo. New 4K 31
Glenwood Clo. Stoke 2G 41
Globe St. Stoke 4H 27
Gloucester Grange. New 1F 39
Gloucester Rd. Kid 1C 20
Glover St. Stoke 7C 28
Glyn Pl. Stoke 1J 27
Goddard St. Stoke 2H 41
Godfrey Rd. Stoke 2G 35
Godleybarn La. Dil 1A 44
Godleybrook. 1A 44
Godley La. Dil 2A 44
Golborn Av. Stoke 3B 48
Golborn Clo. Stoke 3B 48
Goldcrest Way. Bid 2D 14
Goldenhill. 4F 21
Goldenhill Rd. Stoke 2G 41
Goldfinch Clo. Cong 6G 9
Goldfinch Dri. Als 7C 10
Goldsmith Pl. Stoke 2J 41
Gold St. Stoke 3G 41
Golf Links Clo. Stoke 4F 21
Goms Mill Rd. Stoke . . . . . 5F 41 (Drubbery La.)
Goms Mill Rd. Stoke . . . . . 4G 41 (Ladysmith St.)
Goodfellow St. Stoke . . . . . 7G 21 (in two parts)
Goodson St. Stoke 1B 34 (3F 5)
Goodwick Clo. Stoke 2B 46
Goodwin Av. New 3E 32
Goodwin Rd. Stoke 4C 42
Goodwood Av. C'dle 2J 45
Goodwood Pl. Stoke 7K 39
Goosemoor Gro. Stoke 7C 42
Goose St. New 5E 32 (5D 6)
Goostrey Ct. Cong . . . . . 4H 9 (off Brunswick St.)
Gordale Clo. Cong 2J 9
Gordan Clo. Leek 5D 16
Gordon Av. C'dle 3E 44
Gordon Av. Stoke 5B 28
Gordon Banks Dri. Stoke 3C 40
Gordon Ct. New 2B 32
Gordon Cres. Stoke 5D 28
Gordon Rd. Stoke 5F 21
Gordon St. New 2B 32
Gordon St. Stoke 3A 28
Gorse St. Stoke 2D 40
Gorsey Bank. Stoke 5D 22
Gorsty Bank. 2K 31
Gort Rd. New 1C 32
Gosforth Gro. Stoke 7D 42
Gosling Way. Cong 4C 8
Govan Rd. Fen I 5D 34
Gowan Av. Stoke 7K 21
Gower St. New 4F 33 (2F 7)
Gower St. Stoke 3H 41
Gowy Clo. Als 7A 10
Grace Rd. Stoke 7B 40
Grace St. Leek 3D 16
Graffam Gro. C'dle 2J 45
Grafton Av. Stoke 3A 28
Grafton Rd. Stoke 2H 41
Grafton St. Stoke 7C 28 (1G 5)
Graham St. Stoke 2F 35
Granby Wlk. Stoke 7J 33
Granchester Clo. Stoke 1C 48
Grange Ct. Bid 2J 15
Grangefields. Bid 1K 15
Grange Gdns. Leek 5E 16
Grange La. New . . . . . 1G 33 (in two parts)
Grange Pk. Dri. Bid 1K 15
Grange Rd. Bid 1K 15
Grange Rd. Stoke 1A 48
Grange St. Stoke 6A 28
Grange, The. Stoke 4B 42
Grangewood Av. Stoke 1A 48
Grangewood Rd. Stoke 6B 42
Granstone Clo. Stoke 4K 21
Grantham Pl. Stoke 6F 29
Grantley Clo. Stoke 5F 41
Grant St. Stoke 6B 34
Granville Av. New 3F 33 (1F 7)
Granville Av. Stoke 5C 28
Granville Rd. Stoke 1G 35
Grasmere Av. Cong 5B 8
Grasmere Av. New 2E 38
Grasmere Ter. Stoke 1K 27
Grass Rd. Dray 7B 44
Grass Rd. Stoke 6F 23
Grassygreen La. A'ly 3E 24
Gratton La. End 1K 23
Gratton Rd. Stoke 2J 35
Gravelly Bank. Stoke 7A 42
Grayling Gro. Stoke 1A 28
Grayling Willows. Mad 2B 30
Gray's Clo. Sch G 3E 12
Grayshott Rd. Stoke 6H 21
Greasley Rd. Stoke 6G 29
Greatbatch Av. Stoke 6J 33
Great Chell. 5K 21
Great Eaves. 7H 29
Gt. Fenton Bus. Pk. Stoke 2C 40
Greatoak Rd. Big E 7G 19
Greenacres Av. B Bri 6D 42
Greenacres Rd. Cong 5B 8
Greenbank Rd. New 2F 33
Greenbank Rd. Stoke 1J 27
Greenbirches Ind. Est. Stoke 7G 21
Greenbrook Ct. New 2E 32
Green Clo. B'stn 6C 46
Green Clo. B Bri 7E 42
Greendale Dri. New 3A 26
Greendock St. Stoke 3G 41
Green Dri. Als 6E 10
Greenfield. Bid 4C 14
Greenfield Av. Brn E 4H 23
Greenfield Clo. Brn E 4H 23
Greenfield Ct. Cong 4D 8
Greenfield Cres. C'dle 2H 45
Greenfield Farm Trad. Est. Cong 3D 8
Greenfield Pl. Brn E 4H 23
Greenfield Rd. Cong 4D 8
Greenfield Rd. End 3K 23
Greenfield Rd. Stoke 6H 21
Greenfields Dri. Als 7F 11
Greengate Rd. Chu L 5G 11
Greengates St. Stoke 7H 21
Greenhead St. Stoke 4J 27
Green Health & Fitness. 3C 40
Greenhill Rd. Stoke 5D 22
Green La. B Bri 1H 49
Greenlea Clo. Stoke 2B 46
Greenmeadow Gro. End 5K 23
Greenmeadows Rd. Mad 1B 30
Greenmoor Av. Stoke 3K 21
Greenock Clo. New 5C 32
Green Pk. Ful 6F 49
Green Rd. Stoke 3H 39
Greenside. New 4D 32 (2B 6)
Greenside Av. Stoc B 1H 29
Greenside Clo. Kid 4D 20
Green's La. Stoke 2K 35
Green, The. Brn E 4G 23
Green, The. Cav 3E 42
Green, The. C'dle 4E 44
Green, The. Chu L 5H 11
Green, The. Cong 5E 8
Green, The. New 3F 39
Green, The. Stoc B 1G 29
Green, The. Stoke 5H 33 (5H 7)
Greenway. Als 5C 10
Greenway. Cong 4D 8
Greenway. L'tn 3D 40
Greenway. Tren 7H 39
Greenway Av. Stoke 2A 28
Greenway Bank. B Frd 1B 22
Greenway Bank. L Oaks 2H 29
Greenway Bank Country Pk. 6E 14
Greenway Clo. Rode H 2G 11
Greenway Hall Rd. L Oaks 2J 29
Greenway Hall Rd. Stoc B 1H 29
Greenway Pl. Stoke 5G 29
Greenway Rd. Bid 2K 15
Greenways. Big E 2G 25
Greenways. C'dle 4E 44
Greenways Dri. C'dle 2G 45
Greenway, The. New 2F 33
Greenwood Av. Cong 4H 9
Greenwood Av. Stoke 4H 39
Greenwood Rd. For 6H 43
Greeting St. Stoke 5K 27
Gregory St. Stoke 3G 41
Gregson Clo. Stoke 3F 41
Grenadier Clo. Stoke 3B 46
Grendon Grn. Stoke 3H 35
Gresley Way. Big E 2G 25
Gresty St. Stoke 6K 33
Greville St. Stoke 7C 28 (1G 5)
Greyfriars Rd. Stoke 7F 29
Greyhound Ct. Mad 2B 30
Greyhound Way. Stoke 7K 27 (1B 4)
Greysan Av. Pac 3J 21
Greystones. New . . . . . 5F 27 (off First Av.)
Greyswood Rd. Stoke 3H 39
Grice Rd. Stoke 5H 33
Griffin St. Stoke 2G 41
Grig Pl. Als 5D 10
Grindley Hill Ct. Stoke 6G 33
Grindley La. B Bri 7F 43
Grindley La. Stoke 2B 48
Grindley Pl. Stoke 7J 33
Grisedale Clo. Stoke 7B 42
Gristhorpe Way. Stoke 4J 35
Gritter St. Stoke 2G 27
Grosvenor Av. Als 5E 10
Grosvenor Av. Stoke 2J 39
Grosvenor Clo. Als 5E 10
Grosvenor Clo. End 1K 23
Grosvenor Gdns. New 5F 33 (5E 7)
Grosvenor Pl. New 7F 27
Grosvenor Pl. Stoke 7G 21
Grosvenor Rd. Cong 4C 8
Grosvenor Rd. New 5F 33 (5E 7)
Grosvenor Rd. Stoke 5A 42
Grosvenor St. Leek 4G 17
Grosvenor St. Stoke 3G 41
Grove Av. Chu L 6H 11
Grove Av. Kid 2B 20
Grove Av. Stoke 2D 40
Grovebank Rd. Stoke 3H 39
Grove Ct. Als 6F 11
Grove Pk. Av. Chu L 6H 11
Grove Pl. Stoke 3A 34 (6C 4)
Grove Rd. Stoke 2C 40
Grove Rd. Ind. Est. Stoke 2C 40
Grove St. Leek 3E 16
Grove St. New 2B 32
Grove St. Stoke 6K 27
Grove Ter. Leek . . . . . 3E 16 (off Westwood Gro.)
Grove, The. B Bri 1F 49
Grove, The. Chu L 6H 11
Grove, The. New 7E 32
Grove, The. Stoke 2A 28
Guernsey Clo. Cong 6J 9
Guernsey Dri. New 2B 38
Guernsey Wlk. Stoke . . . . . 3F 41 (off Anglesey Dri.)
Guildford St. Stoke 5B 34
Gun Battery La. Bid M 2F 15
Gunderson Clo. B Bri 6J 43
Gunn St. Bid 2B 14
Guy St. Stoke 1G 35
Gwenys Cres. Stoke 2D 40
Gwyn Av. Knyp 5C 14

H

Hackett Clo. Stoke 2J 41
Hackwood Clo. B'stn 3E 46
Hadden Clo. Werr 3C 36
Haddon Gro. New 6C 26
Haddon Pl. Stoke 7H 29
Hadfield Grn. Stoke 2C 28
Hadleigh Clo. New 4E 38
Hadleigh Rd. Stoke 6G 29
Hadrian Way. New 7A 26
Haig Rd. Leek 2H 17
Haig St. Stoke 4J 41
Hailsham Clo. Stoke 6J 21
Hales Hall Rd. C'dle 2J 45
Hales Pl. Stoke 5H 41
Halesworth Cres. New 4F 39
Halfway Pl. New 4B 32
Halifax Clo. Stoke 7D 42
Haliford Av. Stoke 5C 28
Hallahan Gro. Stoke 5K 33
Hallam St. Stoke 7C 34
Hall Av. Leek 2H 17
Halldearn Av. Cav 3E 42
Hall Dri. Als 7D 10
Hall Dri. Stoke 2C 42
Hallfield Gro. Stoke 6H 21
Hall Green. 5B 12
Hall Hill Dri. Stoke 5J 35
Hall Orchard. C'dle 3G 45
Hall Pl. New 7G 27
Halls Rd. Bid 1B 14
Halls Rd. Mow C 3F 13
Hall St. A'ly 2E 24
Hall St. New 4E 32 (2C 6)
Hall St. Stoke 4H 27
Hallwater. End 1K 23

60 A-Z Stoke

Halmer End—High St.

Halmer End. 6F 25
Halton Grn. Stoke 6D 40
Hambleton Pl. Knyp 5A 14
Hamble Way. Stoke 4J 35
Hambro Pl. Stoke 4A 22
Hamil Dri. Leek 3E 16
Hamil Rd. Stoke 3K 27
Hamilton Ct. New 4F 39
Hamilton Ind. Cen. Stoke 1D 40
Hamilton Ri. Stoke 2G 29
Hamilton Rd. Stoke 4J 41
Hamilton St. Stoke 1B 40
Hamlett Pl. Stoke 1D 28
Hammersley Hayes Rd. C'dle 1H 45
Hammersley St. Stoke 6D 28
Hammerton Av. Stoke 3E 34
Hammond Av. Brn E 4G 23
Hammond Ho. Stoke 3C 34
Hammond Rd. P West 4B 26
Hammoon Gro. Stoke 3G 35
Hamner Grn. Stoke 5J 35
Hampshire Clo. Cong 3F 9
Hampshire Clo. End 2K 23
Hampshire Cres. Stoke 6H 41
Hampstead Gro. Stoke 7B 40
Hampton Ct. Leek 4E 16
Hampton St. Join I 3C 34 (6G 5)
Hams Clo. Bid 3B 14
Hanbridge Av. New 6D 26
Hanchurch. 7E 38
Hanchurch La. Han 7E 38
Hancock Rd. Cong 3H 9
Hancock St. Stoke 6B 34
Handel Gro. Stoke 6F 29
Handley Banks. Cav 3F 43
Handley Dri. B Frd 1A 22
Handley St. Pac 1K 21
Handsacre Rd. Stoke 1J 41
Hand St. Stoke 2H 27
Hanford. 5J 39
Hanley. 1B 34 (3F 5)
Hanley Bus. Pk. Stoke 3B 34 (6D 4)
Hanley Mall. Stoke 2F 5
Hanley Rd. Stoke 3B 28
Hanover Ct. New 2E 7
Hanover St. New 4F 33 (2E 7) (in three parts)
Hanover St. Stoke 1B 34 (1E 5)
Harber St. Stoke 3H 41
Harborne Cotts. C'dle 2H 45
Harborne Cres. C'dle 2H 45
Harborne Rd. C'dle 2G 45
Harcourt Av. Stoke 5A 42
Harcourt St. Stoke 3A 34
Hardewick Clo. Werr 2C 36
Hardinge St. Stoke 7C 34
Harding Rd. Stoke 3B 34 (6F 5)
Hardings Bank. 3J 9
Hardings Row. Mow C 3G 13
Hardings Wood. 1A 20
Hardingswood. Kid 1B 20
Hardingswood Ind. Est. Kid 1B 20
Hardingswood Rd. Kid 1B 20
Harding Ter. Stoke 7K 33
Hardman St. Stoke 3F 29
Hardwick Clo. Stoke 3B 46
Hardy Clo. C'dle 4F 45
Hardy St. Stoke 7G 21
Harebell Gro. Pac 2J 21
Harecastle Av. Tal 2B 20
Harecastle Vs. Kid 1B 20
Haregate. 1H 17
Haregate Rd. Leek 2H 17
Haregate Ter. Leek 2H 17
Hareshaw Gro. Stoke 3K 21
Harewood Clo. C'dle 2G 45
Harewood Est. C'dle 1E 44
Harewood Rd. Stoke 2G 27
Harewood St. Stoke 2G 27
Hargreave Clo. Stoke 7D 42
Harington Dri. Stoke 1K 41
Harlech Av. Stoke 5K 41
Harlech Dri. Knyp 4B 14
Harlequin Dri. Stoke 2B 28
Harley St. Stoke 2C 34 (5G 5) (in two parts)
Harold St. Stoke 3B 28
Harper Av. New 1D 32
Harper Gro. Cong 3G 9
Harper St. Stoke 5H 27
Harpfield Rd. Stoke 7H 33
Harplow La. C'dle 5D 44
Harptree Wlk. Stoke 4J 39
Harpur Cres. Als 5C 10
Harrier Clo. Stoke 1B 48
Harriseahead. 5G 13
Harriseahead La. Har 6F 13
Harrison Clo. Halm 6E 24
Harrison Ct. New 6F 33 (6F 7) (off Occupation St.)
Harrison Rd. Stoke 1D 28
Harrison St. New 5F 33 (5F 7)
Harris St. Stoke 5K 33
Harrogate Gro. New 3G 31
Harrop St. Stoke 6C 28
Harrowby Dri. New 2C 38
Harrowby Rd. Stoke 6B 42
Hart Ct. New 4E 32 (2C 6)
Hartill St. Stoke 5B 34
Hartington Clo. Leek 5F 17
Hartington St. Leek 4F 17
Hartington St. New 7E 26
Hartland Av. Stoke 7B 22
Hartley Gdns. Cong 7K 9
Hartshill. 5H 33 (3H 7)
Hartshill Rd. Stoke 4G 33 (3G 7)
Hartwell. 5G 47
Hartwell. New 2C 38
Hartwell La. Stone & R'gh C 5F 47
Hartwell Rd. Stoke 6B 42
Harvey Rd. Cong 2J 9
Harvey Rd. Stoke 4B 42
Haslemere Av. Stoke 3G 29
Haslington Clo. New 3A 26
Hassall Green. 1A 10
Hassall Rd. Has G & Als 2A 10
Hassall St. Stoke 2C 34 (4G 5)
Hassam Av. New 3D 32
Hassam Pde. New 7E 26
Hassell St. New 5E 32 (4D 6)
Hatfield Cres. Stoke 6D 40
Hathersage Clo. Stoke 1H 41
Hatherton Clo. New 2A 26
Hatrell St. New 5F 33 (5D 6)
Hatter St. Cong 4G 9
Havannah. 2J 9
Havannah La. Cong 3J 9
Havannah La. Hav 1H 9
Havannah St. Cong 3H 9
Havelet Dri. New 3C 38
Havelock Gro. Bid 3B 14
Havelock Pl. Stoke 3A 34 (6C 4)
Haven Av. Stoke 4C 28
Haven Cres. Werr 1C 36
Haven Gro. New 5F 27
Havergal Wlk. Stoke 1H 41
Hawes St. Stoke 7G 21
Hawfinch Rd. C'dle 3H 45
Hawk Clo. Stoke 7B 42
Hawkins St. Stoke 7B 34
Hawksdale Clo. Stoke 7B 42
Hawksmoor Clo. Stoke 7A 42
Hawkstone Clo. New 5F 33 (5F 7)
Hawksworth Av. Leek 5E 16
Hawksworth Clo. Leek 5E 16
Haworth Av. Cong 2H 9
Hawthorne Av. Big E 3G 25
Hawthorne Av. Stoke 1H 39
Hawthorne Clo. Cong 3C 8
Hawthorne Ct. Als 6E 10
Hawthorne Ter. Leek 3G 17
Hawthorn Gdns. Tal 3A 20
Hawthorn Gro. Bid 3D 14
Hawthorn Pl. Stoke 6A 42
Hawthorn Rd. New 3B 26
Hawthorns, The. K'le 5G 31
Hawthorn St. Stoke 6K 27
Hawthorn Vs. Als 7H 11
Haydock Clo. C'dle 1H 45
Haydock Ct. Sil 4K 31
Haydon Ct. Stoke 3H 33
Haydon St. Stoke 3H 33
Hayes. 6D 24
Hayes Clo. Leek 3G 17
Hayes St. Stoke 2B 28
Hayeswood La. Halm 6F 25
Hayfield Cres. Stoke 6D 34
Hayfield Rd. New 4J 31
Hayhead Clo. Kid 1E 20
Hayling Pl. Stoke 3E 40
Haymarket. Stoke 1G 27
Hayner Gro. Stoke 2C 42
HAYWOOD AND STANFIELD HOSPITAL. 1K 27
Haywood Rd. Stoke 2J 27
Haywood St. Leek 4G 17
Haywood St. Stoke 4A 34
Hazel Clo. Kid 7E 12
Hazel Clo. Stoke 1J 39
Hazeldene Rd. Stoke 7B 40
Hazel Gro. Als 7H 11
Hazel Gro. Bid M 1G 15
Hazel Gro. Leek 5D 16
Hazel Gro. Stoke 4A 42
Hazelhurst Rd. Stoke 5J 21
Hazelhurst St. Stoke 3C 34 (6H 5)
Hazel Rd. New 4A 26
Hazelwood Clo. Stoke 6B 28
Hazelwood Rd. End 5K 23
Hazlitt Way. Stoke 1K 41
Headlingley Gro. Stoke 6C 40
Heakley Av. Stoke 7E 22
Healey Av. Knyp 5A 14
Heanor Pl. Stoke 3F 41
Heath Av. New 2F 33
Heath Av. Rode H 2F 11
Heath Av. Werr 1F 37
Heathcote Ct. Stoke 1J 41
Heathcote Ri. Stoke 2C 42
Heathcote Rd. Halm 5F 25
Heathcote Rd. Stoke 3F 41 (in two parts)
Heathcote St. Kid 2D 20
Heathcote St. New 4B 26
Heathcote St. Stoke 7H 35
Heath Ct. Chu L 4G 11
Heathdene Clo. Stoke 2G 41
Heath End Rd. Als 4C 10
Heather Clo. Werr 1B 36
Heather Cres. Stoke 3B 48
Heather Glade. Mad 1A 30
Heather Hills. Stoc B 6J 23
Heatherlands Clo. R'gh C 2A 48
Heatherleigh Gro. Stoke 6E 28
Heatherside. Mow C 5F 13
Heather Vw. Stoke 5D 22
Heathfield Clo. Cong 4B 8
Heathfield Ct. Stoke 4F 21
Heathfield Dri. New 3A 26
Heathfield Gro. Stoke 1A 48
Heathfield Rd. Stoke 6B 22
Heath Gro. Stoke 2B 48
Heath Ho. La. Stoke 1E 34
Heath Pl. New 2F 33
Heath Rd. Cong 5C 8
Heath Row. Mad H 5B 30
Heathside La. Stoke 4E 20
Heath's Pas. Stoke 3J 41
Heath St. Bid 3B 14
Heath St. Ches 6C 26
Heath St. New 4E 32 (2D 6)
Heath St. Stoke 4F 21
Heath View. Als 5F 11
Heathwood Dri. Als 5C 10
Heaton Ter. New 6E 26
Heaton Ter. Werr 1K 23
Heaton Vs. Brn E 4G 23
Heber St. Stoke 2H 41
Hedley Pl. New 5C 32 (4A 6)
Heighley. 7A 24
Heighley Castle Way. Mad 4A 30 & 1B 30
Heighley La. Bet 7A 24
Heights, The. Leek 7C 16
Hellyar-Brook Rd. Als 6C 10
Helston Av. Stoke 3K 41
Hem Heath. 1B 46
Hem Heath Wood Nature Reserve. 1B 46
Heming Pl. Stoke 2F 35
Hemingway Rd. Stoke 2J 41
Hemlock Rd. Stoke 2J 41
Hempstalls Ct. New 3E 32 (1D 6)
Hempstalls Gro. New 2E 32
Hempstalls La. New 3E 32 (2D 6)
Hemsby Way. New 4E 38
Hencroft. Leek 3F 17
Henderson Gro. Stoke 3C 42
Henley Av. Knyp 4K 13
Henley Clo. B'stn 3D 46
Henrietta St. Cong 4E 8
Henry St. Stoke 7G 21
Henshall Hall Dri. Cong 6K 9
Henshall Pl. Stoke 5G 21
Henshall Rd. P West 4B 26
Herbert St. Cong 4H 9
Herbert St. Stoke 7C 34
Herd St. Stoke 3J 27
Hereford Av. New 2F 39
Hereford Gro. Stoke 3J 35
Herm Clo. New 2B 38
Hermes Clo. Stoke 7D 42
Heron Clo. Mad 6A 30
Heron Cross. 2D 40
Heron St. Stoke 1D 40
Hertford Clo. Cong 3G 9
Hertford Gro. New 2G 39
Hertford St. Stoke 2D 40
Hesketh Av. Stoke 6C 22
Heskin Way. Stoke 5K 21
Hester Clo. Stoke 7H 35
Hethersett Wlk. Stoke 3J 35
Hewitt Cres. Werr 2C 36
Hewitt St. Stoke 5J 21
Heyburn Cres. Stoke 4H 27
Heyfield Cotts. T'sor 7A 46
Heysham Clo. Stoke 2C 42
Heywood St. Cong 5E 8
Hickman St. New 4E 32 (3C 6)
Hick St. New 4D 6
Hidden Hills. Mad 5A 30
Hide St. Stoke 6A 34
Higginson Clo. Cong 6K 9
High Bank Pl. Stoke 3A 28
Highbury Rd. Werr 1D 36
High Carr. 2C 26
High Carr Bus. Pk. New 2C 26
Highcroft Av. Cong 5H 9
Highcroft Wlk. Stoke 2A 28
Higher Ash Rd. Tal 2A 20
Higherland. New 5D 32 (5B 6)
Higherland Ct. Kid 1D 20 (off Attwood St.)
Higher Woodcroft. Leek 5E 16
Highfield Av. C'dle 2G 45
Highfield Av. Kid 1E 20
Highfield Av. New 1G 33
Highfield Av. Stoke 5A 42
Highfield Clo. B Bri 7E 42
Highfield Ct. New 7F 33
Highfield Cres. C'dle 2G 45
Highfield Dri. Stoke 2D 40
Highfield Grange. New 1H 33
Highfield Pl. Bid 2C 14
Highfield Ri. Stoke 6J 39
Highfield Rd. Cong 6G 9
Highfield Rd. E. Bid 3C 14
Highfield Rd. W. Bid 3C 14
Highgate Clo. Stoke 1D 28
Highgrove Rd. Stoke 3J 39
Highland Clo. Bid M 2G 15
Highland Clo. B Bri 1F 49
Highland Dri. Stoke 5J 41
High La. Als B 7G 25
High La. Brn E 5F 23
High La. Stoke 5K 21
High Lowe Av. Cong 3J 9
High St. Bid 2B 14
High St. Big E 3H 25
High St. Cav 3F 43
High St. C'dle 3G 45
High St. Ches 5B 26
High St. Cong 5F 9
High St. Dil 2K 43

A-Z Stoke 61

High St. *Halm* 5D **24**
High St. *Har* 6H **13**
High St. *Kid* 7F **13**
High St. *Knut* 2B **32**
High St. *Leek* 3F **17**
High St. *Mow C* 3G **13**
High St. *New* 2G **33**
(May Bank)
High St. *New* 4E **32** (3C **6**)
(Newcastle-under-Lyme,
in three parts)
High St. *N'cpl* 1H **21**
High St. *Sand* 4F **21**
High St. *Sil* 3H **31**
High St. *Tal P* 5A **20**
High St. *Tun* 6G **21**
High St. *Wol* 6F **27**
Highton St. *Stoke* 3H **29**
Hightown. 6K **9**
Highup Rd. *Leek* 1C **16**
High View. *Mow C* 5E **12**
High Vw. *Stoke* 2B **48**
High Vw. Rd. *End* 1K **23**
Highview Rd. *Ful* 7F **49**
High Vw. Rd. *Leek* 4J **17**
Highway La. *K'le* 7E **30**
Higson Av. *Stoke* 5K **33**
Hilderstone Rd.
Stoke & Spot A 3A **48**
Hilgreen Rd. *Stoke* 1J **41**
Hillary Av. *Cong* 5J **9**
Hillary Rd. *Kid* 7E **12**
Hillary St. *Stoke* 6A **28**
Hillberry Clo. *Stoke* 3F **35**
Hillchurch St. *Stoke* . .1B **34** (2F **5**)
Hillcott Wlk. *Stoke* 3J **41**
Hill Cres. *Als B* 6G **25**
Hillcrest. *Leek* 3E **16**
Hillcrest Ho. *Stoke* . . .1C **34** (3G **5**)
Hillcrest St. *Stoke* 1C **34** (3G **5**)
Hillesden Ri. *Cong* 5H **9**
Hillfield Av. *Stoke* 2H **39**
Hillfields. *Cong* 3F **9**
Hill Fields Clo. *Cong* 3F **9**
Hillman St. *Stoke* 3H **29**
Hillport Av. *New* 5E **26**
Hillport Ho. New 5F **27**
(off Claremont Clo.)
Hillside. *New* 5D **32** (5A **6**)
Hillside Av. *End* 1K **23**
Hillside Av. *For* 6H **43**
Hillside Av. *Kid* 4D **20**
Hillside Av. *Stoke* 5A **42**
Hillside Clo. *Bid M* 1G **15**
Hillside Clo. *Ful* 7F **49**
Hillside Clo. *Mow C* 3G **13**
Hillside Clo. *Stoke* 1H **29**
Hillside Dri. *Leek* 5D **16**
Hillside Rd. *Stoke* 1H **29**
Hillside Rd. *Werr* 1C **36**
Hillside Wlk. *Stoke* . . .5G **33** (5H **7**)
Hill St. *New* 3D **32** (1B **6**)
Hill St. *Stoke* 6K **33**
Hillswood Av. *Leek* 3D **16**
Hillswood Clo. *End* 4K **23**
Hillswood Dri. *End* 3K **23**
Hill Ter. *A'ly* 2E **24**
Hill Top. 2G **23**
Hilltop Av. *New* 3H **33**
Hilltop Clo. *Brn E* 2G **23**
Hill Top Cres. *Stoke* 2B **48**
Hillview. *Leek* 4H **17**
Hill Vw. *Stoke* 2G **29**
Hill Village Rd. *Werr* 1D **36**
Hillwood Rd. *Mad H* 5B **30**
Hilton Ho. *Stoke* 6H **33**
Hilton Rd. *Stoke* 6G **33** (6H **7**)
Hincho Pl. *Stoke* 7D **22**
Hinckley Ct. *Cong* 4C **8**
Hinckley Gro. *Stoke* 2A **46**
Hinde St. *Stoke* 3B **34** (6E **5**)
Hines St. *Stoke* 1D **40**
Hinton Clo. *Stoke* 6E **40**
Hitchman St. *Stoke* 7D **34**
Hobart St. *Stoke* 5K **27**
Hobby Clo. *Stoke* 7B **42**
Hobson St. *Stoke* 4K **27**

Hodgefield. 1G **23**
Hodgkinson St. *New* 6C **26**
Hodnet Gro. *Stoke* 7A **28**
Hogarth Pl. *New* 6B **26**
Holbeach Av. *Stoke* 3F **35**
Holborn. *New* 4E **32** (3C **6**)
Holborn, The. *Mad* 3B **30**
Holbrook Wlk. *Stoke* 4H **35**
Holdcroft Dwellings. Stoke 1J **27**
(off Queens Av.)
Holdcroft Rd. *Stoke* 7G **29**
Holden Av. *New* 2G **33**
Holden Av. N. *Stoke* 4C **28**
Holden Av. S. *Stoke* 4C **28**
Holder St. *Stoke* 7A **28**
Holding Cres. *Halm* 5E **24**
Holditch Ind. Est. *New* 7C **26**
Holditch Rd. *New* 7C **26**
Holecroft St. *Stoke* 4K **27**
Holehouse La. *Brn E & End* . . .1H **23**
Holehouse La. *Sch G* 3K **11**
Holehouse Rd. *Stoke* 6G **29**
Holford St. *Cong* 4F **9**
Holland St. *Stoke* 1G **27**
Hollies Dri. *Stoke* 2B **48**
Hollies, The. *New* 3F **33** (1E **7**)
Hollings St. *Stoke* 1F **41**
Hollington Dri. *Stoke* 3K **21**
Hollins. 3A **20**
Hollins Cres. *Tal* 2B **20**
Hollins Grange. *Tal* 3A **20**
Hollinshead Av. *New* 1D **32**
Hollinshead Clo. *Sch G* 3C **12**
Hollinwood Clo. *Kid* 3B **20**
Hollinwood Rd. *Kid* 3B **20**
Hollinwood Pl. *Stoke* 6D **22**
Hollowood Wlk. *Stoke* 6C **22**
Hollow, The. *Cav* 4F **43**
Hollow, The. *Mow C* 5E **12**
Holly Bank. *Stoke* 7H **39**
Holly Bank Cres. *Stoke* 1K **39**
Hollybush. 3D **40**
Hollybush Cres. *Stoke* 2D **40**
Hollybush Rd. *Stoke* 3D **40**
Holly Cross. *K'le* 7H **31**
Holly Dri. *Stoke* 2B **36**
Holly La. *Als* 7F **11**
Holly La. *Har* 5H **13**
Holly M. *K'le* 6G **31**
Holly Pl. *Stoke* 2D **40**
Holly Rd. *New* 3A **26**
(Birch Ho. Rd.)
Holly Rd. *New* 3B **26**
(Cedar Rd.)
Holly Tree Dri. *Gil H* 2H **15**
Holly Wall. 6F **21**
Hollywall La. *Stoke* 7E **20**
(in two parts)
Hollywood La. *New* 4D **30**
Holmes Chapel Rd. *Cong* 3A **8**
Holmesfield Wlk. *Stoke* 3J **41**
Holmesville Av. *Cong* 5D **8**
Holmes Way. *Stoke* 3A **22**
Holm Oak Rd. *Mad* 1B **30**
Holst Dri. *Stoke* 6F **29**
Holyhead Cres. *Stoke* 2C **42**
Holywell Clo. *Knyp* 4D **14**
Homer Pl. *Stoke* 6A **22**
Homer St. *Stoke* 1D **34** (3H **5**)
Homeshire Ho. *Als* 7E **10**
Homestead St. *Stoke* 5J **35**
Homestead, The. *New* 3F **33**
Homestead, The. *Stoke* 1H **29**
Honeysuckle Av. *B Bri* 1G **49**
Honeywall. *Stoke* 6K **33**
Honeywall Ho. *Stoke* 6K **33**
Honeywall La. *Mad H* 5C **30**
Honeywood. *New* 2E **32**
Honiton Wlk. *Stoke* 3J **41**
Hood & Broomfield Fine
Art Gallery. 4G **33** (2G **7**)
Hoon Av. *New* 1E **32**
Hoover St. *Stoke* 1G **27**
Hopedale Clo. *New* 3E **38**
Hopedale Clo. *Stoke* 6G **35**
Hope St. *Big E* 1G **25**
Hope St. *Stoke* 1B **34** (2E **5**)

Hopkins Clo. *Cong* 4D **8**
Hopton Way. *Stoke* 3K **21**
Hopwood Pl. *Stoke* 2G **35**
Horace Lawton Ct. *Cong* 4F **9**
Horatius Rd. *New* 6A **26**
Hordley St. *Stoke* 2C **34** (4G **5**)
Hornby Dri. *Cong* 4C **8**
Hornby Row. *Stoke* 6K **33**
Horsecroft Cres. *Leek* 1H **17**
Horsecroft Gro. *Leek* 2H **17**
Horsley Gro. *Stoke* 6D **40**
Horton Dri. *Stoke* 2B **42**
Horton St. *Leek* 3G **17**
Horton St. *New* 4G **33** (2G **7**)
Horwood. *K'le* 7K **31**
Horwood Gdns. *Stoke* 3B **28**
Horwood Hall. *K'le* 6K **31**
Hose St. *Stoke* 1G **27**
Hoskins Rd. *Stoke* 6H **21**
Hot La. *Bid M* 1G **15**
Hot La. *Hot I & Stoke* 5A **28**
Hot La. Ind. Est. *Stoke* 4A **28**
Hougher Wall Rd. *A'ly* 3E **24**
Hough Hill. *Brn E* 2G **23**
Houghton St. *Stoke* . . .3B **34** (6F **5**)
Houghwood. 1K **29**
Houghwood La. *Stoc B* 7J **23**
Houldsworth Dri. *Stoke* 4A **22**
Housefield Rd. *Stoke* 5J **35**
Houseman Dri. *Stoke* 1A **42**
Houston Av. *End* 3K **23**
Hoveringham Dri. *Stoke* 4E **34**
Howard Clo. *Leek* 5D **16**
Howard Clo. *Werr* 1C **36**
Howard Cres. *Stoke* 3D **34**
Howard Gro. *New* 7D **32**
Howard Pl. *New* 7D **32**
Howard Pl. *Stoke* 3A **34**
Howard St. *Stoke* 4H **41**
Howard Wlk. *Stoke* 4H **41**
Howe Gro. *New* 3B **32**
Howey Hill. *Cong* 6F **9**
Howey La. *Cong* 5F **9**
Howson St. *Stoke* 2C **34** (5G **5**)
Hudson Wlk. Stoke 2H **41**
(off Caroline St.)
Hugh Bourne Pl. *B Frd* 1A **22**
Hughes Av. *New* 3E **32**
Hughes St. *Stoke* 5K **27**
Hughson Gro. *Stoke* 1D **28**
Hugo St. *Leek* 4F **17**
Hulland Clo. *New* 4J **31**
Hullock's Pool Rd. *Big E* 6E **18**
Hulme. 5B **36**
Hulme Clo. *New* 4J **31**
Hulme La. *Werr & Hul* 3B **36**
Hulme Rd. *Stoke* 1A **42**
Hulme St. *Stoke* 5H **33**
Hulme Walfield. 1D **8**
Hulse St. *Stoke* 7G **35**
Hulton Clo. *Cong* 6K **9**
Hulton Rd. *Stoke* 6G **29**
Hulton St. *Stoke* 7C **28**
Humber Dri. *Bid* 2D **14**
Humbert St. *Stoke* 2J **33**
Humber Way. *New* 3E **38**
Hungerford La. *Mad* 7A **30**
Hunsford Clo. Stoke 2H **41**
(off Goddard St.)
Huntbach St. *Stoke* 1B **34** (3F **5**)
Hunters Clo. *Bid* 2B **14**
Hunters Dri. *Stoke* 7J **33**
Hunters Way. *Stoke* 1J **39**
Huntilee Rd. *Stoke* 1H **27**
Huntingdon Pl. *Stoke* 6E **28**
Huntley. 7F **45**
Huntley Av. *Stoke* 7K **33**
Huntley Clo. *C'dle* 6G **45**
Huntley La. *C'dle* 6E **44**
Huntsbank Dri. *New* 3A **26**
Hunt St. *Stoke* 1H **27**
Huron Gro. *Stoke* 6K **39**
Hurricane Gro. *Stoke* 7F **21**
Hurst Clo. *Tal P* 5A **20**
Hurst St. *Stoke* 3F **41**
Hutchinson Wlk. *Stoke* 3F **41**
Hutton Dri. *Cong* 5J **9**

Hutton Way. *Stoke* 3J **35**
Huxley Pl. *Stoke* 2J **41**
Hyacinth Ct. *New* 3F **33**
Hyacinth Rd. *Stoke* 4H **33**
Hyde Pk. Ind. Est. *Stoke* 7B **34**
Hyndley Clo. *Stoke* 2F **35**
Hyssop Pl. *Stoke* 2C **28**

I

Ian Rd. *N'cpl* 1G **21**
Ibsen Rd. *Stoke* 2B **42**
Ikins Dri. *Big E* 2G **25**
Ilam Clo. *New* 4J **31**
Ilford Side. *Stoke* 6D **40**
Ilkley Pl. *New* 3G **31**
Imandra Clo. *Stoke* 7K **39**
Imex Bus. Pk. *Stoke* 7C **40**
(Bellringer Rd.)
I-Mex Bus. Pk. *Stoke* 1E **40**
(Old Tramway)
Imogen Clo. *Stoke* 7G **35**
Imperial Ct. *Stoke* 3C **34** (6G **5**)
Ingelow Clo. *Stoke* 4F **41**
Ingestre Sq. *Stoke* 6D **40**
Ingleborough Pl. *Stoke* 3J **29**
Ingleby Rd. *Stoke* 6D **40**
Inglefield Av. *Stoke* 3A **28**
Ingleton Gro. *Stoke* 7B **42**
Inglewood Dri. *New* 6F **27**
Inglewood Gro. *New* 6F **27**
Inglis St. *Stoke* 5B **34**
Inkerman Ter. *Leek* 2E **16**
Intake Rd. *Stoke* 7C **22**
Intone Fitness Cen. 7E **10**
Iona Pl. *Stoke* 3E **40**
Ipswich Wlk. *Stoke* 3G **35**
Irene Av. *New* 3G **33**
Irene Av. *Stoke* 1J **27**
Iris Clo. *Stoke* 1D **42**
Ironbridge Dri. *New* 3C **32**
Ironmarket. *New* 4E **32** (3D **6**)
Irvine Rd. *Werr* 1D **36**
Isherwood Pl. *Stoke* 2J **41**
Isis Clo. *Cong* 6H **9**
Islay Wlk. *Stoke* 3F **41**
Ivy Clo. *B Bri* 1G **49**
Ivy Gdns. *Cong* 5E **8**
Ivy Gro. *Stoke* 6J **39**
Ivyhouse Dri. *B'stn* 3D **46**
Ivy Ho. Rd. *Gil H* 2H **15**
Ivy Ho. Rd. *Stoke* 2D **34**
Ivy La. *Als* 1F **19**
Izaac Walton Way. *Mad* 3B **30**

J

Jack Ashley Ct. *Stoke* 7C **34**
Jackfield St. *Stoke* 3A **28**
Jack Haye La. *L Oaks* 3J **29**
Jack Hayes. 4K **29**
Jackson Rd. *Cong* 2G **9**
Jackson St. *Stoke* 4K **27**
Jacqueline St. *Stoke* 7F **21**
Jade Ct. *Stoke* 2J **41**
Jamage Ind. Est. *Tal P* 5K **19**
Jamage Rd. *Tal P* 5A **20**
(in two parts)
James Brindley Clo. *Stoke*
 . . . . .3K **33** (6B **4**)
James Brindley Mus. 3E **16**
James Cres. *Werr* 1D **36**
James St. *Leek* 4E **16**
James St. *New* 7F **27**
James St. *Stoke* 1J **39**
James Way. *Knyp* 4K **13**
Jamieson Clo. *Als* 6F **11**
Janet Pl. *Stoke* 1D **34**
Janson St. *Stoke* 5J **39**
Jasmine Clo. *B Bri* 7G **43**
Jasmine Cres. *N'cpl* 1G **21**
Jasmine Way. *Pac* 1J **21**
Jason St. *New* 3D **32** (1B **6**)
Jasper Clo. *B'stn* 3E **46**
Jasper Clo. *New* 5E **26**

Jasper St. *Stoke* 2B **34** (5F **5**)
Java Cres. *Stoke* 7A **40**
Jaycean Av. *Stoke* 7H **21**
Jean Clo. *Stoke* 2K **27**
Jefferson St. *Stoke* 7G **21**
Jenkinson Clo. *New* 5C **32** (5A **6**)
Jenkins St. *Stoke* 4J **27**
Jerbourg Clo. *New* 2B **38**
Jeremy Clo. *Stoke* 7J **33**
Jersey Clo. *Cong* 5J **9**
Jersey Clo. *New* 2B **38**
Jersey Cres. *Stoke* 5H **41**
Jervison St. *Stoke* 3A **22**
Jervis St. *Stoke* 7C **28** (2H **5**)
    (in two parts)
Jesmond Gro. *Stoke* 6D **40**
Joanhurst Cres. *Stoke*
    . . . . .3A **34** (6C **4**)
Jodrell Vw. *Kid* 3E **20**
John Bright St. *Stoke* . .7C **28** (1H **5**)
John Offley Rd. *Mad* 2A **30**
John O'Gaunt's Rd. *New*
    . . . . .4D **32** (3B **6**)
John Rhodes Way. *Stoke* 6F **21**
Johnson Av. *New* 1D **32**
Johnson Clo. *Cong* 6J **9**
Johnson Pl. *Stoke* 5A **22**
Johnstone Av. *Werr* 1D **36**
John St. *Bid* 3B **14**
John St. *Ches* 4B **26**
John St. *Cong* 5E **8**
John St. *Knut* 3B **32**
John St. *Leek* 4F **17**
John St. *New* 4G **33** (3G **7**)
John St. *Stoke* 2B **34** (4F **5**)
Joiner's Square. 3D **34**
Joiner's Sq. Ind. Est. *Stoke* . . .6G **5**
Jolley St. *Stoke* 3B **28**
Jolliffe St. *Leek* 4F **17**
    (off Cornhill St.)
Jolyon Clo. *Stoke* 7G **35**
Jonathan Rd. *Stoke* 3B **46**
Jordan St. *Stoke* 3A **34** (6C **4**)
Joseph Cres. *Als* 1G **19**
Joseph St. *Stoke* 4H **27**
Josiah Wedgwood St.
    Stoke 2K **33** (4B **4**)
Joyce Av. *Stoke* 2A **28**
Jubilee Av. *Stoke* . . .2K **33** (5B **4**)
Jubilee Clo. *Bid* 3C **14**
Jubilee Rd. *Cong* 5G **9**
Jubilee Rd. *New* 2G **33**
Jubilee Rd. *Stoke* 6J **39**
Jubilee Ter. *Leek* 3E **16**
Judgefield La. *Brn E* 1E **22**
Judith Gro. *Stoke* 1B **40**
Jug Bank. *Stoke* 6A **28**
June Rd. *Stoke* 7G **35**
Juniper Clo. *New* 3B **26**
Juniper Clo. *Stoke* 1B **48**
Jupiter St. *Stoke* 3B **28**
Justin Clo. *New* 6G **27**

K

Kara Pl. *Stoke* 6A **40**
Kaydor Clo. *Werr* 1C **36**
Kearsley Way. *Stoke* 6D **40**
Keary St. *Stoke* 7A **34**
Keates St. *Stoke* 4J **27**
Keats Dri. *Rode H* 2F **11**
Keats Gdns. *Kid* 3D **20**
Keble Way. *Stoke* 4E **40**
Kedleston Rd. *Stoke* 2K **27**
Keele. 6G **31**
Keele By-Pass. *K'le* 5F **31**
Keele Observatory. 6K **31**
Keele Rd. *K'le & New* . . .6H **31** (5A **6**)
Keele Rd. *Mad H* 5C **30**
Keele Science Pk. *Uni K* 6J **31**
Keele St. *Stoke* 7G **21**
Keele University Leisure Cen.
    . . . . .6J **31**
Keeling Rd. *C'dle* 3H **45**
Keelings Dri. *Stoke* 2H **39**
Keelings Rd. *Stoke* 7C **28** (1H **5**)

Keeling St. *New* 6F **27**
Keene Clo. *Stoke* 1D **28**
Keepers Clo. *B Bri* 1H **49**
Kelly Grn. *Stoke* 5A **22**
Kelman Rd. *Stoke* 7F **35**
Kelmore Clo. *Stoke* 2G **41**
Kelsall St. *Cong* 4G **9**
Kelsall St. *Stoke* 3A **28**
Kelsall Way. *A'ly* 3E **24**
Kelvin Av. *Stoke* 6C **28**
Kelvin St. *New* 1G **33**
Kemball Av. *Stoke* 2B **40**
Kemball Av. *Stoke* 3A **22**
Kempthorne Rd. *Stoke*
    . . . . .3C **34** (6H **5**)
Kempton Gro. *C'dle* 1H **45**
Kendal Ct. *Cong* 5C **8**
Kendal Gro. *Stoke* 3J **35**
Kendal Pl. *New* 7E **32**
Kendrick St. *Stoke* 3H **41**
Kenelyn Cres. *Stoke* 2D **40**
Kenilworth Gro. *New* 2H **33**
Kenilworth Gro. *Stoke* 5A **42**
Kenilworth Wlk. *C'dle* 4E **44**
Kenley Av. *End* 1K **23**
Kennedy Rd. *Stoke* 7A **40**
Kennedy Wlk. *Werr* 1C **36**
Kennermont Rd. *Stoke* 7H **29**
Kennet Clo. *New* 3E **38**
Kennington Oval. *Stoke* 6B **40**
Kennet Dri. *Cong* 6H **9**
Kensington Ct. *Als* 6A **10**
Kensington Ct. *Stoke* 3H **39**
    (Trent Vale)
Kensington Ct. *Stoke* 7H **21**
    (Tunstall)
Kensington Rd. *Stoke* 2J **39**
Kensworth Clo. *New* 3D **38**
Kent Dri. *Cong* 3F **9**
Kent Dri. *End* 5K **23**
Kent Gro. *New* 4A **26**
Kentmere Clo. *New* 1G **41**
Kentmere Pl. *New* 7E **32**
    (in two parts)
Kent Pl. *Stoke* 7D **34**
Kents Row. *B'stn* 5D **46**
Kenworthy St. *Stoke* 7H **21**
Kersbrook Clo. *Stoke* 1B **46**
Kervis Gro. *Stoke* 1C **46**
Kesteven Rd. *Stoke* 2G **35**
Kestrel Av. *Stoke* 7D **42**
Kestrel Clo. *Cong* 6G **9**
Kestrel Clo. *Knyp* 4A **14**
Kestrel La. *C'dle* 3H **45**
Keswick Ct. *Cong* 5C **8**
Keswick Pl. *New* 7E **32**
Kettering Dri. *Stoke* 3E **34**
Ketton Clo. *Stoke* 3A **22**
Keynsham Wlk. *Stoke* 2C **28**
Keyworth Wlk. *Stoke* 3F **35**
Kibworth Gro. *Stoke* 7B **28**
Kidbrooke Pl. *Stoke* 6C **40**
Kidsgrove. 2C **20**
Kidsgrove Bank. *Kid* 3E **20**
Kidsgrove Rd. *Stoke* 3F **21**
Kidsgrove Sports Cen. 2C **20**
KIDSGROVE STATION. RAIL
    . . . . .2C **30**
Kilburn Pl. *Stoke* 3E **34**
Kildare St. *Stoke* 4H **41**
    (in two parts)
Kilndown Clo. *Stoke* . .3K **33** (6B **4**)
Kiln La. *Leek* 3D **16**
Kilsby Gro. *Stoke* 2G **29**
Kimberley Grange.
    New 3E **32** (1C **6**)
Kimberley Rd. *New* . . .3E **32** (1C **6**)
Kimberley Rd. *Stoke* . .2K **33** (5A **4**)
Kimberley St. *Stoke* 4G **41**
Kimberly Pl. *New* 4J **31**
King Charles Clo. *Stoke* 7B **42**
King Edward St. *C'dle* 2H **45**
Kingcross St. *Stoke* 3H **41**
Kingfisher Clo. *Cong* 6G **9**
Kingfisher Clo. *Mad* 6A **30**
Kingfisher Cres. *C'dle* 3J **45**

Kingfisher Cres. *Ful* 7F **49**
Kingfisher Gro. *Stoke* 1B **28**
King George St. *Stoke*
    . . . . .7C **28** (1H **5**)
King's Av. *New* 7F **27**
Kingsbridge Av. *New* 1E **38**
Kingsbury Gro. *Stoke* 6E **28**
Kingsclere Gro. *Stoke* 5D **28**
King's Cft. *Stoke* 4G **33** (3H **7**)
Kingsdale Clo. *Stoke* 7B **42**
Kingsdown M. *New* 2F **39**
Kingsfield Cres. *Bid* 2C **14**
Kingsfield Oval.
    Stoke 4G **33** (2G **7**)
Kingsfield Rd. *Bid* 2C **14**
Kingsfield Rd. *Stoke* . .4G **33** (2H **7**)
Kingsford Pl. *Stoke* 6B **42**
Kingside Gro. *Stoke* 2B **46**
Kingsland Av. *Stoke* 2J **39**
Kingsley Clo. *Tal P* 5A **20**
Kingsley Rd. *Stoke* 4J **9**
Kingsley Rd. *Tal P* 5A **20**
Kingsley Rd. *Werr & Dil* 1G **37**
Kingsley St. *Stoke* 5B **42**
Kingsmead Rd. *Stoke* 7A **42**
Kingsnorth Pl. *Stoke* 1C **48**
Kings Pl. *Stoke* 3G **33** (1H **7**)
Kings Rd. *Stoke* 5K **39**
Kings Ter. *Stoke* 4G **33** (2H **7**)
Kingston Av. *Stoke* 5D **28**
Kingston Pl. *Bid* 2K **15**
Kingston Rd. *Stoke* 1D **28**
King St. *C' H'th* 2D **32**
King St. *A'ly* 3E **24**
King St. *Bid* 2B **14**
King St. *Bug* 3H **9**
King St. *Ches* 5B **26**
King St. *Kid* 1D **20**
King St. *Leek* 4F **17**
King St. *New* 4F **33** (3E **7**)
King St. *Tal P* 5A **20**
    (in two parts)
Kingsway. *Stoke* 6A **34**
Kingsway E. *New* 7E **32**
Kingsway W. *New* 7D **32**
Kingswell Rd. *Stoke* . . .4G **33** (3H **7**)
Kingswinford Pl. *Stoke* 5C **28**
Kingswood. *Kid* 2E **20**
King William St. *Stoke* 1H **27**
Kinnersley Av. *Kid* 3C **20**
Kinnersley St. *Kid* 1D **20**
Kinsey St. *Cong* 5G **9**
Kinsey St. *New* 4J **31**
Kinver St. *Stoke* 3B **28**
Kipling Way. *Stoke* 4J **35**
Kirby St. *Stoke* 6K **27**
Kirkbride Clo. *Stoke* 2J **41**
Kirkham St. *Stoke* 7K **33**
Kirkland La. *Stoke* 6K **33**
Kirk St. *Stoke* 2B **28**
Kirkstall Pl. *New* 2E **38**
Kirkstone Ct. *Cong* 6C **8**
Kirkup Wlk. *Stoke* 3F **41**
Kirkwall Gro. *Stoke* 2G **29**
Kite Gro. *Kid* 7G **13**
Kite Gro. *Stoke* 7B **42**
Knarsdale Clo. *Stoke* 1J **41**
Knebworth Ct. *Cong* 7K **9**
Knenhall. 7K **47**
Knenhall Bk. *Knen* 6J **47**
Knenhall Bk. La. *Knen* 7K **47**
Knightley. *Mad* 7A **30**
Knightsbridge Way. *Stoke* . . .1G **27**
    (off Madeira Pl.)
Knights Cft. *K'le* 6G **31**
Knight St. *Stoke* 7G **21**
Kniveden La. *Leek* 4H **17**
Knowl Bank. 6A **24**
Knowlbank Rd. *A'ly* 6A **24**
Knowle Rd. *Bid* 3B **14**
Knowle St. *Stoke* 5K **33**
Knowle Style. 3B **14**
Knowle Wood Vw. *Stoke* 3E **40**
Knowsley La. *Chu L* 6B **12**
Knutsford Old Rd. *Chu L* 5G **11**
Knutsford Rd.
    Chu L & Rode H 5G **11**

Knutton. 2B **32**
Knutton La. *New* 3C **32** (2A **6**)
Knutton Recreation Cen. . . .3B **32**
Knutton Rd. *New* 7F **27**
Knype Clo. *New* 5D **26**
Knypersley. 4B **14**
Knypersley Gdns. *Knyp* 5C **14**
Knypersley Rd. *Stoke* 6D **40**
Knype Way. *Knyp* 4A **14**
Knype Way. *New* 5D **26**
Kyffin Rd. *Stoke* 6G **29**

L

Laburnum Clo. *B Bri* 1H **49**
Laburnum Clo. *Cong* 3B **8**
Laburnum Clo. *Kid* 3B **20**
Laburnum Gro. *Stoke* 3D **40**
Laburnum Pl. *New* 3A **26**
Laburnum Pl. *Stoke* 6A **42**
Lacy Ct. *Cong* 5H **9**
Ladderedge. *Leek* 7B **16**
Ladderedge Country Pk. 6E **16**
Lad La. *New* 4E **32** (3D **6**)
Lady Bennett Ct. *Stoke* 3F **41**
    (off Grosvenor St)
Ladydale Clo. *Leek* 5G **17**
Ladymoor Gate. 6G **15**
Ladymoor La. *Brn E* 6G **15**
Ladysmith Rd. *Stoke*
    . . . . .2K **33** (5A **4**)
Ladysmith St. *Stoke* 4G **41**
Ladywell Rd. *Stoke* 1G **27**
    (in two parts)
Lagonda Clo. *Knyp* 5A **14**
Lakeside. *Stoke* 7J **27**
Lake Vw. *Als* 1D **18**
Lake Vw. *Cong* 5D **8**
Lakewood Dri. *B'stn* 3D **46**
Lakewood Gro. *Stoke*
    . . . . .1K **33** (3A **4**)
Lally Pl. *B Frd* 1A **22**
Lambert's La. *A'bry* 6D **8**
    (in three parts)
Lambert's La. *Cong* 7G **9**
Lambert St. *Stoke* 1H **27**
Lambourne Dri. *Stoke* 3H **29**
Lambourn Pl. *Stoke* 6C **40**
Lamb St. *Kid* 1D **20**
Lamb St. *Stoke* 1B **34** (3F **5**)
Lamerton Gro. *Stoke* 4A **42**
Lamotte Clo. *Stoke* 1G **41**
Lanark Walks. *New* 6C **32**
Lancaster Av. *Ful* 6F **49**
Lancaster Av. *Leek* 2G **17**
Lancaster Av. *New* . . .5G **33** (4G **7**)
Lancaster Bldgs. *New*
    . . . . .4E **32** (3D **6**)
    (off Ironmarket)
Lancaster Cres. *Stoke*
    . . . . .5G **33** (5G **7**)
Lancaster Dri. *Stoke* 7E **22**
Lancaster Rd. *New* . . .5G **33** (4G **7**)
Lanchester Clo. *Knyp* 4A **14**
Lancia Clo. *Knyp* 5A **14**
Lander Pl. *Stoke* 5B **22**
Landon St. *Stoke* 3H **41**
Landrake Gro. *Stoke* 4J **21**
Landseer Pl. *New* 6B **26**
Lane Ends. 1J **21**
La. Farm Gro. *Stoke* 5D **28**
Lanehead Rd. *Stoke* . . .2J **33** (5A **4**)
Langdale Ct. *Cong* 6C **8**
Langdale Cres. *Stoke* 5C **28**
Langdale Rd. *New* 1E **38**
Langford Rd. *New* 2D **38**
Langford St. *Stoke* 2G **35**
Langford St. *Leek* 4E **16**
Langham Rd. *Stoke* 3F **29**
Langland Dri. *Stoke* 4E **40**
Langley Clo. *New* 2A **26**
Langley St. *Stoke* 4G **33** (2H **7**)
Langton Ct. *Werr* 1B **36**
Lansbury Gro. *Stoke* 3C **42**
Lansdell Av. *New* 6D **26**

Lansdowne Clo. *Leek* 4C 16
Lansdowne Cres. *Werr* 1C 36
Lansdowne Rd. *Stoke*
........5H 33 (4H 7)
Lansdowne St. *Stoke* 5G 41
Lapwing Clo. *Pac* 2H 21
Lapwing Rd. *Kid* 7G 13
Larch Clo. *Kid* 3D 20
Larch Ct. *Stoke* 5K 27
(off Commercial St.)
Larch Gro. *Stoke* 4D 40
Larchmount Clo. *Stoke* 7A 40
Larch Pl. *New* 4B 26
Larchwood. *K'le* 7H 31
Lark Av. *Kid* 7G 13
Larkfield. *Kid* 2E 20
Larkin Av. *Stoke* 2J 41
Larksfield Rd. *Stoke* 3C 28
Larkspur Gro. *New* ...3F 33 (1E 7)
Lascelles St. *Stoke* 1G 27
Lask Edge. 3J 15
Laski Cres. *Stoke* 4C 42
Latebrook. 5E 20
Latebrook Clo. *Stoke* 4F 21
Latham Gro. *Stoke* 4A 22
Latimer Way. *Stoke* 3H 35
Lauder Pl. N. *Stoke* 5K 35
Lauder Pl. S. *Stoke* 5K 35
Laurel Cres. *Werr* 2B 36
Laurel Dri. *Har* 7H 13
Laurel Gro. *Stoke* 4C 40
Lauren Clo. *Stoke* 7D 34
Lavender Av. *B Bri* 1G 49
Lavender Clo. *Stoke* 1D 42
Laverock Gro. *Mad* 2B 30
Lawley St. *Stoke* 3J 41
Lawn Farm Cres. *Stoke* 6J 35
Lawrence St. *Stoke* 3A 34 (6D 4)
Lawson Ter. *Knut* 2B 32
Lawson Ter. *New* 6E 26
Lawton Av. *Chu L* 7A 12
Lawton Coppice. *Chu L* 6B 12
Lawton Cres. *Bid* 2C 14
Lawton-gate. 5H 11
Lawtongate Est. *Chu L* 5H 11
Lawton Heath. 4G 11
Lawton Heath End. 4E 10
Lawton Heath Rd. *Chu L* 4F 11
Lawton Rd. *Als* 6E 10
Lawton St. *Bid* 2C 14
Lawton St. *Cong* 5G 9
Lawton St. *Rook* 6F 13
Lawton St. *Stoke* 2K 27
Laxey Rd. *New* 3D 32
Laxton Gro. *Stoke* 3B 46
Leacroft Rd. *Stoke* 6B 42
Leadbeater Av. *Stoke* 1J 39
Leadendale. 4A 48
Leadendale La. *R'gh C* 4K 47
Leadendale M. *Stoke* 6A 42
Leaford Wlk. *Stoke* 3E 34
Leaks All. *Stoke* 4G 41
Leamington Gdns. *New* 2H 33
Leamington Rd. *Cong* 4B 8
Lea Pl. *Stoke* 4C 42
Leaside Rd. *Stoke* 1H 39
Leason Rd. *Stoke* 4B 42
Leason St. *Stoke* 6A 34
Leaswood Clo. *New* 4F 39
Leaswood Pl. *New* 4F 39
Lea, The. *Stoke* 7A 40
Lea Way. *Als* 7E 10
Leawood Rd. *Stoke* 3H 39
Ledbury Cres. *Stoke* 7E 28
Ledstone Way. *Stoke* 2K 41
Leech Av. *New* 6C 26
Leech St. *New* 5F 33 (5F 7)
Leeds St. *Stoke* 1E 40
Lee Gro. *New* 2E 38
Leek. 3F 17
LEEK MOORLANDS HOSPITAL.
........4H 17
Leek New Rd.
Stoke & Stoc B (ST2,ST9)
........2F 29
Leek New Rd. *Stoke* (ST6,ST1)
........5A 28

Leek Rd. *Brn E* 4H 23
Leek Rd. *C'dle* 1E 44
Leek Rd. *Cong* 7H 9
Leek Rd. *Stoc B & End* 6J 23
Leek Rd. *Stoke* (ST1)
........3C 34 (6H 5)
Leek Rd. *Stoke* (ST2) 7F 29
Leek Rd. *Stoke* (ST4) 5B 34
Leek Rd. *W Coy & Werr* 7C 36
Leek Rd. *Wet R & C'dle* 1J 37
Leek Town F.C. (Harrison Pk.)
........3D 16
Leese St. *Stoke* 6A 34
Legge St. *New* 5F 33 (5F 7)
Leicester Av. *Als* 5D 10
Leicester Clo. *New* 1F 39
Leicester Pl. *Stoke* 3H 35
Leigh La. *Stoke* 3F 27
Leigh Rd. *Cong* 2K 9
Leigh St. *Stoke* 2K 27
Leighton Clo. *Stoc B* 7H 23
Lennox Rd. *Stoke* 4J 41
Lenthall Av. *Cong* 7H 9
Leonard Av. *Bad G* 1G 29
Leonard Dri. *Brn E* 5G 23
Leonard St. *Leek* 4G 17
Leonard St. *Stoke* 2A 28
Leonora St. *Stoke* 5J 27
Leopold St. *Stoke* 7D 34
Lessways Clo. *New* 4E 26
Lessways Wlk. *Stoke* 5J 27
Lester Clo. *Als* 6E 10
Leveson Rd. *Stoke* 5J 39
Leveson St. *Stoke* 4H 41
Levita Rd. *Stoke* 2J 39
Lewisham Dri. *Stoke* 4F 21
Lewis St. *Stoke* 5A 34
Lexham Pl. *Stoke* 4K 41
Leycett. 3D 30
Leycett La. *Mad H & Ley* 5C 30
Leycett Rd. *S Hay* 1E 30
Leyfield Rd. *Stoke* 1A 46
Ley Gdns. *Stoke* 4F 41
Leyland Grn. *Stoke* 4K 21
(off Coppull Pl.)
Leys Dri. *New* 2B 38
Leys La. *Stoke* 2H 29
Liberty La. *Stoke* 1B 28
(off Bradeley Village)
Libra Pl. *Stoke* 5J 21
Lichfield Clo. *New* 3A 32
Lichfield Rd. *Tal* 4A 20
Lichfield St. *Stoke* 2B 34 (4F 5)
Liddle St. *Stoke* 7K 33
Lidgate Clo. *Stoke* 4E 40
Lidgate Wlk. *New* 4F 39
Lid La. *C'dle* 3F 45
(in two parts)
Light Oaks. 3J 29
Light Oaks Av. *L Oaks* 3J 29
Lightwater Gro. *Stoke* 3E 28
Lightwood. 7K 41
Lightwood Rd. *New* 3A 26
Lightwood Rd.
Stoke & R'gh C 4H 41
Lilac Clo. *New* 3A 26
Lilac Clo. *Stoke* 1D 42
Lilac Ct. *Cong* 5G 9
Lilac Gro. *Stoke* 3D 40
Lilleshall Rd. *New* 1G 39
Lilleshall St. *Stoke* 4H 41
Lillydale Rd. *Stoke* 2G 35
Lily St. *New* 7F 27
Lime Clo. *Stoke* 1D 42
Lime Gro. *Als* 7F 11
Lime Gro. *B'stn* 3E 46
Limes, The. *New* 5F 27
Lime Kiln La. *Chu L* 1B 20
Lime St. *Cong* 5F 9
Lime St. *Stoke* 1A 40
Lime Tree Av. *Cong* 4D 8
Limewood Clo. *B Bri* 1H 49
Linacre Way. *Stoke* 1K 41
Lincoln Av. *New* 1F 39
Lincoln Gro. *New* 1F 39

Lincoln Rd. *Kid* 1C 20
Lincoln Rd. *Stoke* 5K 27
Lincoln St. *Stoke* 2C 34 (4H 5)
Lindale Clo. *Cong* 2J 9
Lindale Gro. *Stoke* 7C 42
Linda Rd. *Stoke* 6H 21
Linden Clo. *Cong* 7J 9
Linden Clo. *New* 2E 32
Linden Dri. *Gil H* 1B 14
Linden Gro. *Gil H* 2H 15
Linden Gro. *New* 2E 32
Linden Pl. *Stoke* 5E 40
Lindley Pl. *Stoke* 3B 48
Lindley St. *Stoke* 5A 28
Lindop Ct. *Stoke* 3G 5
Lindops La. *Mad* 6A 30
Lindop St. *Stoke* 1C 34 (3G 5)
Lindsay Hall. *K'le* 7J 31
Lindsay St. *Stoke* 2A 34 (5D 4)
Lindsay Way. *Als* 6B 10
Lindum Av. *Stoke* 7B 40
Line Houses. 5E 20
Linfield Rd. *Stoke* 1C 34 (3G 5)
Lingard St. *Stoke* 4K 27
Lingfield Av. *Brn E* 3F 23
Linhope Gro. *Stoke* 7C 42
Linkend Clo. *Stoke* 7E 28
Links Av. *New* 1E 32
Linksway. *Cong* 7G 9
Linksway Clo. *Cong* 7H 9
Linley Gro. *Als* 7G 11
Linley La. *Als* 6G 11
Linley Rd. *Als* 7G 11
Linley Rd. *Stoke* 5H 33 (4H 7)
Linley Rd. *Tal* 2J 19
Linley St. *Stoke* 2K 19
Linley Trad. Est. *Tal* 2K 19
Linnburn Rd. *Stoke* 2J 41
Linnet Way. *Bid* 2D 14
Linwood Way. *Stoke* 6H 21
Lionel Gro. *Stoke* 6H 33
Lion Gro. *New* 4B 26
Lion St. *Cong* 5F 9
Lion St. *Stoke* 6K 33
Lisbon Pl. *New* 6B 32
Liskeard Clo. *Stoke* 4F 35
Litley Dri. *C'dle* 6G 45
Little Chell. 6J 21
Lit. Chell La. *Stoke* 6J 21
Lit. Cliffe Rd. *Stoke* 2D 40
Lit. Eaves La. *Stoke* 6H 29
Little-Field. *Stoke* 2H 39
Little La. *R'gh C* 3K 47
Little Madeley. 6B 30
Little-moss. 5B 12
Lit. Moss Clo. *Sch G* 5B 12
Lit. Moss La. *Sch G* 5B 12
Little Row. *Fen I* 5E 34
Little Row. *Kid* 1E 20
(off Brights Av.)
Little St. *Cong* 5F 9
Littondale Clo. *Cong* 2H 9
Liverpool Rd. *Kid* 1C 20
Liverpool Rd. *New* 7D 26 (1C 6)
(in two parts)
Liverpool Rd. *Red S* 1A 26
Liverpool Rd. *Stoke* 6A 34
Liverpool Rd. E.
Chu L & Kid 7A 12
Liverpool Rd. W. *Chu L* 6G 11
Livingstone St. *Leek* 4G 17
Livingstone St. *Stoke* 2B 28
Lloyd St. *Stoke* 4H 41
Loachbrook Av. *Cong* 5C 8
Lockerbie Clo. *Leek* 4J 17
Locketts La. *Stoke* 4H 41
(Lightwood Rd.)
Locketts La. *Stoke* 4J 41
(Normacot Rd.)
Lockett St. *Stoke* 6C 28
Lockington Av. *Stoke* 3J 35
Lockley St. *Stoke* 7D 28
Lockwood St. *New* 4G 33 (3G 7)
Lockwood St. *Stoke* 1G 29
Lodge Barn Rd. *Knyp* 4E 14
Lodge Gro. *New* 6F 27
Lodge Rd. *Als* 6D 10
Lodge Rd. *Stoke* 6H 33 (6H 7)

Lodge Rd. *Tal P* 5A 20
Loftus St. *Stoke* 7A 28 (1D 4)
Loganbeck Gro. *Stoke* 1J 41
Lomas St. *Stoke* 3K 33
Lombardy Gro. *Stoke* 4B 42
Lomond Gro. *C'dle* 2H 45
Lomond Wlk. *Stoke* 7E 40
London Rd. *Ches & New* 4B 26
London Rd. *New* 5F 33 (5E 7)
London Rd. *Stoke* 3H 39
London St. *Leek* 4G 17
Longbridge Hayes Rd.
Stoke 4F 27
Longbrook Av. *Stoke* 4E 40
Longclough Rd. *New* 2A 26
Longdoles Av. *Stoke* 3K 41
Longdown Rd. *Cong* 4A 8
Longfield Rd. *Stoke* ...5G 33 (5H 7)
Longford Wlk. *Stoke* 3F 35
Long La. *Ful* 7F 49
Long La. *Har* 6H 13
Longley Rd. *Stoke* 1H 41
Long Mdw. *New* 3F 39
Longnor Pl. *Stoke* 3F 35
Longport. 4G 27
Longport Rd. *Stoke* 5G 27
LONGPORT STATION. RAIL
........5G 27
Long Row. *Cav* 3E 42
Long Row. *Kid* 2D 20
Longsdon. 7A 16
Longsdon Clo. *New* 3K 25
Longsdon Gro. *Stoke* 2K 41
Longshaw Av. *New* 5E 26
Longshaw St. *Stoke* 4G 27
Longton. 3H 41
Longton Exchange. *Stoke* 3G 41
(off Strand, The)
Longton Hall Rd. *Stoke* 4E 40
LONGTON COTTAGE HOSPITAL.
........5J 41
Longton Rd. *B'stn* 6D 46
Longton Rd. *Knen* 7J 47
Longton Rd. *Stoke* 7K 39
LONGTON STATION. RAIL 2G 41
Long Valley Rd. *Gil H* 2H 15
Longview Av. *Als* 6F 11
Longview Clo. *Stoke* 1J 41
Lonsdale St. *Stoke* 7A 34
Loomer Rd. *New* 7A 26
Loomer Rd. Ind. Est. *New* 7B 26
Lords Clo. *Stoke* 7C 40
Lordship La. *Stoke* 6B 34
Lordshire Pl. *Pac* 2J 21
Lord St. *Bid* 3C 14
Lord St. *Stoke* 3B 28
Lorien Clo. *Leek* 5D 16
Loring Rd. *New* 6E 26
Loring Ter. S. *New* 6F 27
Lorne St. *Stoke* 3K 27
Lorraine St. *Pac* 2J 21
Lotus Av. *Knyp* 4A 14
Loughborough Wlk. *Stoke* 2H 41
Louise Dri. *Stoke* 3E 40
Louise St. *Stoke* 3K 27
Louvain Av. *Stoke* 5C 28
Lovatt Av. *New* 1D 32
Lovatt St. *Stoke* 6A 34
Loveage Dri. *Stoke* 2G 35
Love La. *B'ton* 1D 10
Loveston Gro. *Stoke* 2J 41
Love Av. *Cong* 5G 9
Lowe Hill. 6J 17
Lowell Dri. *Stoke* 2K 41
Lwr. Ash Rd. *Kid* 3B 20
Lwr. Bedford St.
Stoke 3K 33 (6A 4)
Lwr. Bethesda St.
Stoke 2B 34 (5F 5)
Lwr. Bryan St. *Stoke* ...7B 28 (1E 5)
Lwr. Cross St. *L'tn* 2H 41
Lwr. Foundry St.
Stoke 1B 34 (3E 5)
Lower Hadderidge. *Stoke* 4J 27
Lower Heath. 2G 9
Lower Heath. *Cong* 3G 9

Lwr. Heath Av. *Cong* 2G **9**
Lwr. Heath Ter. *Cong* 3G **9**
Lwr. High St. *Mow C* 3G **13**
Lwr. Mayer St. *Stoke* . . .7C **28** (1G **5**)
Lwr. Milehouse La. *Knut* 3C **32**
Lwr. Oxford Rd. *New*
. . . . .3H **33** (1H **7**)
Lwr. Park St. *Cong* 4G **9**
Lwr. Spring Rd. *Stoke* 4J **41**
(in two parts)
Lower St. *New* 4E **32** (2C **6**)
Lower St. *Stoke* 5K **27**
Lowe's Pas. *Stoke* 4J **41**
Lowe St. *Stoke* 6A **34**
Lowfield Dri. *New* 7H **27**
Lowhurst Dri. *Stoke* 4J **21**
Lowlands Rd. *Stoke* 7D **20**
Lowndes Clo. *Stoke* 7J **33**
Low St. *Rode H* 2F **11**
Lowther Pl. *Leek* 4H **17**
Lowther St. *Stoke* 7A **28** (1C **4**)
Lowthorpe Way. *Stoke* 4K **35**
Loxley Pl. *Stoke* 7A **42**
Lucas St. *Stoke* 5H **27**
Lucerne Pl. *New* 6B **32**
Ludbrook Rd. *Stoke* 1G **41**
Ludford Clo. *New* 2A **26**
Ludlow St. *Stoke* 1C **34** (3H **5**)
Ludwall Rd. *Stoke* 5K **41**
Lugano Clo. *New* 7C **32**
Lukesland Av. *Stoke* 7H **33**
Luke St. *Stoke* 5H **27**
Lulworth Gro. *Stoke* 5J **21**
Lumpy St. *Cong* 4E **8**
Lundy Rd. *Stoke* 3E **40**
Lune Clo. *Cong* 6H **9**
Lunt Moss **3A 12**
Lydford Pl. *Stoke* 3A **42**
Lydia Dri. *Stoke* 6E **28**
Lyme Brook Pl. *Stoke* 3H **39**
Lyme Ct. *New* 6F **7**
Lymedale Pk. *New* 7B **26**
Lymedale Small Firms Cen.
Lyme B 7C **26**
Lyme Dri. *Park* 7G **33**
Lyme Gro. *New* 2F **33**
Lyme Rd. *Stoke* 5C **42**
Lymes Rd. *But* . . . . . .7G **31** & 2A **38**
Lymes, The. **3A 38**
Lyme Valley Rd. *New* . . .6E **32** (5D **6**)
Lymewood Clo. *New* . . .5E **32** (5C **6**)
Lymewood Gro. *New* . . .6E **32** (6C **6**)
Lyminster Gro. *Stoke* 3G **29**
Lynam St. *Stoke* 6K **33**
Lynam Way. *Mad* 1B **30**
Lyndhurst Dri. *Brn L* 4K **13**
Lyndhurst St. *Stoke* 4H **27**
Lyneside Rd. *Knyp* 4A **14**
Lynmouth Clo. *Bid* 4B **14**
Lynmouth Gro. *Stoke* 4J **21**
Lynn Av. *Tal* 3K **19**
Lynn St. *Stoke* 1C **42**
Lynsey Clo. *Halm* 5F **25**
Lynton Gro. *Stoke* 6A **42**
Lynton Pl. *Als* 6E **10**
Lynton Rd. *New* 1C **38**
Lysander Rd. *Stoke* 7B **42**
Lytton St. *Stoke* 6B **34**

M

Macclesfield Rd. *Cong* 2G **9**
Macclesfield Rd. *Leek* 1C **16**
Macclesfield St. *Stoke* 3A **28**
Macdonald Cres. *Stoke* 3B **42**
Mace St. *Stoke* 2J **39**
McGough St. *Stoke* 1G **27**
Machin Cres. *New* 5D **26**
Machin St. *Stoke* 7H **21**
Macintyre St. *Stoke* 5K **27**
McKellin Clo. *Big E* 2F **25**
Mackenzie Cres. *C'dle* 5H **45**
McKinley St. *Stoke* 1G **27**
(in two parts)

Maclagan St. *Stoke* 7A **34**
Maddock St. *A'ly* 3E **24**
Maddock St. *Stoke* 5H **27**
Madeira Pl. *Stoke* 1G **27**
Madeley. **2B 30**
Madeley Heath. **5C 30**
Madeley St. *New* 4J **31**
Madeley St. *Stoke* 7G **21**
Madeley St. N. *New* 3J **31**
Madison St. *Stoke* 7G **21**
Mafeking St. *Stoke* 4G **41**
Magdalen Rd. *Stoke* 6D **40**
Magdalen Wlk. *Stoke* 7D **40**
Magenta Dri. *New* 3B **32**
Magnolia Dri. *Stoke* 2E **28**
Magnus St. *Stoke* 5J **27**
Magpie Cres. *Kid* 1E **20**
Maidstone Gro. *Stoke* 3H **35**
Main St. *Stoke* 1C **42**
Maitland Gro. *Stoke* 1A **46**
Majors Barn. **4F 45**
Majors Barn. *C'dle* 4F **45**
Malam St. *Stoke* 7B **28** (1E **5**)
Malcolm Clo. *Stoke* 2G **29**
Malcolm Ct. *Stoke* 7H **29**
Malcolm St. *Stoke* 7H **29**
Malhamdale Rd. *Cong* 2J **9**
Malham Rd. *New* 2B **32**
Malkin Way. *Stoke* 6H **27**
Mallard Way. *Stoke* 1B **28**
Mallard Way. *Stoke* 7C **22**
Mallory Ct. *Cong* 4B **8**
Mallory Way. *C'dle* 3J **45**
Mallowdale Clo. *Stoke* 1B **46**
Malpas Wlk. *Stoke* 4F **21**
Malstone Av. *Stoke* 2H **29**
Malthouse La. *B'stn* 5D **46**
Malthouse La. *Stoke* 5C **36**
Malthouse Rd. *Stoke* 2G **35**
Malt La. *Stoke* 4J **41**
Malton Gro. *Stoke* 6G **21**
Malvern Av. *New* 3G **31**
Malvern Clo. *Cong* 4B **8**
Malvern Clo. *Stoke* 7K **39**
Manchester Rd. *Cong* 1G **9**
Mandalay Way. *Stoke* 4J **41**
Mandeville Clo. *Stoke* 1B **28**
Manifold Clo. *New* 4J **31**
Manifold Rd. *For* 6G **43**
Manifold Wlk. *Stoke* 4H **35**
Mannin Clo. *Stoke* 2B **42**
Mann St. *Stoke* 4D **42**
Manor Clo. *Cong* 6J **9**
Manor Clo. *Dray* 1K **49**
Manor Ct. *Stoke* 7J **33**
Manor Rd. *Mad* 3B **30**
Manor Rd. *Mow C* 3G **13**
Manor St. *Stoke* 7D **34**
Mansfield Clo. *New* 4F **39**
Mansfield Dri. *Brn L* 5K **13**
Mansion Clo. *C'dle* 4H **45**
Maple Av. *Als* 1F **19**
Maple Av. *New* 3B **26**
Maple Av. *Tal* 3A **20**
Maple Clo. *C'dle* 4J **45**
Maple Clo. *Cong* 3B **8**
Maple Clo. *Stoke* 6F **23**
Maples Cres. *B Bri* 1H **49**
Maplehurst Clo. *Hot I* 4A **28**
Maple Pl. *Rode H* 3G **11**
Maple Pl. *Stoke* 4C **42**
Maples Clo. *Stoke* 2K **41**
Marcel Clo. *Stoke* 4K **39**
March La. *Werr* 2H **37**
March Rd. *Stoke* 2G **41**
Marchwood Ct. *Stoke* 7H **33**
Marcus Ind. Est. *Stoke* 2E **34**
Mardale Clo. *Cong* 2J **9**
Margaret Av. *Stoke* 6J **39**
Margaret St. *Stoke* . . .1D **34** (3H **5**)
Margaret Way. *Sch G* 3B **12**
Margill Clo. *Stoke* 2A **34** (5D **4**)
Maries Way. *Sil* 4A **32**
Marina Dri. *New* 1F **33**
Marina Rd. *Stoke* 3J **39**
Marina Way. *Stoke* 1J **33** (4A **4**)

Market La. *New* 4E **32** (3D **6**)
Market La. *Stoke* 1B **34** (3F **5**)
Market Pas. *Stoke* 4J **27**
Market Pl. *C'dle* 3G **45**
Market Pl. Leek *3F 17*
(off Church St.)
Market Pl. *Stoke* 4J **27**
Market Sq. *Cong* 5F **9**
Market Sq. *Stoke* 1B **34** (3F **5**)
Market Sq. Arc. *Stoke* 3F **5**
Market St. *Cong* 5F **9**
Market St. *Kid* 2D **20**
Market St. *Leek* 3G **17**
Market St. *Stoke* 2H **41**
Marlborough Cres. *End* 3K **23**
Marlborough Rd. *Stoke* 2H **41**
Marlborough St. *Stoke* 1C **40**
Marldon Pl. *Stoke* 5F **21**
Marlow Clo. *Stoke* 1J **41**
Marlow Rd. *Stoke* 1J **41**
Marney Wlk. *Stoke* 2A **28**
Marriott St. *Stoke* 1F **41**
Marsden St. *Stoke* 1C **34** (2G **5**)
Marshall Av. *Brn E* 4G **23**
Marshall Gro. *Cong* 6K **9**
Marshall St. *Stoke* 3J **27**
Marsh Av. *New* 7F **27**
Marsh Av. *N'cpl* 1H **21**
Marsh Av. *Stoke* 2A **28**
Marsh Clo. *Als* 7B **10**
Marsh Clo. *Werr* 1B **36**
Marshfield La. *Gil H* 2H **15**
Marsh Grn. Clo. *Bid* 2J **15**
Marshgreen Rd. *Bid* 1J **15**
Marsh Grn. *Gil H* 1H **15**
Marshland Gro. *Stoke* 3K **21**
Marsh La. *Als* 7B **10**
Marsh Pde. *New* 5F **33** (4F **7**)
Marsh St. N. *Stoke* 1B **34** (2E **5**)
Marsh St. S. *Stoke* 1B **34** (3E **5**)
Marsh Vw. *Stoke* 2B **48**
Marsh Way. *New* 7F **27**
Mars St. *Stoke* 3B **28**
Marston Gro. *Stoke* 4C **28**
Martindale Clo. *Stoke* 6A **42**
Martin St. *Stoke* 5A **28**
Marton Clo. *Cong* 2G **9**
Marychurch Rd. *Stoke* 2G **35**
Maryhill Clo. *Kid* 7D **12**
Maryrose Clo. *Stoke* 2G **35**
Masefield Clo. *C'dle* 1G **45**
Masefield Rd. *Stoke* 4F **41**
Maskery Pl. *Cong* 4F **9**
Mason Dri. *Bid* 2A **14**
Mason St. *Stoke* 1E **40**
Masterson St. *Stoke* 7C **34**
Mathews Wlk. *Stoke* 3G **5**
Matlock Pl. *New* 3H **31**
Matlock St. *Stoke* 3B **34**
Matrix Health & Leisure Club.
. . . . .3G **27**
Matthews Ct. *Stoke* 4H **5**
Matthews Pl. *Cong* 5J **9**
Maud St. *Stoke* 6D **34**
Maunders Rd. *Stoke* 3F **29**
Maureen Av. *Stoke* 5G **21**
Maureen Gro. *New* 2F **33**
Mawdesley St. *Stoke* 6A **28**
Mawdsley Clo. *Als* 7A **10**
Mawson Gro. *Stoke* 4C **34**
Maxton Way. *Stoke* 4C **42**
Maxwell Pl. *Stoke* 6H **33**
Maxwell Rd. *Cong* 7J **9**
May Av. *New* 2G **33**
May Av. *Stoke* 1H **27**
May Bank. **2G 33**
May Bank. *New* 2G **33**
Maybury Way. *Stoke* 3F **29**
Mayer Av. *New* 3E **32**
Mayer Bank. *Stoke* 4K **27**
Mayers Ct. *Leek* 4E **16**
Mayer St. *Stoke* 1C **34** (2F **5**)
Mayfair Gdns. Stoke 1C **40**
(off Wesley St.)
Mayfair Gro. *End* 3K **23**
Mayfield Av. *New* 5D **32** (5A **6**)

Mayfield Av. *Stoke* 7D **28**
Mayfield Clo. *Leek* 4C **16**
Mayfield Cres. *Stoke* 7D **28**
Mayfield Dri. *B Bri* 6E **42**
Mayfield Pl. *New* 1F **33**
Mayfield Pl. E. *Stoke* 1H **39**
Mayfield Pl. W. *Stoke* 1H **39**
Mayfield Rd. *Bid* 4C **14**
Maylea Cres. *Stoke* 5B **28**
Mayneford Pl. *Stoke* 5J **39**
Mayne St. *Stoke* 4J **39**
May Pl. *New* 2F **33**
May Pl. *Stoke* 1G **41**
May St. *New* 4K **31**
May St. *Stoke* 3A **28**
Maythorne Rd. *Stoke* 5F **41**
Mead Av. *Sch G* 3B **12**
Meadow Av. *Cong* 6E **8**
Meadow Av. *New* 1D **32**
Meadow Av. *Stoke* 6H **41**
Meadow Clo. *B Bri* 1F **49**
Meadow Clo. *For* 6F **43**
Meadow Clo. *Leek* 4H **17**
Meadow Cotts. Cong 4F **9**
(off Stonehouse Grn.)
Meadow Ct. *B'stn* 5B **46**
Meadow Ct. *N'cpl* 1H **21**
Meadow Cft. *Als* 1F **19**
Meadowcroft Av. *Stoke* 6D **42**
Meadow Dri. *C'dle* 3G **45**
Meadow Dri. *Stoke* 6F **41**
Meadow La. *Ful* 7F **49**
Meadow La. *New* 1D **32**
Meadow La. *Stoke* 7B **40**
Meadow Pl. *Stoke* 5C **42**
Meadow Rd. *B'stn* 5C **46**
Meadow Rd. *Brn E* 5G **23**
Meadow Rd. *Stoke* 6B **22**
Meadow Side. *Knyp* 4A **14**
Meadowside. *Sav G* 5J **49**
Meadowside. *Stoke* 7A **40**
Meadowside Av. *A'ly* 3D **24**
Meadowside La. *Sch G* 3E **12**
Meadows Rd. *Kid* 2C **20**
Meadows, The. *Cong* 4F **9**
Meadows, The. *End* 2K **23**
Meadows, The. *Kid* 2C **20**
Meadows, The. *Stoke* 4G **35**
Meadow Stile Cvn. Site.
Brn L 4K **13**
Meadow St. *New* 6C **26**
Meadow St. *Stoke* 3G **29**
Meadowview. *Stoke* 1D **28**
Meadow Way. *Chu L* 5H **11**
Meads Rd. *Als* 6E **10**
Mead, The. *Stoke* 7A **40**
Meaford Dri. *Stoke* 4D **40**
Meaford Rd. *B'stn & Knen* 6C **46**
Meakin Av. *New* 3E **38**
Meakin Clo. *C'dle* 5F **45**
Meakin Clo. *Cong* 6K **9**
Meakins Row. *Stoke* 1E **40**
Medina Way. *Kid* 1E **20**
Medway Dri. *Bid* 1C **14**
Medway Pl. *New* 2E **38**
Medway Wlk. *Stoke* 7K **21**
Meerbrook Clo. *Stoke* 2A **46**
Meere Clo. *Stoke* 1D **28**
Mega Bowl. 1K **33** (3A **4**)
Megacre. **3H 25**
Megacre. *Big E* 2H **25**
Meigh Rd. *Ash B & Werr* 2B **36**
Meigh St. *Stoke* 1B **34** (3G **5**)
Meiklejohn Pl. *Stoke* 5K **21**
Meir. **5B 42**
Meir Hay. **2J 41**
Meirhay Rd. *Stoke* 4J **41**
Meir Heath. **2B 48**
Meir Rd. *Stoke* 5K **41**
Meir St. *Stoke* 7G **21**
Meir Vw. *Stoke* 4B **42**
Melbourne St. *Stoke* 1J **41**
Melchester Gro. *Stoke* 5K **41**
Melfont St. *Stoke* 1H **27**
Meliden Way. *Stoke* 7J **33**
Mellard St. *A'ly* 3E **24**
Mellard St. *New* 3D **32** (1B **6**)

Mellors Bank. *Mow C* 4G 13
Mellor St. *Pac* 2J 21
Melrose Av. *Meir H* 3B 48
Melrose Av. *New* 1D 38
Melrose Av. *S Grn* 5C 28
Melrose Pl. *Leek* 4C 16
Melstone Av. *Stoke* 1J 27
Melton Clo. *Cong* 4B 8
Melton Dri. *Cong* 4B 8
Melville Ct. *New* 5F 39
Melville Rd. *Stoke* 4K 41
Melville St. *Stoke* 2D 34 (5H 5)
Melvyn Cres. *New* 5F 27
Menai Dri. *Knyp* 4C 14
Menai Gro. *Stoke* 1H 41
Mendip Grn. *Stoke* 3F 29
Mendip Pl. *New* 2B 32
Menzies Ho. *Stoke* 6A 42
Mercer St. *Stoke* 5G 41
Mercia Cres. *Stoke* 6K 27
Mercury Pl. *Stoke* 3C 28
Mere Ct. *Als* 6E 10
Merelake. 3G 19
Merelake Rd. *Tal P* 2F 19
Merelake Way. *Als* 1G 19
Meremore Dri. *New* 2A 26
Mereside Av. *Cong* 5D 8
Merevale Av. *Stoke* 3F 35
Meriden Rd. *New* 4F 39
Merino Clo. *Stoke* 6H 41
Merlin Clo. *Stoke* 3K 21
Merlin Grn. *Mad* 2B 30
Merlin Way. *Kid* 7G 13
Merrial St. *New* 4E 32 (3D 6)
Merrick St. *Stoke* 7C 28
Merrion Dri. *Stoke* 2A 28
Mersey Rd. *New* 3D 38
Mersey St. *Stoke* 1A 34 (4D 4)
Merthyr Gro. *Knyp* 4D 14
Merton St. *Stoke* 2H 41
Metcalfe Rd. *Stoke* 1K 27
Metro Bus. Pk. *Stoke* . .2K 33 (4B 4)
Mews Clo. *Stoke* 3F 35
Mews, The. *New* 1G 33
Michael Clo. *Stoke* 3C 42
Michaels Clo. *New* 5F 27
Michigan Gro. *Stoke* 6A 40
Micklea La. *Long* 7A 16
Mickleby Way. *Stoke* 7D 42
Middle Cross St. *Stoke* 2H 41
Middlefield Rd. *Stoke* 5J 35
Middle La. *Cong* 3K 9
Middle Madeley. 6A 30
Middleport. 5J 27
Middleton Clo. *Stoke* 1D 28
Midfield Clo. *Gil H* 2H 15
Midhurst Clo. *Pac* 3J 21
Midway Dri. *B Bri* 1F 49
Midway, The. *New* 5E 32 (4C 6)
Midwinter Clo. *Stoke* 6H 27
Milan Dri. *New* 7B 32
Milborne Dri. *New* 1F 39
Milburn Rd. *Stoke* 5A 28
Milehouse La. *New* 1E 32
Miles Bank. *Stoke* 3F 5
Miles Green. 4F 25
Miles Grn. Rd. *Big E* 4F 25
Milford Av. *Werr* 1C 36
Milford Rd. *New* 6D 32 (6B 6)
Milford St. *Stoke* 1E 40
Milgreen Av. *Stoke* 5C 28
Milk St. *Cong* 4F 9
Milk St. *Leek* 2G 17
Millbank Pl. *New* 4C 32
Millbank St. *Stoke* 3H 41
Millbridge Clo. *Stoke* 1C 48
Millbrook Gro. *Stoke* 3F 29
Millbrook Way. *C'dle* 4H 45
Mill Clo. *Cav* 3D 42
Mill Ct. *Stoke* 7H 39
Millend. 6D 18
Mill End La. *Big E* 6D 18
Millennium Way. *High B* 2C 26
Millers La. *Stoke* 7H 39
Miller St. *New* 4F 33 (2F 7)
Millers Vw. *C'dle* 4J 45
Millers Vw. *Kid* 2D 20

Millers Wharf. *Rode H* 3G 11
Millett Rd. *Stoke* 2F 35
Millfield Cres. *Stoke* 3F 29
Mill Fields. *Cong* 4F 9
Mill Grn. *Cong* 4F 9
Mill Gro. *C'dle* 4H 45
Mill Gro. *Tal* 2A 20
Mill Hayes Rd. *Knyp* 7B 14
Mill Hayes Rd. *Stoke* 3H 27
Mill Hill Cres. *Stoke* 7K 21
Mill Ho. Dri. *C'dle* 5H 45
Millicent St. *Stoke* 7D 34
Mill La. *Mad* 6A 30
Mill La. *Sch G* 3D 12
Millmead. *Rode H* 3G 11
Mill Ri. *Kid* 2D 20
Millrise Rd. *Stoke* 3F 29
Mill Rd. *C'dle* 4H 45
Millstone Av. *Tal* 2B 20
Mill Stream Clo. *C'dle* 4H 45
Mill St. *Cong* 3H 9
. . . .(Buxton Rd.)
Mill St. *Cong* 4F 9
. . . .(Swan Bank)
Mill St. *Leek* 3E 16
Mill St. *New* 4A 32
Milltown Way. *Leek* 5H 17
Mill Vw. *Stoke* 5C 22
Millward Rd. *Stoke* 2H 35
Millwaters. *C'dle* 4H 45
Milner Ter. *Leek* 2H 17
Milnes Clo. *Stoke* 4F 41
Milton. 3G 29
Milton Cres. *Tal* 3K 19
Milton M. Als 7E 10
. . . .(off Crewe Rd.)
Milton Rd. *Stoke* 5C 28
Milton St. *Stoke* 2A 34 (5C 4)
Milvale St. *Stoke* 5H 27
Milverton Pl. *Stoke* 3F 41
Milward Gro. *Stoke* 1A 48
Minard Gro. *Stoke* 2B 42
Minden Gro. *Stoke* 4C 28
Mineal Rd. *Stoke* 6J 35
Minerva Clo. *Knyp* 5A 14
Minerva Rd. *Stoke* 7E 34
Minfield Clo. *Kid* 3D 20
Minshall Ct. Stoke 1B 40
. . . .(off Minshall St.)
Minshall St. *Stoke* 1B 40
Minster St. *Stoke* 3A 28
Minton Clo. *C'dle* 5G 45
Minton Clo. *Cong* 6K 9
Minton Pl. *New* 7G 27
Minton St. *New* 7G 27
Minton St. *Stoke* 5H 33
Miranda Gro. *Stoke* 3C 28
Mistley Wlk. *Stoke* 4F 21
Mitchell Av. *Tal* 2A 20
Mitchell Dri. *Tal* 2A 20
Mitchell Memorial Youth Cen. &
Theatre. 2B 34 (4E 5)
Mitchell St. *Stoke* 3J 27
Moat La. *A'ly* 2B 24
Moat, The. *Stoke* 2B 42
Mobberley. 6G 45
Mobberley Rd. *Stoke* 3F 21
Moddershall Oaks. *Knen* 7A 48
Moffat Clo. *Stoke* 6K 35
Moffatt Way. *New* 3G 31
Mollatts Clo. *Leek* 7C 16
Mollatts Wood Rd. *Leek* 7C 16
Mollison Rd. *Stoke* 6B 42
Monaco Pl. *New* 6B 32
Monkhouse. 2F 45
Monkhouse. *C'dle* 3G 45
Monkleigh Clo. *Stoke* 2A 46
Monks Clo. *New* 7F 33
Monkton Clo. *Stoke* 5F 41
Monmouth Pl. *New* 2G 39
Monsal Gro. *Stoke* 7E 28
Montfort Pl. *New* 7E 32
Montgomery Ct. *New*
. . . . .4D 32 (2A 6)
Montgomery Pl. *Stoke* 4C 42
Montrose St. *Stoke* 1E 40
Monty Pl. *Stoke* 1G 41

Monument Rd. *Tal P* 5A 20
Monument Vw. *Big E* 2G 25
Monument Vw. *Mad H* 5B 30
Monyash Clo. *Stoke* 7D 42
Monyash Dri. *Leek* 4H 17
Moody St. *Cong* 5F 9
Moor Clo. *Bid* 1D 14
Moorcroft Av. *New* 3E 38
Moorcroft Clo. *C'dle* 5F 45
Moorcroft Mus. 5A 28
Moore St. *Stoke* 5K 27
Moorfield Av. *Bid* 2B 14
Moorfields. *Leek* 4G 17
Moor Green. 6H 43
Moorhead Dri. *Bag* 7K 23
Moorhouse Av. *Als* 6E 10
Moorhouse St. *Leek* 4G 17
Moorings. *Cong* 6G 9
Moorland Av. *Werr* 1C 36
Moorland Clo. *Werr* 1C 36
Moorland Rd. *Bid* 1C 14
Moorland Rd. *Leek* 4J 17
Moorland Rd. *Mow C* 3G 13
Moorland Rd. *Stoke* 4K 27
Moorlands Ct. *Bid* 2C 14
Moorland Vw. *Stoke* 1B 28
Moorland Wlk. C'dle 3G 45
. . . .(off High St.)
Moor La. *C'dle* 2J 45
Moorside Rd. *Werr* 1E 36
Moorson Av. *Sch G* 2C 12
Moor St. *Cong* 5G 9
Moorsyde Rd. *Stoke* 1H 39
Moorthorne Cres. *New* 6D 26
Moorview Gdns. *Har* 5H 13
Moran Gro. *Stoke* 5H 27
Moran Rd. *New* 3C 32 (1A 6)
Moresby Clo. *Stoke* 3G 29
Moreton Av. *New* 6G 39
Moreton Clo. *Kid* 3E 20
Moreton Clo. *Werr* 3C 36
Moreton Dri. *Als* 7D 10
Moreton Ho. *New* 1G 33
Moreton Pde. *New* 1G 33
Morgan Way. *Stoke* 5K 21
Morley Dri. *Cong* 6J 9
Morley St. *Leek* 4E 16
Morley St. *Stoke* 2A 34 (4D 4)
Morningside. *Mad* 2B 30
Mornington Rd. *Stoke* 4C 28
Morpeth St. *Stoke* 3H 41
Morris Sq. *New* 7G 27
Morson Dri. *New* 4E 38
Mortimer Pl. *Stoke* 2A 42
Morton St. *Stoke* 5H 27
Morville Clo. *Stoke* 6D 34
Mosedale Av. *Stoke* 6A 42
Moss Clo. *Werr* 1C 36
Mossfield Cres. *Kid* 1E 20
Mossfield Dri. *Bid* 3D 14
Mossfield Rd. *Stoke* 6H 35
Moss Fields. *Als* 7B 10
Moss Grn. Rd. *Stoke* 6J 35
Moss Gro. *New* 1A 26
Moss Hill. 6J 23
Moss Hill. *Stoc B* 6J 23
Mossland Rd. *Stoke* 1H 41
Moss La. *C'dle* 5J 45
Moss La. *Cong* 1G 9
Moss La. *Mad* 2A 30
Moss La. *Sch G* 6B 12
Moss La. *Spot A* 7D 48
Mossley. 7K 9
Mossley Ct. *Cong* 7H 9
Mossley Gth. Clo. *Cong* 6J 9
Moss Pk. Av. *Werr* 1B 36
Moss Pl. *Kid* 7E 12
Moss Ri. *New* 5F 39
Moss Rd. *Cong* 7H 9
Moss Side. *Stoke* 4D 28
Moss St. *Stoke* 6D 22
Moss Way. *Als* 7B 10
Moston Ct. Cong 4H 9
. . . .(off Brunswick St.)
Moston St. *Stoke* 5H 27
Mostyn Clo. *Knyp* 4D 14
Mott Pl. *Stoke* 4H 27

Moulton Rd. *Stoke* 2G 41
Mounfield Pl. *Stoke* 7C 34
Mount Av. *Stoke* 6J 33
Mountbatten Way. *Cong* 4F 9
Mount Clo. *Werr* 1D 36
Mountford St. *Stoke* 3J 27
Mount Pl. *For* 7H 43
Mount Pleasant. 1C 40
. . . .(Fenton)
Mount Pleasant. 4E 12
. . . .(Mow Cop)
Mount Pleasant. *C'dle* 3F 45
Mount Pleasant. *Ches* 6B 26
Mount Pleasant. *Cong* 5G 9
Mount Pleasant. *Kid* 2D 20
Mount Pleasant. *Leek* 3F 17
Mount Pleasant. *New* . . .5F 33 (4F 7)
Mount Pleasant. *Stoke*
. . . . .2A 34 (5C 4)
Mt. Pleasant Dri. Leek 3F 17
. . . .(off Mount Pleasant)
Mt. Pleasant Rd. *Sch G* 3E 12
Mount Rd. *B Bri* 7H 43
Mount Rd. *Kid* 2D 20
Mount Rd. *Leek* 3J 17
Mountside Gdns. *Leek* 3J 17
Mountsorrel Clo. *Stoke* 1B 46
Mount St. *New* 6B 26
Mount St. *Stoke* 7C 28 (1H 5)
Mount, The. *Cong* 5C 8
Mount, The. *Kid* 2D 20
Mount, The. *New* 6B 26
Mount, The. *Sch G* 3B 12
Mousley St. *Stoke* 4H 27
Mowbray Wlk. *Stoke* 4E 28
Mow Cop. 3G 13
Mow Cop. 3G 13
Mow Cop Rd. *Mow C* 5F 13
Mow La. *Mow C & Gil H* 1K 13
Mow La. *Sch G & Mow C* 5D 12
Moxley Av. *Stoke* 5C 28
Mulberry Pl. *New* 4B 26
Mulberry St. *Stoke* 2C 34 (4H 5)
Mulgrave St. *Stoke* 7A 28 (1C 4)
Mullberry Way. *Leek* 5H 17
Mulliner Clo. *Stoke* 2J 35
Munro St. *Stoke* 1K 39
Munster Ter. *Stoke* 1J 39
Murhall St. *Stoke* 4H 27
Murray St. *Stoke* 4F 21
Mustang Clo. *Stoke* 7F 21
Myatt St. *Stoke* 7C 28 (1H 5)
Mynors St. *Stoke* 1C 34 (2H 5)
Myott Av. *New* 6D 32 (5B 6)
Myrtle Av. *Stoke* 3C 42

N

Nabbs Clo. *Kid* 1E 20
Nabbswood Rd. *Kid* 1E 20
Nab Hill Av. *Leek* 3D 16
Nab Hill Ct. *Leek* 3D 16
Nantwich Rd. *A'ly* 3A 24
Napier Gdns. *Kid* 1D 20
Napier St. *Stoke* 7C 34
Naples Dri. *New* 7C 32
Narvik Cres. *Stoke* 2B 28
Naseby Rd. *Cong* 4C 8
Nashe Dri. *Stoke* 4E 40
Nash Peake St. *Stoke* 1F 27
Nash St. *New* 3B 32
Nathan Clo. *Stoke* 3E 42
Navigation Rd. *Stoke* 5J 27
Navigation St. *Stoke* 5H 27
Naylor St. *Stoke* 6J 21
Naylor Yd. Leek 3F 17
. . . .(off Mount Pleasant)
Neale Pl. *Stoke* 7G 29
Neath Clo. *Stoke* 3J 41
Neath Pl. *Stoke* 7H 35
Nelson Bank. *Stoke* 4D 28
Nelson Bldgs. *Kid* 2D 20
Nelson Gro. *Als* 1G 19
Nelson Ind. Est. *Tal* 2K 19
Nelson Pl. *New* 4F 33 (3E 7)

Nelson Pl.—Overland Dri.

Nelson Pl. *Stoke* 2C 34 (4H 5)
Nelson Rd. *Stoke* 5H 33
Nelson St. *Cong* 5F 9
Nelson St. *Leek* 2G 17
Nelson St. *New* 7F 27
Nelson St. *Stoke* 1C 40
Nephew St. *Stoke* 4H 27
Neptune Gro. *Stoke* 6E 28
Ness Gro. *C'dle* 1H 45
Nethercote Pl. *Stoke* 5J 35
Netherset Hey La. *Mad* 7A 30
Netherton Gro. *Stoke* 2G 29
Netley Pl. *Stoke* 7D 40
Nevada La. *Hot I* 4A 28
Neville St. *Stoke* 2J 39
Nevin Av. *Knyp* 5C 14
Newark Gro. *Stoke* 4F 21
New Av. *Dray* 1K 49
Newbold Ct. Cong 4H 9
(off Herbert St.)
Newborough Clo. *Stoke* 6D 28
New Bldgs. *Knyp* 7B 14
Newburn Gro. *Stoke* 6A 40
Newbury Gro. *Stoke* 7D 40
Newby Ct. *Cong* 6C 8
Newcastle Bus. Cen. *P East* 4D 26
Newcastle Crematorium.
New 5F 27
Newcastle La. *Stoke* 7G 33
Newcastle Rd. *A'bry & Cong* 7C 8
Newcastle Rd. *Leek* 6D 16
Newcastle Rd.
Mad & Mad H 1B 30
Newcastle Rd. *New* 6F 39
Newcastle Rd. *Stoke* 7G 33
Newcastle Rd. *Tal* 3A 20
Newcastle St. *New* 3K 31
Newcastle St. *Stoke* 4G 27
Newcastle-under-Lyme. 4E 32 (3D 6)
New Century St. *Stoke*
1A 34 (3C 4)
Newchapel. 1H 21
New Chapel Ct. *Stoke* 7G 21
Newchapel Observatory. 1H 21
Newchapel Rd. *Kid* 7E 12
New Clo. Av. *For* 6J 43
Newcomen Gro. *Stoke* 6J 35
Newcroft Ct. *New* 7F 27
Newcrofts Wlk. *Stoke* 5C 22
Newfield. 7F 21
Newfield St. *Stoke* 7G 21
Newfield Trad. Est. *Stoke* 6G 21
Newfold Cres. *Brn E* 3G 23
Newford Cres. *Stoke* 3E 28
New Forest Ind. Est. *Stoke*
7C 28 (1F 5)
New Haden Rd. *C'dle* 4E 44
New Hall Rd. *Stoke* 4J 41
New Hall St. *Stoke* 1B 34 (2E 5)
Newhaven Gro. *Stoke* 2A 46
New Hayes Rd. *Stoke* 7H 21
Newhouse Ct. *Stoke* 7G 29
Newhouse Rd. *Stoke* 7G 29
Newington Gro. *Stoke* 2B 46
New Inn La. *Stoke* 5J 39
New King St. *A'ly* 3D 24
New Kingsway. *W Coy* 2B 42
Newlands Clo. *New* 1E 38
Newlands St. *Stoke* 4A 34
New La. *Brn E* 2G 23
New Leek La. *Bid* 2F 15
Newleigh St. *Stoke* 3G 29
Newlyn Av. *Cong* 7H 9
Newman Clo. *Cong* 4D 8
Newmarket Way. *C'dle* 1H 45
Newmill St. *Stoke* 3F 29
Newmount Rd. *Stoke* 1G 41
New Pk. Gdns. *Stoke* 2B 46
Newpool. 4A 14
Newpool Cotts. *Bid* 5A 14
Newpool Rd. *Knyp* 4K 13
Newpool Ter. *Brn L* 5A 14
Newport Gro. *New* 2B 26
Newport La. *Stoke* 4H 27
Newport St. *Stoke* 4H 27
Newquay Ct. *Cong* 7G 9
New Rd. *Big E* 2E 24
New Rd. *Dil* 3K 43
New Rd. *Mad* 1B 30
New Rd. *Stoke* 2A 36
New Row. *Mad H* 5B 30
Newshaw Wlk. *Stoke*
1C 34 (3H 5)
Newstead. 7C 40
Newstead Rd. *Stoke* 7G 29
Newstead Trad. Est. *Stoke* 7C 40
New St. *Bid M* 4E 14
New St. *Cong* 5G 9
New St. *Leek* 3G 17
New St. *New* 7G 27
New St. *Stoke* 4J 27
New St. Cotts. *Hav* 1J 9
Newton Ct. *Werr* 1B 36
Newton Pl. *Cong* 5H 9
Newton Rd. *New* 7E 26
Newton St. *Stoke* 3H 33
Newtown. *N'cpl* 1H 21
New Victoria Theatre, The.
3G 33 (1G 7)
Niall Rd. *Stoke* 5J 39
Nicholas Gro. *Leek* 5C 16
Nicholas St. *Stoke* 4J 27
Nicholls St. *Stoke* 1A 40
Nicholson Way. *Leek* 3E 16
Nidderdale Clo. *Cong* 2J 9
Nightingale Way. *Als* 7C 10
Nile St. *Stoke* 4K 27
Noblett Rd. *Stoke* 5D 28
Norbury Av. *Stoke* 3G 29
Norbury Dri. *Cong* 3G 9
Norfolk Clo. *New* 4E 38
Norfolk Gro. *Bid* 1B 14
Norfolk Rd. *Cong* 3G 9
Norfolk Rd. *Kid* 1C 20
Norfolk St. *Stoke* 3A 34
Normacot. 4J 41
Normacot Grange Rd.
Stoke 7A 42
Normacot Rd. *Stoke* 3H 41
(Millbank St.)
Normacot Rd. *Stoke* 4J 41
(Queensberry Rd.)
Norman Av. *Stoke* 1J 27
Normandy Gro. *Stoke* 2F 29
Norman Gro. *New* 3G 33
Normanton Gro. *Stoke* 7J 35
Norris Rd. *Stoke* 1J 27
Northam Rd. *Stoke* 6C 28
North Av. *Leek* 4E 16
Northcliffe. Leek 3E 16
(off Belle Vue Rd.)
Northcote Av. *Stoke* 5K 33
Northcote Ct. *New* 4F 33 (2F 7)
Northcote Pl. *New* 4F 33 (2F 7)
Northcote St. *Stoke* 4A 34
Northesk Pl. *New* 1D 38
Northfield Dri. *Bid* 2K 15
Northfleet St. *Stoke* 2F 35
Northgate Clo. *Stoke* 5J 39
Northolme Gdns. *Als* 6D 10
North Pl. *Stoke* 6G 29
North Rd. *Stoke* 5A 28
NORTH STAFFORDSHIRE HOSPITAL CENTRAL OUTPATIENTS DEPARTMENT. 5H 33
NORTH STAFFORDSHIRE NUFFIELD HOSPITAL. 3F 39
NORTH STAFFORDSHIRE ROYAL INFIRMARY. 6J 33
North St. *Cong* 4F 9
North St. *Leek* 3D 16
North St. *Mow C* 4E 12
North St. *New* 4F 33 (3F 7)
North St. *Stoke* 4J 33
North Ter. *New* 7E 26
North Wlk. *Stoke* 5C 42
N. West Ter. *Stoke* 3B 28
Northwood. 1D 34
(Stoke-on-Trent)
Northwood. 4F 39
(Trentham)
Northwood Clo. *New* 4G 39
Northwood Ct. *Stoke* 3H 5
Northwood Grn. *Stoke* 1D 34
Northwood La. *New* 4F 39
Northwood Pk. Rd. *Stoke*
7C 28 (1H 5)
(in two parts)
Northwood Stadium. 1D 34
Norton Av. *Stoke* 1K 27
Norton Cres. *Stoke* 4C 28
Norton Dri. *Stoke* 3C 28
Norton Green. 6E 22
Norton Hall Clo. *Stoke* 1D 28
Norton Ind. Est. *Stoke* 2D 28
Norton-in-the-Moors. 7D 22
Norton La. *Stoke* 7D 22
Norton St. *Stoke* 3G 29
Norwich Pl. *New* 1F 39
Norwich Rd. *Stoke* 3J 35
Novi La. *Leek* 2H 17
No. 1 Rd. N. *Rad G* 2A 18
No. 1 Rd. S. *Rad G* 2A 18
No. 2 Rd. N. *Rad G* 2A 18
No. 2 Rd. S. *Rad G* 2A 18
Nunn's Clo. *Stoke* 1D 42
Nunn St. *Leek* 3E 16
Nursery Av. *Stoc B* 1H 29
Nursery Clo. Brn E 4G 23
(off High La.)
Nursery Clo. *C'dle* 3F 45
Nursery Clo. *Tal* 2A 20
Nursery Dri. *Gil H* 2H 15
Nursery La. *Cong* 5G 9
Nursery La. *Stoc B* 1H 29
Nursery Rd. *Als* 7A 10
Nursery Rd. *Sch G* 5B 12
Nursery St. *Stoke* 1K 39
Nutbrook Av. *Stoke* 1B 40
Nyewood Av. *Stoke* 1J 41

O

Oak Av. *Als* 1F 19
Oakdale. *New* 3F 39
Oakdene Av. *New* 6D 26
Oakdene Clo. *B Bri* 1J 49
Oakdene Clo. *New* 6D 26
Oakdene Gro. *New* 6D 26
Oakdene Way. *Bid* 3C 14
Oakfield Gro. *Bid* 3D 14
Oakham Way. *Stoke* 3H 35
Oak Hill. 2J 39
Oakhill Av. *Stoke* 2J 39
Oakhill Hall. *Stoke* 2J 39
Oakhurst Cres. *Stoke* 1B 48
Oaklands Av. *New* 6F 27
Oak Lea. *Leek* 5C 16
Oakleigh Ct. *Cong* 4B 8
Oakley Pl. *Stoke* 3K 21
Oakmoor Rd. *C'dle* 2J 45
Oak Mt. Rd. *Werr* 1D 36
Oak Pl. *Stoke* 4A 42
Oak Rd. *New* 2A 32
Oakshaw Gro. *Stoke* 6A 40
Oaks, The. *K'le* 7H 31
Oak St. *C'dle* 3G 45
Oak St. *New* 2G 33
Oak St. *Rode H* 2F 11
Oak St. *Stoke* 6D 28
Oaktree La. *Tal P* 6A 20
Oak Tree Rd. *Stoke* 1A 46
Oakville Av. *Stoke* 2A 28
Oakwell Ct. *Stoke* 5H 41
Oakwell Gro. *Stoke* 5H 41
Oakwood Pl. *New* 4B 26
Oakwood Rd. *Leek* 3D 16
Oakwood Rd. *Rode H* 2G 11
Oakwood Rd. *Stoke* 5D 40
Oban Clo. *New* 5C 32
Obelisk Way. *Cong* 4E 8
Oberon Clo. *Stoke* 3C 28
Occupation St. *New* 6F 33 (6F 7)
Octagon Shop. Pk., The.
Stoke 1K 33 (3B 4)
Odell Gro. *Stoke* 3H 27
Odeon Cinema. 1K 33 (3A 4)
Odger Clo. *Stoke* 4C 42
Ogden Rd. *Stoke* 2B 34 (5F 5)
Ogmore Gro. *Stoke* 6B 42
O'Hare Pl. *Leek* 2H 17
Ohio Gro. *Hot I* 4A 28
Oldacres Rd. *Stoke* 2A 46
Old Butt La. *Tal* 1K 19
Oldcastle Av. *New* 6D 26
Old Chapel Clo. *K'le* 5F 31
Oldcott Cres. *Kid* 3F 21
Oldcott Dri. *Kid* 3F 21
Oldcourt St. *Stoke* 1G 27
Oldfield Av. *Stoke* 6C 22
Oldfield Ind. Est. *Stoke* 2E 40
Oldfield St. *Stoke* 1F 41
Old Hall Dri. *New* 4C 26
Old Hall St. *Stoke* 1B 34 (4F 5)
Oldham St. *Join I* 3C 34 (6H 5)
Oldhill Clo. *Tal P* 6B 20
Old La. *Brn E* 2F 23
Old Man of Mow, The. 2G 13
(National Trust)
Oldmill St. *Stoke* 6B 34
Old Rd. *B'stn* 4B 46
Old Rd. *Big E* 1F 25
Old Rd. *Knen* 7H 47
Old School Clo. *Kid* 2D 20
Old Town Rd. *Stoke* 7B 28 (1F 5)
Old Tramway. *Stoke* 1E 40
Oldway Pl. *Stoke* 1H 41
Old Wharf Pl. *Stoke* 3D 34
Old Whieldon Rd. *Stoke* 7B 34
Olive Gro. *New* 3A 26
Oliver Lodge Ho. Stoke 6K 33
(off Epworth St.)
Oliver Rd. *Stoke* 6H 33
Olof Palme Gro. *Stoke* 4H 41
Omega Way. *Stoke* 6K 39
Onsetter Rd. *Stoke* 6J 35
Onslow Dri. *New* 4E 26
Ontario Clo. *Stoke* 6K 39
Opal Rd. *Stoke* 1D 40
Orb St. *Stoke* 2B 34 (4E 5)
Orchard Ct. *Als* 6F 11
Orchard Cres. *Tal* 2A 20
Orchard Gdns. *Leek* 3D 16
Orchard Pl. *B'stn* 6C 46
Orchard Ri. *B Bri* 7F 43
Orchards, The. *Stoke* 2D 40
Orchard St. *New* 7F 27
Orchard, The. *Brn E* 3F 23
Orchard Way. *Cong* 4C 8
Orchid Gro. *Stoke* 4H 33
Orford Rd. *End* 2K 23
Orford St. *New* 5G 27
Orford Way. *Stoke* 6D 40
Orgreaves Clo. *New* 4E 26
Orgreave St. *Stoke* 5K 27
Oriel St. *Stoke* 6K 33
Orion Ct. *New* 5C 32 (5A 6)
Orion St. *Stoke* 3B 28
Orkney Av. *Pac* 3J 21
Orlestone Pl. *Stoke* 4K 21
Orme Rd. *Knyp* 5C 14
Orme Rd. *New* 4C 32 (3A 6)
Orme St. *Stoke* 4H 27
Ormonde St. *Stoke* 1E 40
Orpheus Gro. *Stoke* 6E 28
Orton Rd. *New* 3D 32
Orwell Dri. *Stoke* 1A 42
Orwell Pl. *New* 2E 38
Osborne Rd. *Stoke* 5H 33
Osborne St. *Leek* 3H 17
Oslo Gro. *Stoke* 6D 28
Osprey Av. *Stoke* 7B 42
Osprey Vw. *Kid* 7G 13
Ostend Pl. *New* 6C 32
Oswald Av. *Stoke* 1B 42
Oulton Dri. *Cong* 4B 8
Oulton Rd. *C'dle* 3J 45
Oulton Rd. *Stoke* 4A 22
Outclough Rd. *B Frd* 1A 22
Outlook, The. *Stoke* 1A 28
Oval, The. *Stoke* 4F 41
Oval, The. *Werr* 1F 37
Overdale Pl. *Leek* 4C 16
Overhouse St. *Stoke* 3J 27
Overland Dri. *Brn E* 3F 23

A-Z Stoke 67

Oversley Rd. *Stoke* 4K 21
Over The Hill. *Bid M* 1F 15
Overton Bank. Leek 3F 17
           (off Mill St.)
Overton Clo. *Cong* 4E 8
Overton Clo. *L'tn* 4F 41
Overwood Pl. *Stoke* 4J 21
Owen Gro. *Stoke* 3K 27
Oxford. 3K 21
Oxford Av. *Stoke* 5C 28
Oxford Cres. *Stoke* 6K 33
Oxford Rd. *New* 2G 33
Oxford Rd. *Stoke* 4A 22
Oxford St. *Stoke* 5K 33
Oxhay Ct. *New* 2F 33
Oxhay Vw. *New* 2F 33
Ox-Hey Cres. *Bid* 1C 14
Ox-Hey Dri. *Bid* 2J 15

P

Pacific Rd. *Stoke* 7K 39
Packett St. *Stoke* 2G 41
Packmoor. 2J 21
Paddock Cotts. *Stoke* 7K 39
Paddock Ri. *Stoke* 7K 39
Paddocks Grn. *Cong* 7H 9
Paddock, The. *C'dle* 4G 45
Paddock, The. *Has G* 1A 10
Padgbury Clo. *Cong* 6C 8
Padgbury La. *Cong* 5B 8
Padlowe St. *Stoke* 3H 27
Padston Dri. *Als* 7C 10
Padstow Way. *Stoke* 2A 46
Padworth St. *Stoke* 3B 42
Page St. *Stoke* 1B 34 (2E 5)
Paisley Clo. *Stoke* 5K 35
Paladin Av. *Stoke* 2C 42
Palatine Dri. *New* 6A 26
Pall Mall. *Stoke* 2B 34 (3E 5)
Palmers Grn. *Stoke* . . .5G 33 (4G 7)
Palmerston St. *Join I* . .3C 34 (6G 5)
Palmerston St. *New* 7F 27
Palmerston Way. *Bid* 2C 14
Palmer St. *Stoke* 2J 41
Palmers Way. *New* . . .5G 33 (4G 7)
Palomino Clo. *Stoke* 6H 41
Pandora Gro. *Stoke* 6E 28
Panturner Rd. *Stoke* 6J 35
Parade, The. *New* 4K 31
Paradise St. *New* 4D 6
Paradise St. *Stoke* 1G 27
Paragon Av. *New* 3E 38
Paragon Clo. *C'dle* 5F 45
Paragon Rd. *Stoke* 3J 41
Paramount Bus. Pk. *Stoke* . . .4K 27
Paris Av. *New* 6B 32
Parish Clo. *Als* 6C 10
Park Av. *C'dle* 4H 45
Park Av. *Kid* 3B 20
Park Av. *New* 7F 27
Park Av. *Werr* 1E 36
Park Av. *W Coy* 1B 42
Park Av. *W. New* 7E 26
Park Bank. *Cong* 5H 9
Park Clo. *Mad* 5A 30
Park Ct. *Ches* 5B 26
Park Dri. *B'stn* 6B 46
Park Dri. *C'dle* 2F 45
Park Dri. *Stoke* 7H 39
Park Dri. *Werr* 1D 36
Park End. 7B 18
Park End. *For* 6J 43
Parker Jervis Rd. *Stoke* 2A 42
Parker St. *Leek* 3H 17
Parker St. *Stoke* 1A 34 (4D 4)
Parker Way. *Cong* 4C 8
Pk. Farm Vw. *Stoke* 4G 21
Parkfields. *End* 2K 23
Parkfields Clo. *B'stn* 6B 46
Parkfields Clo. *New* 3H 31
Pk. Hall Av. *Stoke* 2B 42
Pk. Hall Bus. Village. *Stoke* . . .1K 41
Parkhall Country Pk. 6A 36

Pk. Hall Cres. *Stoke* 2B 42
Pk. Hall Ind. Est. *Stoke* 2H 27
Pk. Hall Rd. *Stoke* 7K 35
        (in two parts)
Pk. Hall St. *Stoke* 2H 41
Parkhead Cres. *Stoke* 3B 42
Parkhead Dri. *Stoke* 2B 42
Parkhead Gro. *Stoke* 3B 42
Parkhouse Ind. Est. E. *New* . . .3C 26
Parkhouse Ind. Est. W. *New* . . .4C 26
Parkhouse Rd. E. *P East* 3C 26
Parkhouse Rd. W. *New* 3B 26
Parkhouse St. *Stoke* . . .3A 34 (6C 4)
Parklands. *Kid* 2E 20
Parklands, The. *Bid M* 1G 15
Parklands, The. *Cong* 5J 9
Park La. *A'ly* 6B 18
Park La. *C'dle* 2F 45
Park La. *Cong* 5G 9
Park La. *End* 1K 23
Park La. *Knyp* 4B 14
Park La. *Stoke* 1E 40
Park La. Clo. *C'dle* 3F 45
Parkleigh. *Cong* 5H 9
Park Pl. *Stoke* 7D 34
Park Rd. *But* 4B 38
Park Rd. *Cong* 4G 9
Park Rd. *Leek* 2E 16
Park Rd. *Sil* 4J 31
        (in two parts)
Park Rd. *Stoke* 3K 27
Park Rd. *Werr* 1D 36
Parkside. *Mad* 6A 30
Parkside. *Stoke* 7A 40
        (Trentham)
Parkside. *Stoke* 2A 42
    (Weston Coyney)
Parkside Cres. *End* 1K 23
Parkside Dri. *New* 2G 33
Parkside Gro. *New* 2G 33
Parkstone Av. *New* 5F 33 (5F 7)
Park St. *Cong* 5G 9
        (Kinsey St.)
Park St. *Cong* 5G 9
        (Moor St.)
Park St. *Stoke* 7E 34
Park Ter. *Leek* 4H 17
Park Ter. *Stoke* 1H 27
Park Vw. *B Bri* 1F 49
Park Vw. *Cong* 4G 9
Pk. View St. *Stoke* 5G 41
Park Vw. Rd. *Kid* 7D 12
Park Way. *For* 6H 43
Parkway. *Tren* 7H 39
Parkway, The. *New* 7E 32
Parkway, The. *Stoke* 3B 34
Parkwood Av. *Stoke* 6J 39
Parliament Row. *Stoke*
         . . . . .1B 34 (3F 5)
Parliament Sq. *Stoke* . .1B 34 (3F 5)
Parnell Sq. *Cong* 5J 9
Parrot's Drumble Nature Reserve.
         . . . . .6J 19
Parsonage St. *Stoke* 7G 21
Parson St. *Cong* 5E 8
Parson Gro. *Stoke* 2B 42
Partridge Clo. *Cong* 6G 9
Partridge Clo. *Stoke* 7B 42
Pastoral Clo. *Mad* 3B 30
Patch Mdw. *C'dle* 3E 44
Patrick Pl. *B Frd* 1A 22
Patterdale St. *Stoke* 1K 27
Pavilion Dri. *Stoke* . . .7K 27 (1A 4)
Pavilion Way. *Cong* 4E 8
Paxton St. *Stoke* 3C 34 (6G 5)
Paynter St. *Stoke* 1E 40
Peacehaven Gro. *Stoke* 2B 46
Peacock Hay. 7B 20
Peacock Hay Rd. *Tal P* 7B 20
Peacock Ho. *Stoke* 7J 39
Peacock La. *New & Han* 6D 38
Peacock Rd. *New* 7C 26
Peacock Vw. *Fen I* 4E 34
Peak Dale Av. *Stoke* 4E 20
Peake St. *New* 2B 32
Peak Vw. *Leek* 4H 17
Pearl Gro. *Stoke* 6B 42

Pear Pl. *Stoke* 6J 35
Pear Tree Clo. *B'stn* 6C 46
Pear Tree Dri. *Mad* 1A 30
Pear Tree La. *New* 4A 26
Pear Tree Rd. *Big E* 3G 25
Peascroft Rd. *Stoke* 7C 22
Pebble Mill St. *Stoke* 2J 33
Peckforton Vw. *Kid* 4D 20
Peck Mill La. *B Frd* 2B 22
Pedley Ct. *Stoke* 6E 40
Pedley Gro. *Stoke* 3C 28
Peebles Grn. *Stoke* 3H 35
Peebles Rd. *New* 3G 31
Peel Ct. *Kid* 1D 20
      (off Attwood St.)
Peel Dri. *A'bry* 7D 8
Peel Hollow. *A'ly* 3B 24
Peel La. *A'bry* 7D 8
Peel St. *Stoke* 5H 41
        (Dresden)
Peel St. *Stoke* 4F 27
        (Longport)
Peel St. *Wol* 7F 27
Pegasus Gro. *Stoke* 3C 28
Peggy's Bank. *Big E* 4G 25
Pegroy Gro. *Stoke* 3C 28
Pelham St. *Stoke* 3C 34 (6G 5)
Pemberton Dri. *Stoke* 2B 48
Pembridge Rd. *Stoke* 7D 40
Pembroke Dri. *New* . . .6D 32 (6A 6)
Pembroke Rd. *Stoke* 3F 29
Penarth Gro. *Stoke* . . .7B 28 (1E 5)
Penarth Pl. *New* 6D 32 (6A 6)
Pendine Gro. *Stoke* 7G 35
Pengrove Clo. *Stoke* 3H 21
Penhale Av. *Stoke* 5B 42
Penkhull. 6K 33
Penkhull Ct. *Stoke* 6K 33
Penkhull New Rd. *Stoke* 7J 33
Penkhull Ter. *Stoke* 6K 33
Penk Rd. *For* 7H 43
Penkville St. *Stoke* 1K 39
Penmark Gro. *Stoke* 6K 41
Penmere Dri. *New* 5F 39
Penmere Dri. *Werr* 2B 36
Pennell St. *Stoke* 1G 35
Pennine Way. *Bid* 2K 15
Pennine Way. *New* 2B 32
Pennington Clo. *Stoke* 4D 42
Pennyfields Av. *Stoke* 3G 27
Pennyfields Rd. *N'cpl* 1F 21
Penny La. Shop. Mall. *C'dle* . . .3G 45
Penport Gro. *Stoke* 4F 41
Penrhyn Av. *Stoke* 3A 28
Penrith Clo. *Stoke* 2B 46
Penrith Ct. *Cong* 5C 8
Penrith Ct. *New* 7E 32
Pensford Gro. *Stoke* 7E 28
Pentland Gro. *New* 2B 32
Penton Pl. *Stoke* 7D 40
Penton Wlk. *Stoke* 7D 40
Pen y Bont Wlk. *Knyp* 4D 14
Pepper St. *K'le* 5F 31
Pepper St. *New* 4E 32 (4C 6)
Perceval St. *Stoke* 7D 28
Percival Dri. *Stoc B* 1H 29
Percy James Clo. *Als* 6F 11
Percy St. *Stoke* 1B 34 (3F 5)
Peregrine Gro. *Stoke* 7B 42
Perivale Clo. *Stoke* 6F 29
Perkins St. *Stoke* 4F 21
Perry Clo. *Stoke* 2C 34 (4G 5)
Perrymount Ct. *Stoke* 7J 33
Persia Wlk. *Stoke* 1G 27
Perth St. *Stoke* 1F 41
Perthy Gro. *Stoke* 7J 39
Perton Wood Vw. *Stoke* 3E 40
Petersfield Rd. *Stoke* 4K 21
Peterson Ho. *Stoke* 6A 42
Petrel Gro. *Stoke* 7C 42
Pevensey Gro. *Stoke* 7H 35
Philip La. *Werr* 1C 36
Philip St. *Stoke* 7D 34
Phillipson Way. *Stoke* 4C 28
Phipp Pl. *Stoke* 6C 40
Phoenix Clo. *Kid* 1F 21

Phoenix St. *Stoke* 1G 27
Picasso Ri. *Stoke* 1C 48
Piccadilly. *Stoke* 2B 34 (4E 5)
Piccadilly Arc. *Stoke* . .1B 34 (3E 5)
Piccadilly St. *Stoke* 1G 27
Pickering Clo. *Stoke* 5F 41
Pickford Pl. *Stoke* 5A 42
Pickmere Clo. *Stoke* 1G 29
Pickwick Pl. *Tal* 1A 20
Pickwood Av. *Leek* 4H 17
Pickwood Clo. *Leek* 4H 17
Picton St. *Leek* 3E 16
Picton St. *Stoke* 2C 34 (4H 5)
Pidduck St. *Stoke* 5H 27
Pierce St. *Stoke* 1G 27
Piggott Gro. *Stoke* 2F 35
Pikemere Rd. *Als* 5C 10
Pilkington Av. *New* 7D 32
Pillar Clo. *Stoke* 6J 35
Pilsbury St. *New* 6G 27
Pilsden Pl. *Stoke* 7D 42
Pine Clo. *Tal* 4A 20
Pine Ct. *Als* 6F 11
Pine Ct. *B Bri* 7E 42
Pinehurst Clo. *New* 3E 38
Pine Rd. *Stoke* 2B 40
Pine Tree Dri. *B Bri* 7E 42
Pinewood Cres. *Stoke* 4C 42
Pinewood Gro. *B Bri* 1H 49
Pinewood Gro. *New* 3B 26
Pinfold Av. *Stoke* 7C 22
Pinhoe Pl. *Stoke* 3K 41
Pinnox St. *Stoke* 2H 27
Pioneer Pl. *Stoke* 1B 28
      (off Brammer St.)
Pippins, The. *New* 3F 39
Pireford Pl. *Stoke* 3D 26
Pirehill Rd. *New* 3E 26
Pirie Clo. *Cong* 3J 9
Pirie Rd. *Cong* 2J 9
Pitcairn St. *Stoke* 1H 27
Pitcher La. *Leek* 4J 17
Pitfield Av. *New* 2G 33
Pitfield House. 3F 33 (1F 7)
        (Arts Cen.)
Pitgreen La. *New* 6F 27
Pit La. *Tal P* 5K 19
Pitlea Pl. *Stoke* 7H 35
Pitsford St. *Stoke* 4J 41
Pitts Hill. 6H 21
Pitts Hill Bank. *Stoke* 6J 21
Pitt St. E. *Stoke* 4K 27
Pitt St. W. *Stoke* 5K 27
Plainfield Gro. *Stoke* 5J 35
Plaisaunce, The. *New* 7E 32
Plane Gro. *New* 3B 26
Plantation Pk. *K'le* 7K 31
Plantation Rd. *Stoke* 1C 46
Plant St. *C'dle* 3H 45
Plant St. *Stoke* 2H 41
Platts Av. *End* 5K 23
Pleasant St. *Stoke* 5J 27
Plex St. *Stoke* 1G 27
Plex, The. *Als* 6E 10
Pleydell St. *Stoke* 5E 28
Plough Cft. *Als* 7B 10
Plough St. *Stoke* 7C 28 (1G 5)
Plover Clo. *Stoke* 7B 42
Plover Dri. *Bid* 2D 14
Plover Fld. *Mad* 2A 30
Plumtree Gro. *Stoke* 6E 28
Plymouth Gro. *New* 5C 26
Pochard Clo. *Stoke* 2C 28
Podmore Av. *Als B* 6G 25
Podmore La. *Halm* 6E 24
        (in two parts)
Podmore St. *Stoke* 5K 27
Podmore Ter. *Halm* 6E 24
Pointon Gro. *Stoke* 6F 23
Polperro Way. *Stoke* 7B 42
Pomona St. *Stoke* 4C 28
Pool Dam. *New* 5E 32 (5C 6)
Poole Av. *Stoke* 6G 29
Poolend. 1C 16
Pooles Rd. *Bid M* 2G 15
Poolfield Av. *New* 5C 32 (5A 6)
Poolfield Av. N. *New* . . .5D 32 (4A 6)

Poolfields—Riley Av.

Poolfields. . . . 5D 32 (5B 6)
Poolfields Clo. New . . . 5C 32
Poolfields Ct. Brn E . . . 4H 23
Poolhill Clo. Stoke . . . 4F 41
Poolside. Mad . . . 2B 30
Poolside. New . . . 4D 32 (3B 6)
Poolside. Sch G . . . 3H 11
Poolside. Stoke . . . 6E 40
Poolside Ct. Als . . . 6F 11
Pool St. New . . . 5D 32 (5B 6)
Pool St. Stoke . . . 7G 35
Poplar Av. New . . . 2D 32
Poplar Clo. B Bri . . . 1H 49
Poplar Clo. Cong . . . 3C 8
Poplar Clo. New . . . 2D 32
Poplar Ct. New . . . 2D 32
Poplar Dri. Als . . . 1F 19
Poplar Dri. Kid . . . 2D 20
Poplar Dri. Stoke . . . 4D 40
Poplar Gro. New . . . 4G 33 (2G 7)
Poplar Gro. Stoke . . . 5F 41
Poppyfields. Als . . . 7C 10
Porlock Gro. Stoke . . . 1A 46
Porthill. . . . 5F 27
Porthill Bank. New . . . 6F 27
Porthill Grange. New . . . 6F 27
Porthill Grn. New . . . 6F 27
Porthill Rd. Stoke . . . 5G 27
Portland Clo. B Bri . . . 7E 42
Portland Dri. Bid . . . 2J 15
Portland Dri. For . . . 6J 43
Portland Dri. Sch G . . . 4B 12
Portland Gro. New . . . 3E 38
Portland M. New . . . 6E 26
Portland Pl. B'stn . . . 3E 46
Portland Rd. Stoke . . . 2G 41
Portland St. Leek . . . 3G 17
Portland St. Stoke . . . 7A 28 (1C 4)
Portland St. N. Leek . . . 3G 17
Portland St. S. Leek . . . 3G 17
Port St. Stoke . . . 5H 27
Port Va. Ct. Stoke . . . 3K 27
Port Vale F.C. (Vale Pk.) . . . 3K 27
Port Va. St. Stoke . . . 5H 27
Post La. End . . . 2K 23
Post Office Sq. Mad . . . 3B 30
Post Office Ter. Ful . . . 7F 49
Potteries Mus. & Art Gallery, The. . . . 2B 34 (4E 5)
Potteries Shop. Cen. Stoke . . . 1B 34 (2F 5)
Potteries Way. Stoke . . . 7B 28 (1E 5) (in two parts)
Potters Barn, The. . . . 1B 10
Potters Barn, The. Has G . . . 1B 10
Potters End. Bid . . . 1A 14
Poulson St. Stoke . . . 6A 34
Pound Gdns. Stoke . . . 7C 22
Poundsgate Gro. Stoke . . . 6A 40
Povey Pl. New . . . 3E 26
Powderham Clo. Stoke . . . 3H 21
Powell St. Stoke . . . 7A 28 (1C 4)
Power Gro. Stoke . . . 2F 41
Powerleague Soccer Cen. . . . 3C 40
Power Wash Trad. Est. Knyp . . . 5A 14
Powy Dri. Kid . . . 1E 20
Premier Gdns. Kid . . . 1C 20
Prestbury Av. New . . . 5E 38
Preston St. Stoke . . . 4B 28
Pretoria Rd. Stoke . . . 2K 33 (6A 4)
Priam Clo. New . . . 3E 26
Price St. Stoke . . . 3J 27
Priestley Dri. Stoke . . . 2J 41
Priesty Ct. Cong . . . 5F 9
Priesty Fields. Cong . . . 5F 9
Prime St. Stoke . . . 7D 28
Primitive St. Mow C . . . 3F 13
Primrose Dell. Mad . . . 2A 30
Primrose Gro. New . . . 3F 33
Primrose Hill. Stoke . . . 4K 39
Primrose Vale. . . . 4J 9
Prince Charles Av. Leek . . . 2J 17
Prince George St. C'dle . . . 3G 45
Prince's Rd. Stoke . . . 5J 33
Princess Av. A'ly . . . 3E 24
Princess Av. Leek . . . 1J 17
Princess Ct. Tal P . . . 6A 20
Princess Dri. Stoke . . . 3B 42
Princes Sq. Stoke . . . 4G 27
Princess St. Bid . . . 3C 14
Princess St. Cong . . . 4F 9
Princess St. New . . . 5F 33 (4F 7)
Princess St. Tal P . . . 6A 20
Prince St. Leek . . . 2G 17
Princetown Clo. Stoke . . . 7B 42
Priorfield Clo. Stoke . . . 2G 41
Priory Av. Leek . . . 1H 17
Priory Clo. Cong . . . 7K 9
Priory Ct. Stoke . . . 7H 29
Priory Pl. Kid . . . 7E 12
Priory Rd. New . . . 6D 32 (6B 6)
Priory Rd. Stoke . . . 6G 29
Priory, The. End . . . 1K 23
Probyn Ct. Stoke . . . 4H 41
Prospect Pl. Leek . . . 4F 17
Prospect Rd. Leek . . . 4H 17
Prospect St. Cong . . . 5E 8
Prospect St. Stoke . . . 6H 27
Prospect Ter. New . . . 4D 32 (2B 6)
Providence Sq. Stoke . . . 1G 5
Providence St. Stoke . . . 7C 28
Provost Pl. Leek . . . 2H 17
Pullman Ct. C'dle . . . 4F 45
Pump Bank. K'le . . . 6G 31
Pump St. Leek . . . 2G 17
Pump St. New . . . 5D 32 (5B 6)
Pump St. Stoke . . . 6K 33
Purbeck St. Stoke . . . 5A 28
Purser Cres. New . . . 7E 26
Pyenest St. Stoke . . . 3A 34

Q

Quabbs La. For . . . 6K 43
Quadrangle, The. End . . . 2K 23
Quadrant Rd. Stoke . . . 1B 34 (2E 5)
Quadrant, The. Stoke . . . 2F 5
Quail Gro. Stoke . . . 7B 42
Quarry Av. Stoke . . . 5J 33
Quarry Bank. . . . 4G 31
Quarry Bank Rd. K'le . . . 4G 31
Quarry Clo. Stoc B . . . 1H 29
Quarry Clo. Werr . . . 1B 36
Quarry Rd. Stoke . . . 5J 33
Quarry Ter. Kid . . . 2D 20
Quarry Wlk. Path. C'dle . . . 6K 45
Quayside. Cong . . . 6G 9
Queen Anne St. Stoke . . . 5A 34
Queen Elizabeth II Ct. Stoke . . . 7C 34
Queen Mary Rd. Stoke . . . 5K 39
Queen Mary's Dri. B'stn . . . 3D 46
Queens Av. Stoke . . . 1H 27
Queensberry Rd. Stoke . . . 4J 41
Queens Clo. B'stn . . . 5E 46
Queens Ct. New . . . 4F 33 (2E 7)
Queens Ct. Stoke . . . 5G 41 (off Queen's Pk. Av.)
Queen's Dri. Bid . . . 4C 14
Queens Dri. Leek . . . 1J 17
Queens Gdns. Tal P . . . 5A 20
Queensmead Rd. Stoke . . . 7A 42
Queen's Pk. Av. Stoke . . . 5G 41
Queen's Rd. Stoke . . . 5J 33
Queens Row. B'stn . . . 5E 46
Queen's Ter. Stoke . . . 1D 34
Queen St. A'ly . . . 3D 24
Queen St. C'dle . . . 3H 45
Queen St. Ches . . . 5B 26
Queen St. Cong . . . 5E 8 (Booth St.)
Queen St. Cong . . . 3H 9 (Havannah St.)
Queen St. Kid . . . 1D 20
Queen St. Leek . . . 3G 17
Queen St. New . . . 6E 26 (Heaton Ter.)
Queen St. New . . . 4F 33 (2E 7) (Nelson Pl.)
Queen St. Stoke . . . 4J 27
Queens Wlk. Stoke . . . 2C 42
Queensway. Als . . . 5C 10
Queens Way. New . . . 7E 32
Queensway Ct. Stoke . . . 5B 42 (off Broadway)
Queensway Ind. Est. Stoke . . . 4F 27
Quinta Rd. Cong . . . 4C 8
Quintin Wlk. Stoke . . . 2B 28
Quinton Gro. New . . . 1E 32

R

Race Course. New . . . 4K 31
Racecourse Rd. Stoke . . . 2K 39
Rachel Gro. Stoke . . . 7G 35
Radford Rd. Stoke . . . 4J 33
Radley Way. Werr . . . 2C 36
Radnor. . . . 1A 8
Radnor Clo. Cong . . . 4D 8
Radnor Pk. Trad. Est. Cong . . . 3C 8
Radstone Ri. New . . . 3E 38
Radway Green. . . . 2A 18
Radway Grn. Rd. Rad G . . . 3A 18
Radway Green Sports & Social Club. . . . 6F 11
Raglan St. Stoke . . . 7C 34
Raglan Wlk. Stoke . . . 7C 34 (off Raglan St.)
Railton Av. Stoke . . . 5F 41
Railway Cotts. Brn L . . . 6A 14
Railway Cotts. Cong . . . 6J 9
Railway Cotts. Stoke . . . 3B 40
Railway Ct. End . . . 2K 23
Railway Enterprise Cen. Stoke . . . 4K 33
Railway Pas. Stoke . . . 2H 41
Railway St. Stoke . . . 2H 27
Railway Ter. B Bri . . . 7F 43
Railway Ter. Stoke . . . 3H 41
Rainford Clo. Pac . . . 2J 21
Rainham Gro. Stoke . . . 3K 21
Rakeway. . . . 5J 45
Rakeway Rd. C'dle . . . 5H 45
Ralph Dri. Stoke . . . 4D 28
Ramage Gro. Stoke . . . 5J 41
Ramsay Clo. B'stn . . . 3D 46
Ramsey Rd. New . . . 3D 32
Ramsey St. Stoke . . . 1B 40
Ramshaw Gro. Stoke . . . 7J 35
Ramshaw Vw. Leek . . . 1H 17
Randel La. Stoke . . . 3E 20
Ranelagh St. Stoke . . . 2B 34 (5E 5)
Rangemore Ter. New . . . 2G 33
Ransome Pl. Stoke . . . 2K 41
Ranworth Clo. New . . . 4E 38
Rathbone Av. New . . . 2G 33
Rathbone St. Stoke . . . 1H 27
Rattigan Dri. Stoke . . . 2A 42
Ratton St. Stoke . . . 1C 34 (2G 5)
Ravenna Way. Stoke . . . 1K 41
Ravenscliffe. . . . 6D 20
Ravenscliffe. New . . . 5F 27 (off First Av.)
Ravenscliffe Rd. Kid . . . 3D 20
Ravens Clo. Big E . . . 1F 25
Ravensdale. . . . 2F 27
Ravenside Retail Pk. Stoke . . . 5C 34
Raven's La. Big E . . . 1G 25
Ravenswood Clo. New . . . 3D 38
Rawle Clo. C'dle . . . 3F 45
Rawlins St. Stoke . . . 7D 28 (1H 5)
Rayleigh Way. Stoke . . . 4J 35
Raymond Av. Stoke . . . 5C 28
Raymond St. Stoke . . . 3B 34 (6E 5)
Reade's La. Cong . . . 7K 9
Reading Way. Stoke . . . 3J 35
Reads Rd. Fen I . . . 5E 34
Rebecca St. Stoke . . . 5A 34
Recorder Gro. Stoke . . . 5A 22
Recreation Rd. Stoke . . . 4K 41
Rectory Gdns. Tal P . . . 5A 20
Rectory Pas. Stoke . . . 3A 34 (6D 4)
Rectory Rd. Stoke . . . 3A 34 (6C 4)
Rectory St. Stoke . . . 3A 34 (6C 4)
Rectory Vw. Tal P . . . 5A 20
Red Bank. Stoke . . . 5H 41
Redbridge Clo. Stoke . . . 5J 39
Red Bull. . . . 7A 12
Redcar Rd. Stoke . . . 7K 39
Redfern Av. Cong . . . 3H 9
Red Hall La. Halm . . . 1C 30
Redheath Clo. New . . . 3H 31
Redheath Cotts. New . . . 3G 31
Redhills Rd. Stoke . . . 4E 28
Red Ho. Cres. Stoke . . . 3F 41
Redland Dri. Stoke . . . 2J 35
Red La. L Oaks . . . 2H 29
Red La. Mad . . . 3B 30
Red Lion Clo. Tal . . . 4A 20
Red Lion Pas. Stoke . . . 2A 34 (5D 4)
Red Lion Sq. Ches . . . 5B 26
Redman Gro. Stoke . . . 5B 28
Redmine Clo. New . . . 1D 32
Red Street. . . . 1A 26
Redwing Dri. Bid . . . 2D 14
Redwing Gro. Pac . . . 2H 21
Redwood Pl. Stoke . . . 5A 42
Reedbed Clo. Stoke . . . 1B 28
Reedham Way. Stoke . . . 3J 35
Reeves Av. New . . . 1E 32
Reeves Av. Stoke . . . 1K 27
Refinery St. New . . . 5F 33 (5E 7)
Regency Clo. Tal P . . . 6A 20
Regency Dri. Stoc B . . . 7G 23
Regent Av. Stoke . . . 1J 27
Regent Ct. New . . . 6E 26
Regent Ho. B Frd . . . 1A 22 (off Outclough Rd)
Regent Rd. Stoke . . . 3B 34 (6E 5)
Regent St. Leek . . . 3G 17
Regent St. Stoke . . . 1J 39
Regent Theatre. . . . 2B 34 (4E 5)
Reginald Mitchell Ct. Stoke . . . 2C 34 (5G 5)
Reginald Mitchell Way. Stoke . . . 7F 21
Reginald St. Stoke . . . 4K 27
Regina St. Stoke . . . 2C 28
Registry St. Stoke . . . 5A 34
Reid St. Stoke . . . 4H 27
Rembrandt Way. Stoke . . . 1C 48
Remer St. Stoke . . . 6A 28
Renard Way. Stoke . . . 7C 42
Renfrew Clo. New . . . 5C 32
Renfrew Pl. Stoke . . . 5K 39
Renown Clo. Stoke . . . 4E 34
Repington Rd. Stoke . . . 4D 28
Repton Dri. New . . . 1C 38
Reservoir Rd. Stoke . . . 4K 41
Reynolds Av. New . . . 6B 26
Reynolds Rd. Stoke . . . 1K 27
Rhodes Ct. New . . . 5F 27
Rhodes St. Stoke . . . 6C 28
Rhondda Av. Stoke . . . 5B 28
Rialto Pl. Stoke . . . 1G 27
Ribble Clo. New . . . 3E 38
Ribble Dri. Bid . . . 1D 14
Ribble Ind. Est. Stoke . . . 5H 27
Ribblesdale Av. Cong . . . 2J 9
Ricardo St. Stoke . . . 5G 41
Riceyman Rd. New . . . 3E 26
Richards Av. Stoke . . . 1J 27
Richardson Pl. Stoke . . . 5A 22
Richmond Av. Stoke . . . 5C 28
Richmond Gro. New . . . 2G 33
Richmond Rd. Stoke . . . 5J 39
Richmond St. Stoke . . . 5K 33
Richmond Ter. Stoke . . . 3A 34
Ridding Bank. Han . . . 7E 38
Ridge Clo. B'stn . . . 7B 46
Ridge Cres. Stoke . . . 1A 48
Ridgefields. Bid M . . . 1G 15
Ridgehill Dri. Mad H . . . 6C 30
Ridgehouse Dri. Stoke . . . 1K 33 (3A 4)
Ridge Rd. Stoke . . . 5G 21
Ridge Wlk. Stoke . . . 7A 42
Ridgeway. Brn E . . . 3C 22
Ridgmont Rd. New . . . 2C 38
Ridgway Dri. B Bri . . . 7E 42
Ridgway Pl. New . . . 6G 27
Ridgway Rd. Stoke . . . 4B 34
Ridley St. Stoke . . . 1B 40
Ridley Wlk. Stoke . . . 1B 40
Rigby Rd. Kid . . . 7E 12
Riley Av. Stoke . . . 2A 28

A-Z Stoke 69

Riley St. N. *Stoke* 4H 27
Riley St. S. *Stoke* 4J 27
Rileys Way. *Big E* 2G 25
Rill St. *Stoke* 2G 41
Rimini Clo. *Stoke* 1K 41
Rindle, The. *C'dle* 3E 44
Ringland Clo. *Stoke* . . .1C 34 (3H 5)
Ripon Av. *New* 5B 26
Ripon Rd. *Stoke* 6E 40
Riseley Rd. *Stoke* 5G 33 (4H 7)
Rists Ind. Est. *New* 1C 32
Rists Rd. *New* 1C 32
Rivendell La. *Leek* 7G 17
Riverdale Dri. *Stoke* 3H 21
Riverdane Rd. *Cong* 3G 9
Riverhead Clo. *Stoke* 6E 22
River Lea M. *Mad* 2B 30
Riverside Ct. *Stoke* 1E 34
Riverside Rd. *Stoke* 3H 39
Riversmead. *New* 2E 38
River St. *Cong* 4F 9
Rivington Cres. *Stoke* 5K 21
Rixdale Clo. *Stoke* 7B 28 (1E 5)
Robert Heath St. *Stoke* 2B 28
Roberts Av. *New* 3D 32 (1B 6)
Roberts Clo. *Als B* 6G 25
Robertson Dri. *New* 2C 32
Robertson Sq. *Stoke* 2H 39
Robert St. *Stoke* 7G 21
Robertville Rd. *Stoke* 2G 35
Robina Dri. *C'dle* 3H 45
Robin Cft. *Stoke* 4J 27
Robin Hill. 2E 14
Robin Hill. *Bid M* 3F 15
Robin Hill Gro. *Stoke* 1G 41
Robinson Av. *Stoke* 4C 28
Robinson Ct. *Stoke* 6E 40
Robinson Rd. *Stoke* 6J 39
Robson St. *Stoke* 2A 34 (5D 4)
Roche Av. *Leek* 1H 17
Rochester Rd. *Stoke* 1G 41
Rochford Clo. *Leek* 4D 16
Rochford Way. *Stoke* 4J 35
Rock End. 4E 14
Rockfield Av. *L Oaks* 3J 29
Rock House Dri. *B'stn* 6C 46
Rockhouse La. *Tal* 3K 19
    (in two parts)
Rockingham Dri. *C'dle* 3J 45
Rocklands. *New* 5F 27
Rockside. *Mow C* 4F 13
Rocks, The. *Brn E* 3G 23
Rode Ct. *Cong* 4H 9
Rode Hall. 3J 11
Rode Heath. 3G 11
Rodehouse Clo. *Rode H* 3G 11
Rode, The. *Als* 6E 10
Rodgers Ct. *Stoke* 4F 21
    (off Rodgers St.)
Rodgers St. *Stoke* 3F 21
Roebuck Shop. Cen., The.
    New 5E 32 (4D 6)
Roebuck St. *Stoke* 5B 34
Roe La. *New* 2D 38
Roe Pk. *Mow C* 1H 13
Roe St. *Cong* 5G 9
Rogate Clo. *Stoke* 7G 35
Rogers Av. *New* 2C 32
Rogerstone Av. *Stoke* 7H 33
Rolfe Clo. *Stoke* 4K 39
Roma Clo. *Stoke* 6J 41
Roman Dri. *New* 7A 26
Romer Side. *Stoke* 5H 35
Romford Pl. *Stoke* 7C 42
Romney Av. *New* 6B 26
Romney Gro. *Stoke* 6H 41
Romsey Clo. *Stoke* 5J 35
Ronald St. *Stoke* 4H 41
    (in two parts)
Ronaldsway Dri. *New* 3D 32
Ronald Wlk. *Stoke* 4H 41
Ronson Av. *Stoke* 2H 39
Rood Hill. *Cong* 4F 9
Rood La. *Cong* 4F 9
Rookery Av. *Stoke* 5F 41
Rookery Ct. *Stoke* 3H 39
Rookery Cres. *C'wll* 5K 49

Rookery La. *Stoke* 3J 39
Rookery Rd. *Kid* 7F 13
Rookery, The. 7F 13
Rookery, The. *New* 4K 31
Rope St. *Stoke* 4G 33 (3G 7)
Rope Wlk. *Cong* 4F 9
Roseacre. *New* 5C 32 (6A 6)
Roseacre Gro. *Stoke* 1A 48
Roseacre La. *B Bri* 1G 49
Rose Bank St. *Leek* 3G 17
Rosebank Ter. *Leek* 3G 17
    (off Rose Bank St.)
Roseberry Dri. *Mad* 1B 30
Roseberry St. *Stoke* 6J 21
Rosebery Clo. *Bid* 2D 14
Rose Cotts. *Werr* 1K 23
Rosehill Clo. *Stoke* 3G 29
Roseland Cres. *Stoke* 3G 29
Rosemary Pl. *Stoke* 5D 28
Rosemary St. *New* 4B 32
Rosendale Av. *New* 6C 26
Roseneath Pl. *Stoke* 3G 29
Rose St. *Stoke* 7D 28 (1H 5)
Rose Tree Av. *Stoke* 4H 39
Rosevale Bus. Pk. *New* 4C 26
Rosevale Clo. *New* 4B 26
Rosevale La. *New* 4B 26
Rosevale Rd. *P West* 4B 26
Rosevale St. *Stoke* 3G 29
Rosevean Clo. *Stoke* . .7B 28 (1E 5)
Roseville Dri. *Cong* 7K 9
Rosewood Av. *Stoc B* 7H 23
Rossall Av. *New* 1C 38
Ross Clo. *Stoke* 2B 42
Rossett Gro. *Stoke* 3J 21
Rosslyn Rd. *Stoke* 4H 41
Rother Wlk. *Stoke* 7K 21
Rothesay Av. *New* 6C 32
Rothesay Ct. *New* 6C 32
Rothesay Ct. *Stoke* 4J 41
Rothesay Rd. *Stoke* 4J 41
Rothley Grn. *Stoke* 6E 40
Rothsay Av. *Stoke* 4C 28
Rothwell St. *Stoke* 7J 33
Rotterdam. *New* 4C 32 (3A 6)
Rotterdam Rd. *New* 4C 32
Rough Close. 4K 47
Roughcote. 7D 36
Roughcote La. *Cav* 7D 36
Roughwood La.
    Has G & Chu L 1B 10
Roundfields. *Stoc B* 1H 29
Roundway. *Stoke* 4D 40
Roundwell St. *Stoke* 1G 27
Rownall Vw. *Leek* 5D 16
Rowanburn Clo. *Stoke* 1J 41
Rowan Clo. *Als* 7E 10
Rowan Clo. *Bid M* 2G 15
Rowan Clo. *Chu L* 4D 10
Rowan Clo. *Kid* 3D 20
Rowan Gro. *Stoke* 3D 40
Rowan Pl. *New* 4B 26
Rowhurst Clo.
    Row I & New 5K 25
    (in two parts)
Rowhurst Clo. Ind. Est.
    Row I 5K 25
Rowhurst Pl. *Stoke* 6B 22
Rowland St. *Stoke* 5G 41
Rowley Av. *New* 5B 26
Rownall Pl. *Stoke* 4B 42
Rownall Rd. *Stoke* 4B 42
Rownall Rd. *Werr* 1E 36
Roxburghe Av. *Stoke* 4J 41
Royal Doulton Hall. *Stoke* . . .5B 34
Royal Doulton Vis. Cen. 4K 27
Royal St. *Stoke* 1F 41
Royal Wlk. *C'dle* 3G 45
Royce Av. *Knyp* 5A 14
Roycroft Clo. *New* 4E 26
Royden Av. *Stoke* 1E 34
Roylance St. *Stoke* 1G 27
Royle Pk. *Cong* 4F 9
Royle St. *Cong* 4F 9
Royston Wlk. *Stoke* 3H 41
Royville Pl. *Stoke* 4C 28

Ruabon Clo. *Knyp* 4D 14
Rubens Way. *Stoke* 7C 42
Rubian St. *Stoke* 7E 34
Rudyard. 1A 16
Rudyard Gro. *New* 1F 33
Rudyard Rd. *Bid M* 1G 15
Rudyard Rd. *Rud* 1A 16
Rudyard Way. *C'dle* 2J 45
Rugby Clo. *New* 1C 38
Rugby Dri. *Stoke* 5G 41
Runnymede Clo. *Stoke* 2G 35
Rupert St. *Bid* 2B 14
Rushcliffe Dri. *Stoke* 7B 42
Rushmoor Gro. *Stoke* 7C 42
Rushton. *New* 2C 38
Rushton Clo. *Brn E* 4G 23
Rushton Gro. *Stoke* 5K 27
Rushton Rd. *Stoke* 5K 27
Rushton Way. *For* 6H 43
Ruskin Clo. *Stoke* 2J 41
Ruskin Rd. *Cong* 5E 8
Rusper Clo. *Stoke* 6E 28
Russell Av. *Als* 5E 10
Russell Clo. *Cong* 7H 9
Russell Gro. *Werr* 1C 36
Russell Pl. *Stoke* 5G 21
Russell Rd. *Stoke* 5G 21
Russell St. *Leek* 4F 17
Russell St. *New* 7F 27
Russell St. *Stoke* 5G 41
Russet Clo. *Stoke* 7B 42
Rustington Av. *Stoke* 3K 41
Ruston Av. *Stoke* 5A 22
Rutherford Av. *New* 3E 38
Rutherford Pl. *Stoke* 6H 33
Ruthin Gro. *Knyp* 4D 14
Ruthin Rd. *Stoke* 3H 35
Rutland Clo. *Cong* 3G 9
Rutland Pl. *New* 2F 39
Rutland Rd. *Kid* 1D 20
Rutland Rd. *Stoke* 2H 41
Rutland St. *Stoke* 7A 28 (1C 4)
Ruxley Ct. *Stoke* 2F 35
Ruxley Rd. *Stoke* 2F 35
Rydal Ct. *Cong* 5C 8
Rydale Way. *Cong* 7K 9
Rydal Way. *Als* 5D 10
Rydal Way. *New* 2E 38
Ryder Rd. *Stoke* 6B 42
Rye Bank. *New* 4E 32 (3D 6)
Rye Bank Cres. *New* . . .4F 33 (2D 6)
Ryebrook Gro. *Stoke* 5J 21
Rye Clo. *Als* 7C 10
Ryecroft. *New* 4E 32 (2C 6)
Ryecroft Rd. *Stoke* 1D 28
Rye Hills. 4E 24
Rye Hills. *Big E* 3F 25
Ryeland Clo. *Stoke* 6H 41
Rylestone Clo. *Stoke* 7C 42

S

Sackville St. *Stoke* . .3H 33 (1H 7)
Saffron Clo. *Stoke* 1B 48
Sage Clo. *Stoke* 3B 34 (6F 5)
St Aidan's St. *Stoke* 7G 21
St Andrews Cres. *Stoke* 5C 28
St Andrews Dri. *Kid* 7F 13
St Andrew's Dri. *New*
    . . . . .5C 32 (4A 6)
St Andrews Gdns. *Als* 1F 19
St Andrews Sq. *Stoke* 6K 33
St Anne's Av. *Brn E* 2G 23
St Ann St. *Stoke* 1C 34 (3H 5)
St Ann Wlk. *Stoke* 3H 5
St Anthony's Dri. *New* 6C 32
St Bartholomews Clo.
    Stoke 7D 22
St Bernard Pl. *Stoke* 7F 29
St Bernard's Rd. *New* 3C 32
St Chads Rd. *Stoke* 1H 27
St Chad's Ter. *New* 2A 26
St Christopher Av. *Stoke* 6H 33
St Clair St. *Stoke* 4H 41
St Davids Way. *Knyp* 4D 14
St Dominic's Ct. *Stoke* 5K 33

St Edmund's Av. *New* 5G 27
St Edward St. *Leek* 4F 17
St Gabriels Ct. *Als* 7D 10
St Georges Av. *End* 5K 23
St Georges Av. *Stoke* 7K 21
St Georges Av. N. *New* 7E 26
St George's Av. S. *New* 7E 26
St George's Av. W. *New* 7E 26
St Georges Cres. *Stoke* 5K 39
St George's Rd. *New*
    . . . . .5D 32 (4A 6)
St Giles Rd. *New* 3C 32
St Gregorys Rd. *Stoke* 3F 41
St Helier Clo. *New* 3C 38
St James Av. *Cong* 5E 8
St James Ct. *A'ly* 2E 24
St James Ct. *Bid* 1K 15
St James Ct. *Cong* 5E 8
St James Pl. *Stoke* 5K 39
St James Stoke 2A 34 (5D 4)
St John's Av. *New* 1F 33
St John's Av. *Stoke* 2H 39
St Johns Pl. *Bid* 3C 14
St John's Rd. *Bid* 4B 14
St John's Rd. *Cong* 3H 9
St John's Sq. *Stoke* 4J 27
St John St. *Stoke* 7C 28 (1G 5)
St John's Wood. *Kid* 2C 20
St Joseph St. *Stoke* 4F 21
St Lucy's Dri. *New* 5F 27
St Luke's Clo. *New* 3J 31
St Luke's Ct. *Stoke* 4B 42
St Luke St. *Stoke* 2C 34 (4H 5)
St Margaret's Ct. *New* 7G 27
St Margaret's Dri. *Stoke* 4D 28
St Margarets Gro. *Stoke* 3D 40
St Mark's Clo. *Stoke* . .3A 34 (6D 4)
St Mark's St. *Stoke* . . .3A 34 (6D 4)
St Martin's La. *Stoke* 3H 41
St Martin's Rd. *New* . . .5C 32 (4A 6)
St Martin's Rd. *Tal P* 5B 20
St Mary's Clo. *Als* 5D 10
St Mary's Ct. *Cong* 5C 8
St Mary's Dri. *New* 5D 32 (4A 6)
St Mary's Rd. *New* 7G 27
St Mary's Rd. *Stoke* 1J 41
St Matthew St. *Stoke* 7E 34
St Saviours St. *Tal* 2A 20
St Stephens Ct. *Bid* 1C 14
    (off Thames Dri.)
St Stephens Ct. *Cong* 4H 9
    (off Herbert St.)
St Thomas Pl. *Stoke* 7J 33
St Thomas St. *Mow C* 3G 13
St Vincent Pl. *New* 3B 32
Salcombe Pl. *Stoke* 5C 28
Salem St. *Stoke* 2J 33 (5A 4)
Salford Pl. *Cong* 4G 9
Salisbury Av. *Stoke* 3B 34
Salisbury Clo. *Mad* 6A 30
Salisbury La. *Leek* 3F 17
Salisbury St. *Stoke* 1H 27
Salkeld Pl. *Stoke* 6A 22
Salop Gro. *New* 2F 39
Salop Pl. *Kid* 7D 12
Saltdean Clo. *Stoke* 4K 41
Salters Clo. *Werr* 2C 36
Salters La. *Werr & Stoke* 2C 36
Salt La. *Has G & Chu L* 1A 10
Sampson St. *Stoke* . . .1A 34 (2D 4)
Samuel St. *Pac* 2J 21

Sancton Grn. *Stoke*	4H 27
Sandbach Rd. *Chu L*	4E 10
Sandbach Rd. *Cong*	5A 8
Sandbach Rd. *Rode H*	1E 10
Sandbach Rd. *Stoke*	5A 28
Sandbach Rd. N. *Als*	6D 10
Sandbach Rd. S. *Als*	7E 10
Sandcrest Pl. *Stoke*	5A 42
Sandcrest Wlk. *Stoke*	5A 42
Sanderson Pl. *New*	6E 26
Sandford Hill.	1H 41
Sandford St. *New*	4B 26
Sandford St. *Stoke*	1H 41
Sandgate St. *Stoke*	3J 41
Sandhurst Av. *Stoke*	5A 42
Sandhurst Clo. *New*	7F 27
Sandiway Pl. *Stoke*	6D 28
Sandon Av. *New*	1D 38
Sandon Clo. *C'wll*	5K 49
Sandon Ct. *Stoke*	7A 42
Sandon Old Rd. *Stoke*	7A 42
Sandon Rd. *C'wll*	5K 49
Sandon Rd. *Stoke*	7A 42
Sandon St. *Leek*	5F 17
Sandon St. *Stoke*	2K 33 (4B 4)
Sandown Clo. *C'dle*	1H 45
Sandown Pl. *Stoke*	2H 29
Sandpiper Ct. *Kid*	1F 21
Sandra Clo. *Stoke*	2K 27
Sandringham Cres. *Stoke*	5K 39
Sandsdown Clo. *Bid*	1B 14
Sandside Rd. *Als*	7C 10
Sands La. *Stoke*	7F 15
Sands Rd. *Har*	4H 13
Sandwell Pl. *Stoke*	6K 41
Sandwick Cres. *Stoke*	6E 28
Sandwood Cres. *Stoke*	1H 41
Sandy Brook Clo. *Leek*	6G 17
Sandybrook La. *Leek*	7G 17
Sandyfield Rd. *Stoke*	7D 28
Sandyford.	5G 21
Sandy Hill. *Werr*	1D 36
Sandylands Cres. *Chu L*	5G 11
Sandy La. *Brn E*	3G 23
Sandy La. *Cong*	3A 8
(Holmes Chapel Rd.)	
Sandy La. *Cong*	5D 8
(Newcastle Rd.)	
Sandy La. *New*	3F 33 (1G 7)
Sandy La. *Stoke*	2H 29
Sandy La. M. *Cong*	2E 8
Sandy Rd. *Gil H*	2H 15
Sandy Rd. *Stoke*	4G 21
Sangster La. *Stoke*	2C 28
Sant St. *Stoke*	4H 27
Saplings, The. *New*	3F 39
Saracen Way. *Stoke*	5B 42
Sargeant Av. *Stoke*	5K 21
Sark Clo. *New*	2B 38
Sark Pl. *Stoke*	7J 35
Sarraine Ind. Pk. *C'dle*	4E 44
Sarver La. *Dil*	2K 43
Saturn Rd. *Stoke*	3B 28
Saunders Rd. *New*	1E 32
Saverley Green.	5J 49
Saverley Grn. Rd. *Ful*	7G 49
Sawpit Yd. *Mad*	6A 30
Sawyer Dri. *Bid*	1B 14
Scarlett St. *New*	5E 32 (4D 6)
Scarratt Clo. *For*	6J 43
Scarratt Dri. *For*	7J 43
Sceptre St. *Stoke*	2B 34 (5E 5)
Scholar Green.	4B 12
School Clo. *Big E*	3H 25
School Clo. *Dil*	1A 44
School Clo. *Leek*	5D 16
School La. *A'bry*	7D 8
School La. *Bid M*	1G 15
School La. *Cav & Stoke*	3E 42
School La. *Long*	6A 16
School La. *Stoke*	6E 40
School Rd. *Bag*	2K 29
School Rd. *Stoke*	7F 29
School St. *Ches*	6C 26
School St. *Leek*	3F 17
School St. *New*	4F 33 (3E 7)

School St. *Stoke*	3H 39
Scot Hay.	2E 30
Scot Hay Rd. *Als B*	1F 31
Scot Hay Rd. *Sil*	2F 31
Scotia Bus. Pk. *Stoke*	2H 27
Scotia Rd. *Stoke*	1H 27
Scotia Clo. *Rode H*	2F 11
Scott Lidgett Ind. Est.	
Stoke	5G 27
Scott Lidgett Rd. *Stoke*	5G 27
Scott Rd. *Stoke*	6J 21
Scott St. *New*	4F 33 (3E 7)
Scragg St. *Pac*	3J 21
Scrimshaw Dri. *Stoke*	1B 28
Scrivener Rd. *Stoke*	4J 33
Seabridge.	3C 38
Seabridge La. *New*	2B 38
Seabridge Rd. *New*	6D 32 (6B 6)
Seaford St. *Stoke*	4A 34
Seagrave Pl. *New*	7D 32
Seagrave St. *New*	4F 33 (3F 7)
Seaton Clo. *Stoke*	6K 41
Sebring Av. *Stoke*	6K 41
Second Av. *Kid*	2B 20
Second Av. *New*	5F 27
Second Av. *Stoke*	1J 35
Sedbergh Clo. *New*	2C 38
Seddon Ct. *Stoke*	3H 5
Seddon Rd. *Stoke*	6A 42
Sedgley Wlk. *Stoke*	2H 41
Seedfields Rd. *Stoke*	3D 40
Sefton Av. *Cong*	6J 9
Sefton Av. *Stoke*	5D 28
Sefton Rd. *Stoke*	4K 41
Sefton St. *Stoke*	2K 33 (4B 4)
Selborne Rd. *Leek*	5F 17
Selbourne Dri. *New*	4J 21
Selby Clo. *New*	1D 38
Selby St. *Stoke*	1C 42
Selby Wlk. *Stoke*	7D 40
Selwood Clo. *Stoke*	5J 41
Selworthy Rd. *Stoke*	6F 23
Selwyn St. *Stoke*	7A 34
Semper Clo. *Cong*	3J 9
Settle Gro. *Stoke*	7B 42
Seven Arches Way. *Stoke*	6B 34
Sevenoaks Gro. *Stoke*	1C 48
Severn Clo. *Bid*	2D 14
Severn Clo. *Cong*	6H 9
Severn Dri. *New*	3E 38
Severn St. *Stoke*	7A 28
Seymour St. *Stoke*	2D 34 (4H 5)
Shackleton Dri. *Stoke*	7F 21
Shackson Clo. *Stoke*	3B 34
Shady Gro. *Als*	6E 10
Shaftesbury Av. *Stoke*	2K 27
Shakerley Av. *Cong*	4H 9
Shakespeare Clo. *Kid*	3C 20
Shakespeare Clo. *Stoke*	2F 29
Shakespeare Ct. *Bid*	3B 14
Shakespeare St. *New*	4E 32 (2C 6)
Shaw St. *New*	4E 32 (2C 6)
Shaw St. *Stoke*	7A 28 (1B 4)
Sheaf Pas. *Stoke*	3H 41
Sheaf St. *Stoke*	3A 34 (6D 4)
Shearer St. *Stoke*	3A 34
Sheep Mkt. *Leek*	3F 17
Sheepwash. *Cav*	6F 37
Shefford Rd. *New*	3C 38
Sheldon Av. *Stoke*	1K 39
Sheldon Av. *Cong*	6J 9
Sheldon Gro. *New*	6C 26
Sheldrake Gro. *Stoke*	7G 35
Shelford Rd. *Stoke*	5G 21
Shelley Clo. *Kid*	3D 20
Shelley Clo. *Rode H*	2F 11

Shelley Dri. *C'dle*	4F 45
Shelley Rd. *Stoke*	6G 29
Shelsley Rd. *C'dle*	2J 45
Shelton.	4A 34
Shelton Farm Rd.	
Stoke	3A 34 (6D 4)
Shelton New Rd.	
Stoke	4G 33 (3G 7)
Shelton Old Rd. *Stoke*	5K 33
Shelton Pool.	4A 34
Shemilt Cres. *Stoke*	1B 28
Shendon Ct. *New*	5D 26
Shenfield Grn. *Stoke*	3J 35
Shenton St. *Stoke*	1J 41
Shepherd St. *Bid*	3B 14
Shepley Gro. *Stoke*	7D 40
Sheppard St. *Stoke*	7K 33
Sherborne Clo. *Stoke*	7D 40
Sherborne Dri. *New*	1D 38
Sheridan Gdns. *Stoke*	4E 40
Sheriden Way. *New*	3B 32
Sheringham Pl. *New*	1G 33
Sherratt Clo. *Cong*	5G 9
Sherratt St. *Stoke*	1B 28
Sherwin Rd. *Stoke*	1J 27
Sherwood Rd. *Stoke*	7A 42
Shetland Rd. *Stoke*	3E 40
Shillingford Dri. *Stoke*	6A 40
Shilton Clo. *Stoke*	1J 39
Shinwell Gro. *Stoke*	6B 42
Shipley Pl. *Stoke*	2B 28
Shirburn Rd. *Leek*	3H 17
Shirburn Ter. *Leek*	4H 17
Shirebrook Clo. *Stoke*	7D 40
Shirley Av. *Werr*	1C 36
Shirley Rd. *Stoke*	3B 34 (6E 5)
Shirley St. *Leek*	4E 16
Shirley St. *Stoke*	4G 27
Shoobridge St. *Leek*	4G 17
Shop La. *Cong*	6G 9
Short Bambury St. *Stoke*	7J 35
Short St. *Stoke*	3H 41
Shorwell Gro. *Stoke*	3H 21
Shotsfield Pl. *Stoke*	3F 29
Shotsfield St. *Stoke*	3F 29
Showan Av. *New*	2G 33
Shraleybrook.	4B 24
Shraleybrook Rd.	
A'ly & Halm	4B 24
Shrewsbury Dri. *New*	2B 26
Shugborough Clo. *Werr*	3B 36
Shutlanehead.	5A 38
Sidcot Pl. *Stoke*	5C 28
Sideway.	3A 40
Sideway. *Stoke*	3A 40
Sideway Rd. *Stoke*	2A 40
Sidings Pl. *Stoke*	2G 41
Sidings, The. *C'dle*	4G 45
Sidmouth Av. *New*	4F 33 (2E 7)
Silk St. *Cong*	5F 9
Silk St. *Leek*	3F 17
Sillitoe Pl. *Stoke*	7K 33
Silsden Gro. *Stoke*	4D 42
Silver Clo. *Bid*	2B 14
Silverdale.	3K 31
Silverdale. *New*	3K 31
Silverdale Bus. Pk. *Sil*	4A 32
Silverdale Pk. *New*	3K 31
(off Silverdale)	
Silverdale Rd. *New*	4A 32 (2A 6)
Silverdale Rd. *Wol*	7F 27
Silverdale St. *New*	2B 32
Silvergate Ct. *Cong*	7G 9
Silvermine Clo. *Kid*	1E 20
Silver Ridge. *B'stn*	7B 46
Silverstone Av. *C'dle*	2H 45
Silverstone Cres. *Stoke*	3H 21
Silver St. *C'dle*	1H 45
Silver St. *Cong*	5G 9
Silver St. *Stoke*	7D 22
Silverton Clo. *New*	4D 26
Silverwood. *Kid*	2E 20
Simister Ct. *Stoke*	1G 27
(off Wesley St.)	
Simonburn Av. *Stoke*	6H 33
Simon Pl. *Stoke*	4A 34
Simpson St. *New*	7E 26

Simpson St. *Stoke*	3C 34
Sinclair Av. *Als*	7C 10
Sir Stanley Matthews Sports Cen.	
	5B 34
Siskin Pl. *Stoke*	7C 42
Sitwell Gro. *Stoke*	2J 41
Skellern Av. *Stoke*	1B 28
Skellern St. *Tal*	1A 20
Skipacre Av. *Stoke*	3C 28
Skye Clo. *Stoke*	3K 41
Slacken La. *Tal*	1A 20
Slaidburn Gro. *Stoke*	7C 28
Slaney St. *New*	6F 33 (6F 7)
Slapton Clo. *Stoke*	4E 34
Slater St. *Bid*	3B 14
Slater St. *Stoke*	5H 27
Sleeve, The. *Leek*	5D 16
Sleigh Gro. *Leek*	4F 17
Slindon Gro. *New*	3A 26
Slippery La. *Stoke*	2A 34 (4D 4)
Sloane Way. *Stoke*	7G 35
Smallthorne.	2A 28
Smallwood Clo. *New*	3A 26
Smallwood Ct. *Cong*	4H 9
(off Brunswick St.)	
Smallwood Gro. *Stoke*	6E 28
Smith Child St. *Stoke*	7G 21
Smith Clo. *Als*	6C 10
Smithfield Cen., The. *Leek*	4G 17
Smithfield Clo. *Stoke*	6E 5
Smithfield Ct. *Stoke*	1K 33 (3A 4)
(off Marina Way)	
Smithpool Rd. *Stoke*	1B 40
Smiths Bldgs. *Stoke*	5B 42
(off Weston Rd.)	
Smiths Pas. *Stoke*	1F 41
Smith St. *Stoke*	2H 41
Smithyfield Rd. *Stoke*	7C 22
Smithy La. *Bid*	2J 15
Smithy La. *Has G*	1A 10
Smithy La. *C'dle*	6G 45
Smithy La. *Hul W*	1D 8
Smithy La. *Stoke*	3H 41
Smokies Way. *Bid*	1B 14
Sneyd Av. *Leek*	4F 17
Sneyd Av. *New*	6C 32
Sneyd Cres. *New*	6C 32
Sneyd Green.	5C 28
Sneyd Hill. *Stoke*	4A 28
Sneyd Hill Trad. Est. *Stoke*	3A 28
Sneyd Ind. Est. *Stoke*	4A 28
Sneyd Pl. *Stoke*	5F 21
Sneyd St. *Leek*	4F 17
Sneyd St. *Stoke*	6A 28
Sneyd Ter. *New*	3J 31
Sneyd Wood Vw. *Stoke*	5B 28
Snowden Way. *Stoke*	4C 42
Snow Hill. *Stoke*	3A 34 (6D 4)
Soames Cres. *Stoke*	7G 35
Solly Cres. *Cong*	5C 8
Solway Gro. *Stoke*	2K 41
Somerford Ct. *Cong*	4H 9
(off Brunswick St.)	
Somerley Rd. *Stoke*	6E 28
Somerset Av. *Kid*	1C 20
Somerset Clo. *Cong*	3F 9
Somerset Rd. *Stoke*	1D 34
Somerton Rd. *Werr*	2B 36
Somerton Way. *Stoke*	1J 41
Somerville Av. *New*	2G 33
Sonnet, The. *C'dle*	4E 26
Sophia Way. *New*	4E 26
Sorrel Clo. *Stoke*	2K 41
Sorrento Clo. *Stoke*	2K 41
Souldern Way. *Stoke*	2J 41
Southall Way. *Stoke*	4F 35
Southampton St. *Stoke*	
	7C 28 (1G 5)
S. Bank Gro. *Cong*	5H 9
Southbank St. *Leek*	4G 17
Southborough Cres. *Stoke*	7A 22
South Clo. *Als*	6B 10
Southdown Clo. *Stoke*	6H 41
Southdown Ct. *Stoke*	6K 33
Southern Way. *Stoke*	3C 28
Southfields. Leek	
	(off Westfields)

Southgate Av. Stoke 1B 46
Southlands. New 7F 27
Southlands Av. Stoke 5G 41
Southlands Clo. Leek 3D 16
Southlands Rd. Cong 6J 9
Southlow. 1G 37
Southlow Av. Werr 1F 37
Southlow Rd. Werr 1F 37
South Moorlands Leisure Cen.
. . . . .4H 45
South Pl. Stoke 5C 22
South Rd. Stoke 7G 29
South St. Cong 4F 9
South St. Mow C 4E 12
South St. Stoke 5C 22
South Ter. New 7F 27
South Ter. Stoke 1K 39
South Vw. Bid 2B 14
South Vw. Stoke 3A 48
South Vw. Cotts. Chu L 5G 11
South Wlk. Stoke 5C 42
S. Wolfe St. Stoke 6A 34
Spalding Pl. Stoke 5K 35
Sparch Av. New 1F 33
Sparch Gro. New 1F 33
Sparch Hollow. New 1F 33
Spark St. Stoke 6K 33
Spark Ter. Stoke 6K 33
Sparrow Butts Gro. Kid 1F 21
Sparrow St. Stoke 2C 28
Sparrow Ter. New 6E 26
Spa St. Stoke 5B 28
Speakman St. Stoke 4J 41
Spedding Rd. Fen I 5D 34
Spedding Way. Bid 2D 14
Speedwall St. Stoke 1H 41
Speedwell Rd. P East 3C 26
Spencer Av. End 5K 23
Spencer Av. Leek 4F 17
Spencer Clo. Als 6A 10
Spencer Pl. New 6B 26
Spencer Rd. Stoke 5B 34
Spencroft Rd. New 7C 26
Spens St. Stoke 4J 27
Spey Dri. Kid 1F 21
Spindle St. Cong 4G 9
Spinney Clo. End 3K 23
Spinney, The. Chu L 6B 12
Spinney, The. Mad H 5B 30
Spinney, The. New 4F 39
Spire Clo. Stoke 1D 28
Spitfire Way. Stoke 7F 21
Spode Clo. C'dle 4F 45
Spode Gro. New 3E 38
Spode Mus. & Vis. Cen. 6A 34
Spode St. Stoke 1A 40
Spoutfield Rd. Stoke 4J 33
Spout Hollow. Tal P 5A 20
Spout La. L Oaks 3H 29
Spragg Ho. La. Stoke 1D 28
Spragg St. Cong 4G 9
Spratslade Dri. Stoke 4G 41
Spring Bank. Sch G 2D 12
Springbank Av. End 5K 23
Spring Clo. Rode H 2F 11
Spring Cres. Brn E 4H 23
Springcroft. B Bri 1G 49
Springfield Clo. Leek 4H 17
Springfield Clo. New 6C 26
Springfield Ct. Leek 3H 17
Springfield Cres. Stoke 4G 41
Springfield Dri. Cong 4F 9
Springfield Dri. For 6H 43
Springfield Dri. Kid 3A 20
Springfield Dri. Leek 3H 17
Springfield Gro. Bid 3C 14
Springfield Rd. Bid 3C 14
Springfield Rd. Leek 4H 17
Springfields. 1H 39
Springfields. B Bri 1F 49
Springfields Pk. Stoke 1H 39
Springfields Rd. Stoke 7H 33
Spring Garden Rd. Stoke 4G 41
Spring Gdns. For 6J 43
Spring Gdns. Leek 4E 16
Springhead Dri. Tal P 5A 20

Springpool. K'le 7K 31
Spring Rd. Stoke 4K 41
Springside Pl. Stoke 7D 40
Spring St. Stoke 4G 33 (3G 7)
Spring Vw. Brn E 4H 23
Springwood. 3K 25
Springwood Rd. New 4K 25
Sprink Bank Rd. Stoke 6K 21
Sprinkwood Gro. Stoke 3B 42
Sproston St. Stoke 6J 21
Spruce Gro. Rode H 3G 11
Spur St. Stoke 3C 34 (6H 5)
Square, The. Cav 4F 43
Square, The. New 7D 32
Square, The. Stoke 4C 42
Squires Vw. Stoke 6B 34
Squirrel Hayes Av. Knyp 4D 14
Squirrels, The. New 3F 39
Stadium Ct. Stoke 6K 27
Stadmorslow La. Har 6J 13
Stafford Av. New 1F 39
Stafford Cres. New 2F 39
Stafford La. Stoke 1B 34 (3F 5)
Staffordshire University. 5A 34
Stafford St. New 5E 32 (4D 6)
Stafford St. Stoke 1B 34 (3E 5)
Stallington. 3E 48
Stallington Clo. B Bri 3E 48
Stallington Gdns. B Bri 1G 49
Stallington Rd. Stoke & Ful 5C 48
Stamer St. Stoke 7A 34
Standard St. Stoke 7C 34
Standersfoot Pl. Stoke 5A 22
Standon Av. New 2K 25
Stanfield. 2J 27
Stanfield Cres. C'dle 5G 45
Stanfield Rd. Stoke 3K 27
Stanhope St. Stoke 3A 34 (6C 4)
Stanier St. New 4D 32 (3B 6)
Stanier St. Stoke 7D 34
Stanley Ct. Als 6D 10
Stanley Dri. New 3K 25
Stanley Grn. Stoke 2F 29
Stanley Gro. New 3G 33 (1H 7)
Stanley Matthews Way.
Stoke 3B 40
Stanley Moor. 7K 23
Stanley Moss. 5K 23
Stanley Moss La. Stoc B 6K 23
Stanley Moss Rd. Stoc B 6K 23
Stanley Rd. Gil H 2H 15
Stanley Rd. New 3G 33
Stanley Rd. Stoc B 7J 23
Stanley Rd. Stoke 5H 33 (4H 7)
Stanley St. Bid 2B 14
Stanley St. Leek 4F 17
Stanley St. Stoke 7H 21
Stansgate Pl. Stoke 7A 28 (1C 4)
Stansmore Rd. Stoke 4C 42
Stanton Clo. New 3C 32
Stanton Rd. Stoke 5B 42
Stanway Av. Stoke 5B 28
Stapleton Cres. Stoke 5F 41
Star & Garter Rd. Stoke 5K 41
Starling Clo. Kid 7G 13
Starwood Rd. Stoke 6K 41
Statham St. Stoke 2A 34 (5D 4)
Station Bri. Rd. Stoke 1D 40
Station Cres. Stoke 2C 28
Station Dri. K'le 5E 30
Station Gro. Stoke 3F 29
Station Rd. Als 7D 10
Station Rd. B'stn 6C 46
Station Rd. Bid 1B 14
(in two parts)
Station Rd. C'dle 4G 45
Station Rd. End 2K 23
Station Rd. Halm 5E 24
Station Rd. K'le 5D 30
(in two parts)
Station Rd. Kid 2C 20
Station Rd. Mad 3B 30
Station Rd. Mow C 2E 12
Station Rd. N'cpl 2H 21
Station Rd. Sch G & Mor 3B 12

Station Rd. Sil 3J 31
Station Rd. Stoke 5A 34
Station St. Leek 4E 16
Station St. Stoke 5G 27
Station Vw. Stoke 5B 42
Station Walks. Halm 5E 24
Station Walks. New 4E 32 (2D 6)
(in two parts)
Station Yd. Cong 6J 9
Staveley Clo. Stoke 2F 35
Staveley Pl. New 4H 31
Stedman St. Stoke 7C 28
Steele Av. Stoke 2A 28
Steel St. Stoke 5H 33
Stellar St. Stoke 3B 28
Stephens Way. Big E 2G 25
Step Row. Leek 4F 17
(off Cornhill St.)
Sterndale Dri. New 3E 38
Sterndale Dri. Stoke 7G 35
Stevenson Rd. Stoke 1F 35
Steventon Pl. Stoke 4J 27
Stewart Ct. Stoke 4J 35
Stewart St. Stoke 7C 34
Stile Clo. Brn L 5A 14
Stirling Clo. Stoke 6K 35
Stirling Ho. Stoke 5K 27
(off Bleak Pl.)
Stirling St. Stoke 4K 27
Stockfield Rd. Stoke 7A 42
Stockholm St. Stoke 5E 28
Stockwell Gro. Stoke 3J 41
Stockwell St. Leek 3F 17
Stockwell Vs. Leek 3F 17
Stockwood Rd. New 2C 38
Stoke Bus. Pk. Stoke 7B 34
Stoke City F.C. (Britannia Stadium)
. . . . .3B 40
Stoke Gymnastics Cen. 4H 27
Stoke Old Rd. Stoke 4G 33 (3H 7)
Stoke-on-Trent. 1B 34 (3F 5)
Stoke-on-Trent Repertory Theatre.
. . . . .4C 34
Stoke-on-Trent Ski Cen.
. . . . .7J 27 (1A 4)
STOKE-ON-TRENT STATION.
RAIL 5A 34
Stoke Recreation Cen. 7A 34
Stoke Rd. Stoke 4A 34
Stokesay Dri. Stoke 3J 45
Stokesay Gro. Stoke 5K 27
Stoke-upon-Trent. 6A 34
Stone Bank Rd. Kid 3D 20
Stone Chair La. Sch G 2B 12
Stonehaven Gro. Stoke 3C 34
Stonehouse Cres. Werr 2C 36
Stonehouse Grn. Cong 4F 9
Stonehouse La. Brn E 2F 23
Stone House Rd. Werr 2C 36
Stonehouses. 1J 49
Stoneleigh Rd. Stoke 6K 21
Stone Rd. R'gh C 5K 47
Stone Rd. Stoke 3H 39
Stone Rd. T'sor 5A 46
Stone St. Stoke 6K 33
(in two parts)
Stonewall Ind. Est. New 3A 32
Stonewall Pl. New 3A 32
Stonewood Clo. Stoke 3H 39
Stoneycroft. Stoke 2G 29
Stoneyfields. Bid M 2G 15
Stoneyfields Av. Stoke 2G 29
Stoneyfields Ct. New . . .3G 33 (1G 7)
Stoney La. End 4K 23
Stonor St. Stoke 6K 27
Stony La. A'bry 6E 8
Stopsley Clo. Cong 3B 8
Stormont Clo. Stoke 2B 28
Stowford Gro. Stoke 6A 40
Stradbroke Dri. Stoke 5F 41
Strand Clo. Stoke 3F 35
Strand Pas. Stoke 2G 41
(off Strand, The)
Strand, The. Stoke 3G 41
Strangman St. Leek 4F 17
Stranraer Clo. Stoke 2C 42

Stratford Av. New 2G 33
Stratford Clo. For 6H 43
Stratford Clo. Stoke 3E 28
Stratheden Rd. Stoke 2A 28
St. Anthony's Ct. Stoke 1A 40
Street La. Rode H 1G 11
Stretton Rd. New 3G 31
Stringer Ct. Stoke 1G 27
Stringer St. Bid 2B 14
Stroma Clo. Stoke 5J 27
Stross Av. Stoke 6J 21
Stroud Clo. Stoke 7C 42
Stuart Av. Dray 1K 49
Stuart Av. Stoke 7K 39
Stuart Gro. New 1F 39
Stuart Rd. Stoke 3C 34 (6H 5)
Stubbsfield Rd. New 6F 33 (6F 7)
Stubbs Ga. New 5F 33 (5E 7)
Stubbs La. Stoke 2C 34 (5G 5)
Stubbs St. New 5E 32 (4D 6)
Stubbs St. Stoke 4H 27
Stubbs' Walks. New 5F 33 (4F 7)
Sturgess St. Stoke 7K 33
Sudbourne Clo. Stoke 3H 21
Sudbury Pl. New 4E 38
Sudgrove Pl. Stoke 7C 42
Sudlow St. Stoke 5A 28
Suffolk Clo. Cong 3F 9
Suffolk Clo. New 2G 39
Suffolk Rd. Stoke 6H 41
Summerbank Rd. Stoke 7G 21
Summerfield. Kid 2E 20
Summerhill Dri. New 3A 26
Summer Row. Stoke 4G 41
Summer St. Stoke 1K 39
Summerville Rd. Stoke 3H 39
Sunbury Clo. Stoke 1B 46
Sundorne Rd. Stoke 3G 35
Sunningdale Clo. Stoke 1A 28
Sunningdale Gro. New 4A 26
Sunny Bank. Stoke 6H 27
Sunnybank Ct. Stoke 1K 27
Sunnycroft Av. Stoke 5F 41
Sunnyfield Oval. Stoke 3H 29
Sunny Hollow. New 2F 33
Sunnyside. Als 6B 10
Sunnyside Av. Stoke 1J 27
Sunridge Clo. Stoke 2G 29
Sun St. C'dle 3H 45
Sun St. Stoke 3K 33 (6B 4)
Sunwell Gdns. C'dle 3H 45
Surrey Dri. Cong 3G 9
Surrey Rd. Kid 1D 20
Surtees Gro. Stoke 1G 41
Sussex Dri. Kid 1C 20
Sussex Pl. Cong 2G 9
Sussex Pl. Stoke 5J 41
Sutherland Av. Stoke 5G 41
Sutherland Cres. B Bri 7F 43
Sutherland Dri. New 1C 38
Sutherland Rd. Long 7B 16
Sutherland Rd. Stoke 3H 41
Sutherland St. Stoke 7B 34
Sutton Dri. Stoke 2J 39
Sutton Pl. Stoke 6A 22
Sutton St. Ches 6B 26
Swaffham Way. Stoke 3J 35
Swainsley Clo. New 5K 27
Swaledale Av. Cong 2J 9
Swallow Clo. Kid 1D 20
Swallow Clo. Stoke 7B 42
Swallow Cft. Leek 6D 16
Swallow Dri. Als 7C 10
Swallowmore Vw. Tal 3K 19
Swallow Wlk. Bid 3C 14
Swanage Clo. Stoke 7C 42
Swan Bank. 5B 30
Swan Bank. Cong 5F 9
Swan Bank. Mad H 5B 30
Swan Bank. Tal 4A 20
Swan Clo. Tal 3A 20
Swanland Gro. Stoke 2J 41
Swan La. Stoke 3H 39
Swan Sq. Stoke 4J 27
Swan St. Cong 5F 9
Swan St. Stoke 5K 33

Swanton Pl. *Stoke* 7J **39**
Swaythling Gro. *Stoke* 4J **35**
Swettenham Clo. *Als* 7D **10**
Swift Clo. *Kid* 1E **20**
Swift Dri. *Bid* 2D **14**
Swift Ho. *Stoke* 2E **5**
Swift Pl. *Stoke* 1A **42**
Swinburne Clo. *Stoke* 4E **40**
Swingle Hill Rd. *Stoke* 3E **40**
Swithin Dri. *Stoke* 7G **35**
Sycamore Av. *Als* 1F **19**
Sycamore Av. *Cong* 3B **8**
Sycamore Av. *Rode H* 3G **11**
Sycamore Clo. *Bid* 2K **15**
Sycamore Clo. *Kid* 3B **20**
Sycamore Clo. *Stoke* 2B **48**
Sycamore Gdns. Stoke 4G **27**
(off Station St.)
Sycamore Gro. *New* 2G **33**
Sycamore Gro. *Stoke* 3D **40**
Sydenham Pl. *Stoke* 5J **35**
Sydney St. *New* 3G **33**
Sylvan Gro. *Stoke* 3H **39**
Sylvester St. *Stoke* 4K **27**
Sytch Rd. *Brn E* 4G **23**

T

Talbot St. *Leek* 4G **17**
Talbot St. *Stoke* 3C **34** (6G **5**)
Talke. 4K **19**
Talke Pits. 6A **20**
Talke Rd. *Als* 7F **11**
Talke Rd. *High B* 7B **20**
Talke Rd. *P East & New* 4C **26**
Talke Rd. *Red S & Tal P* 1A **26**
Tall Ash Av. *Cong* 3J **9**
Tallis Gro. *Stoke* 7E **28**
Tally Clo. *Stoke* 6J **35**
Talsarn Gro. *Stoke* 1B **46**
Tamar Clo. *Cong* 6H **9**
Tamar Gro. *C'dle* 5H **45**
Tamar Rd. *Kid* 1E **20**
Tame Clo. *Bid* 1C **14**
Tame Wlk. *Stoke* 2B **42**
Tanners Rd. *Stoke* 5G **29**
Tanner St. *Cong* 5G **9**
Tansey Clo. *Stoke* 2F **35**
Tape St. *C'dle* 3G **45**
Tara Gro. *Stoke* 1F **29**
Target Clo. *Tal P* 5B **20**
Tarleton Rd. *Stoke* . . .1D **34** (3H **5**)
Tarporley Gro. *Stoke* 1H **39**
Tarvin Gro. *Stoke* 5J **21**
Tasman Sq. *Stoke* 7D **28**
Tatton Clo. *Als* 7D **10**
Tatton Clo. *Leek* 4C **16**
Tatton St. *Stoke* 4H **41**
Taunton Pl. *New* 5C **26**
Taunton Way. *Stoke* 3J **35**
Taurus Gro. *Stoke* 5J **21**
Tavistock Cres. *New* 1D **38**
Tavistock Pl. *Stoke* . . .4H **33** (2H **7**)
Tawney Clo. *Kid* 1E **20**
Tawney Cres. *Stoke* 3C **42**
Tay Clo. *Bid* 1D **14**
Tay Clo. *C'dle* 1H **45**
Tay Clo. *Stoke* 1H **41**
Taylor Av. *New* 1F **33**
Taylor Rd. *Stoke* 6G **29**
Taylor St. *New* 1F **33**
Taylor St. *Stoke* 4F **21**
Taynton Clo. *Stoke* 3K **21**
Teal Vw. *Stoke* 2C **28**
Teanford. 7G **45**
Tean Rd. *C'dle* 5G **45**
Telford Clo. *Cong* 6J **9**
Telford Clo. *Kid* 3B **20**
Telford Way. *Stoke* 7K **21**
Tellwright Gro. *New* 5D **26**
Tellwright St. *Stoke* 3K **27**
Temperance Pl. Stoke 4G **21**
(off Willoughby St.)
Templar Cres. *New* 6E **26**
Templar Ter. *New* 6E **26**

Temple St. *Stoke* 7C **34**
Templeton Av. *Stoke* 5H **35**
Tenbury Grn. *Stoke* 4H **35**
Tenby Gro. *New* 5C **26**
Tennant Pl. *New* 5E **26**
Tennyson Av. *Kid* 3D **20**
Tennyson Clo. *C'dle* 4E **44**
Tennyson Clo. *Rode H* 2F **11**
Tennyson Gdns. *Stoke* 4E **40**
Tercel Gro. *Stoke* 7B **42**
Terence Wlk. *B Frd* 1A **22**
Tern Av. *Kid* 1F **21**
Tern Clo. *Bid* 2D **14**
Terrace, The. *C'dle* 3G **45**
Terrington Dri. *New* 4E **38**
Terry Clo. *Stoke* 3C **42**
Tetton Ct. *Cong* 4H **9**
Tewkesbury Gro. *Stoke* 1F **35**
Tewson Dri. *Stoke* 5B **28**
Thackeray Dri. *Stoke* 4F **41**
Thames Clo. *Cong* 6H **9**
Thames Dri. *Bid* 1C **14**
Thames Dri. *C'dle* 5H **45**
Thames Rd. *New* 3D **38**
Thanet Gro. *Stoke* 3F **41**
Thatcham Grn. *Stoke* 7D **40**
Thatcher Gro. *Bid* 2A **14**
Thelma Av. *Brn E* 4G **23**
Theodore Rd. *Stoke* 2G **35**
Theresa Clo. *Stoke* 4K **39**
Third Av. *Kid* 2B **20**
Third Av. *Stoke* 1J **35**
Thirlmere Ct. *Cong* 5C **8**
Thirlmere Gro. *Stoke* 3K **41**
Thirlmere Pl. *New* 1E **38**
Thirsk Pl. *New* 3H **31**
Thistleberry Av. *New* . .6C **32** (6A **6**)
Thistleberry Ho. *New* 5C **32**
Thistleberry Vs. *New* . .5D **32** (5A **6**)
Thistles, The. *New* 6C **32**
Thistley Hough. *Stoke* 7J **33**
Thomas Av. *New* 1D **32**
Thomas Clo. *Als* 6F **11**
Thomas St. *Bid* 1C **14**
Thomas St. *Cong* 4G **9**
Thomas St. *Leek* 3E **16**
Thomas St. *Pac* 2J **21**
Thomas St. *Tal* 3A **20**
Thompstone Av. *New* 2C **32**
Thorley Dri. *C'dle* 4J **45**
Thornburrow Dri.
Stoke 6H **33**
Thorncliffe Rd. *Thor* 2J **17**
Thorncliffe Vw. *Leek* 1J **17**
Thorncliff Gro. *Stoke* 7D **28**
Thorndyke St. *Stoke* . .3A **34** (6C **4**)
Thorne Pl. *Stoke* 3C **42**
Thorneycroft Av. *Stoke* 2A **28**
Thornfield Av. *Leek* 4J **17**
Thornham Clo. *New* 4E **38**
Thornham Grn. *Stoke* 4H **35**
Thornhill Dri. *Mad* 1B **30**
Thornhill Rd. *Leek* 5D **16**
Thornhill Rd. *Stoke* 5K **35**
Thornley Rd. *Stoke* 1J **27**
Thornton Rd. *Stoke* 5B **34**
Thorpe Grn. *Stoke* 7E **40**
Thorpe Ri. *C'dle* 1H **45**
Three Fields Clo. *Cong* 4C **8**
Three Mile La. *K'le* 7F **31**
Thursfield Av. *Kid* 7F **13**
Thursfield Pl. *Stoke* 7C **22**
Thursfield Wlk. *Stoke* 6C **22**
Thurston Way. *Stoke* 5H **35**
Thyme Gro. *Stoke* 1C **48**
Tibb St. *Big E* 2G **25**
Tiber Dri. *New* 7A **26**
Tickhill La. *Dil* 1G **43**
Tidebrook Pl. *Stoke* 4H **21**
Tideswell Rd. *Stoke* 1H **41**
Tidnock Av. *Cong* 2G **9**
Tierney St. *Stoke* 7C **28** (1H **5**)
Tilbrook Clo. *Stoke* 5H **35**
Tilehurst Pl. *Stoke* 5D **40**

Tilery La. *Stoke* 5C **40**
(in two parts)
Tilewright Clo. *Kid* 1E **20**
Tillet Grn. *Stoke* 3C **42**
Till Wlk. *Stoke* 7J **35**
Tilson Av. *Stoke* 6J **33**
Tilstone Clo. *Kid* 3D **20**
Timble Clo. *Stoke* 5H **35**
Times Sq. Stoke 2G **41**
(off Market St.)
Timmis St. *Stoke* 2K **33** (5B **4**)
Timor Gro. *Stoke* 6A **40**
Tintagel Clo. *Stoke* 7H **35**
Tintagel Pl. *Stoke* 5J **35**
Tintern Pl. *New* 5C **26**
Tintern St. *Stoke* 2D **34** (4H **5**)
Tipping Av. *Stoke* 5C **42**
Tirley St. *Stoke* 1D **40**
Tissington Pl. *Stoke* 7D **42**
Titterton St. *Stoke* 5H **35**
Titterton St. *Stoke* 5H **35**
Tittensor Rd. *New* 1F **39**
Tittensor Rd. *T'sor & B'stn* . . .7A **46**
Tittesworth Av. *Leek* 2H **17**
Tiverton Rd. *Stoke* 4H **35**
Toft End Rd. *New* 3E **26**
Tolkien Way. *Stoke* 5K **33**
Toll Bar Rd. *Werr* 1E **36**
Tollgate Clo. *Tal* 3K **19**
Tollgate Ct. *Stoke* 6E **40**
Tomfields. *Big E* 4G **25**
Tomlinson St. *Stoke* 4G **27**
Tommy's La. *Cong* 3H **9**
Tonbridge Av. *Stoke* 7A **22**
Toney Pl. *Stoke* 2E **34**
Tongue La. *Brn E* 3D **22**
Tontine Sq. *Stoke* 1B **34** (3F **5**)
Tontines, The. *Stoke* 3F **5**
Tontine St. *Stoke* 1B **34** (3F **5**)
(in two parts)
Tony Waddington Pl. *Stoke* . . .2B **40**
Top Chapel La. *Brn E* 2G **23**
Top Heath's Row. *Brn E* 3G **23**
Top Sta. Rd. *Mow C* 3F **13**
Torres Wlk. *Stoke* 7D **28**
Torridon Clo. *Stoke* 1B **46**
Tor St. *Stoke* 5C **28**
Torville Dri. *Bid* 2D **14**
Total Fitness. 7G **33**
Tourist Info. Cen.
(Congleton)
Tourist Info. Cen. 3F **17**
(Leek)
Tourist Info. Cen. 4E **32** (3D **6**)
(Newcastle-under-Lyme)
Tourist Info. Cen. 1B **34** (2F **5**)
(Stoke-on-Trent)
Tower Clo. *Brn L* 4A **14**
Tower Hill Ct. *Cong* 4D **8**
Tower Hill Rd.
Mow C & Brn L 2H **13**
Tower Sq. *Stoke* 1G **27**
Townend. 7F **49**
Town End. *C'dle* 3F **45**
Townend. *Ful* 7G **49**
Townfield Clo. *Tal* 1A **20**
Townfield Rd. *Stoke* . .7B **28** (2F **5**)
Townsend. 2G **35**
Townsend La. *Sch G* 2H **11**
Townsend Pl. *Stoke* 2G **35**
Townsend Rd. *Cong* 5G **9**
Trade St. *Stoke* 6A **34**
Trafalgar Ct. *Stoke* 5K **27**
(off Waterloo St.)
Trafalgar Rd. *Stoke* 5H **33**
Trafalgar St. *Stoke* . . .7B **28** (1E **5**)
Trafford Clo. *Leek* 4J **17**
Transport La. *Stoke* 3G **41**
Tranter Rd. *Stoke* 6G **29**
Travers Ct. *Stoke* 7C **34**
Travers St. *Stoke* 5H **27**
Trecastle Gro. *Stoke* 5K **41**
Tregaron Ct. *Ash B* 2B **36**
Tregenna Clo. *Stoke* 7B **42**
Tregew Pl. *New* 3A **32**
Tregowan Clo. *Stoke* 1A **28**

Trent Clo. *C'dle* 5H **45**
Trentfields Rd. *Stoke* 2F **29**
Trent Gro. *Bid* 4C **14**
Trent Gro. *New* 3D **38**
Trentham. 7K **39**
Trentham Bus. Cen.
Stoke 7C **40**
Trentham Ct. *Stoke* 7H **39**
Trentham Gardens &
Pleasure Grounds. 7H **39**
Trentham Gdns. Cvn. Pk.
Stoke 7H **39**
Trentham Gdns. Clo.
Stoke 7J **39**
Trentham Golf Course. 2A **46**
Trentham Gro. *New* 1F **33**
Trentham Lakes N. *Stoke* 4C **40**
Trentham Lakes S. *Stoke* 7C **40**
Trentham M. *Stoke* 7K **39**
Trentham Rd. *But* 6A **38**
Trentham Rd. *Hem H* 7B **40**
Trentley Dri. *Bid M* 2G **15**
Trentley Rd. *Stoke* 7J **39**
Trentmill Nature Pk. 3D **34**
Trentmill Rd. *Stoke* . . .3D **34** (6H **5**)
Trent Rd. *For* 6H **43**
Trentside Bus. Pk. *Stoke* 2A **40**
Trentside Rd. *Stoke* 6F **23**
Trent St. *Stoke* 2E **34**
Trent Ter. *Stoke* 6F **23**
Trent Vale. 3H **39**
Trent Valley Rd. *Stoke* 2J **39**
Trent Wlk. *Stoke* 3C **34** (6H **5**)
Trentway Clo. *Stoke* 2F **35**
Trevithick Clo. *Stoke* 6J **35**
Trevor Dri. *Cav* 3E **42**
Trimley Way. *Stoke* 3G **35**
Trimpos. *Dil* 1C **44**
Triner Pl. *Stoke* 7D **22**
Tring Clo. *Stoke* 5H **35**
Trinity Ct. *Cong* 6K **9**
Trinity Ct. *New* 4B **26**
Trinity Pde. *Stoke* 1B **34** (2F **5**)
(off Trinity St.)
Trinity Pl. *Cong* 7K **9**
Trinity Pl. *Stoke* 1G **35**
Trinity St. *Stoke* 1A **34** (3D **4**)
Triton Wlk. *Stoke* 3C **28**
Troutbeck Av. *Cong* 5C **8**
Troutdale Clo. *Stoke* 6G **35**
Trowbridge Cres. *Stoke* 2H **35**
Trubshaw. 7G **13**
Trubshaw Ct. *Kid* 7F **13**
Trubshawe Cross. *Stoke* 4G **27**
Trubshawe St. *Stoke* 4G **27**
Trubshaw Pl. *Kid* 7E **12**
Truro Clo. *Cong* 7G **9**
Truro Pl. *Stoke* 3G **35**
Tudor Clo. *Stoke* 7K **33**
Tudor Ct. *Ful* 6F **49**
Tudor Ct. *New* 6E **26**
Tudor Gro. *New* 1F **33**
Tudor Hollow. *Ful* 6F **49**
Tudor Rose Way. *Stoke* 2C **28**
Tudors, The. *Stoke* 7H **21**
Tudor Way. *Cong* 6F **9**
Tulip Gro. *New* 3F **33** (1E **7**)
Tulley Pl. *Stoke* 2F **35**
Tulsa Clo. *Stoke* 4F **35**
Tunbridge Dri. *New* 3G **31**
Tunnel Ter. *Stoke* 6E **20**
Tunnicliffe Clo. *Stoke* 3K **41**
Tunstall. 1H **27**
Tunstall Greenway. *Stoke* 7H **21**
(Boulevard, The)
Tunstall Greenway. *Stoke* 6H **21**
(Furlong Rd.)
Tunstall Pool. 1H **27**
Tunstall Rd. *Knyp & Bid* 5B **14**
Tunstall Rd. Ind. Est. *Knyp* . . .6A **14**
Tunstall Western By-Pass.
Stoke 2E **26**
Turin Dri. *New* 7B **32**
Turnberry Dri. *Stoke* 6J **39**
Turner Av. *Big E* 3H **25**
Turner Cres. *New* 5H **31**
Turner St. *Stoke* 7C **28** (1H **5**)

Turnhill Gro. *New* 5E **26**
Turnhurst. 4J **21**
Turnhurst Rd. *Pac* 2J **21**
Turnlea Clo. *Knyp* 4A **14**
Turnock St. *Stoke* 1H **35**
Tuscan Clo. *C'dle* 5F **45**
Tuscan Ho. *Stoke* 4G **41**
Tuscan St. *Stoke* 2H **41**
Tuscan Way. *New* 6A **26**
Tutbury Gro. *Stoke* 2J **41**
Tweed Gro. *New* 2D **38**
Tweed St. *Stoke* 2D **40**
Twemlow St. *Stoke* ...2K **33** (4B **4**)
Twigg St. *Stoke* 3G **35**
Twyning Grn. *Stoke* 7E **40**
Tyler Gro. *Stoke* 4H **27**
Tyndall Pl. *Stoke* 6H **33**
Tyneham Gro. *Stoke* 2F **29**
Tyne Way. *New* 2D **38**
Tynwald Grange. *New* 3D **32**
Tyrell Gro. *Stoke* 4E **28**
Tyson St. *Stoke* 5J **35**

U

Ubberley. 4H **35**
Ubberley Grn. *Stoke* 3H **35**
Ubberley Rd. *Stoke* 3G **35**
Uffington Pde. *Stoke* 4H **35**
Ufton Clo. *Stoke* 1E **46**
Ullswater Av. *Stoke* 4H **27**
Ullswater Dri. *C'dle* 2H **45**
Ullswater Rd. *Cong* 5B **8**
Ulster Ter. *Stoke* 1K **39**
Ulverston Rd. *Stoke* 7E **40**
Umberleigh Rd. *Stoke* 7D **40**
Under The Hill. *Bid M* 1F **15**
Underwood Rd. *New* 4G **31**
Unicorn Ind. Est. *Stoke* 4G **27**
Unicorn Pl. *Stoke* 6J **21**
Union Clo. *Cong* 4F **9**
Union Ct. *Stoke* 7B **28** (1E **5**)
Union St. *Cong* 4F **9**
Union St. *Leek* 3G **17**
Union St. *Stoke* 7B **28** (1E **5**)
Unity Av. *Stoke* 5C **28**
Unity Way. *Tal* 3A **20**
University of Keele. 6J **31**
Unwin St. *Stoke* 1A **28**
(in two parts)
Uplands Av. *Stoke* 5J **21**
Uplands Av. *Werr* 2B **36**
Uplands Clo. *Werr* 1B **36**
Uplands Cft. *Werr* 2B **36**
Uplands Dri. *Werr* 2B **36**
Uplands Rd. *Stoke* 5G **29**
Uplands, The. *Bid* 2K **15**
Uplands, The. *New* 3F **33** (1E **7**)
Up. Belgrave Rd. *Stoke* 5J **41**
Upper Cres. *Stoke* 5H **33** (5H **7**)
Up. Cross St. *Stoke* 2H **41**
Up. Furlong St. *Stoke* 7C **34**
Up. Hillchurch St. *Stoke*
. . . . .1C **34** (2G **5**)
Up. Huntbach St. *Stoke*
. . . . .1C **34** (2G **5**)
Up. Market Sq. *Stoke*
. . . . .1B **34** (3F **5**)
Up. Marsh. *New* 2G **33**
Up. Normacot Rd. *Stoke* 4J **41**
(Lwr. Spring Rd.)
Up. Normacot Rd. *Stoke* 4J **41**
(Uttoxeter Rd)
Urmston Pl. *Stoke* 7E **40**
Utterby Side. *Stoke* 5H **35**
Uttoxeter Rd. *B Bri* 6D **42**
Uttoxeter Rd. *Dray* 1K **49**
Uttoxeter Rd. *Stoke* 3H **41**

V

Vale Gdns. *Als* 6F **11**
Valentine Rd. *Kid* 2D **20**
Vale Pleasant. *New* 3K **31**
Valerian Way. *Stoke* 1B **48**
Vale St. *New* 4B **26**

Vale St. *Sil* 3J **31**
Vale St. *Stoke* 6A **34**
Vale Ter. *Cong* 5F **9**
Vale, The. *Cong* 5F **9**
(off Priesty Fields)
Vale Vw. *New* 5G **27**
Vale Wlk. *Cong* 5F **9**
Valley Clo. *Als* 7A **10**
Valley Dri. *Leek* 4C **16**
Valley Pk. Way. *Stoke* 3E **40**
Valley Rd. *W Coy* 3C **42**
Valley Vw. *Cong* 4E **8**
Varey Rd. *Eat T* 3H **9**
Vaudrey Cres. *Cong* 4H **9**
Venice Ct. *New* 6B **32**
Venn Pl. *Stoke* 3D **34**
Ventnor Gro. *Stoke* 1E **46**
Venton Clo. *Stoke* 7D **22**
Venture Way. *Stoke* 1B **28**
(off Bradeley Village)
Verney Way. *Stoke* 7E **40**
Vernon Av. *A'ly* 2D **24**
Vernon Av. *Cong* 7H **9**
Vernon Clo. *A'ly* 2E **24**
Vernon Gro. *Stoke* 1K **41**
Vessey Ter. *New* ...5F **33** (5E **7**)
Vicarage Cres. *Cav* 3E **42**
Vicarage Cres. *New* ...6F **33** (6F **7**)
Vicarage Cres. *T'sor* 6A **46**
Vicarage La. *B'stn* 5D **46**
Vicarage La. *Mad* 3B **30**
Vicarage La. *Stoke* 2H **39**
Vicarage Rd. *Leek* 3G **17**
Vicarage Rd. *Stoke* 5J **33**
Vichy Clo. *New* 6B **32**
Vickers Rd. *Stoke* 6K **21**
Victoria Av. *Halm* 5F **25**
Victoria Av. *Kid* 1C **20**
Victoria Av. *Stoke* 3B **34** (6E **5**)
Victoria Clo. *Sil* 3K **31**
Victoria Cotts. *Stoke* 4K **41**
Victoria Ct. *Kid* 1D **20**
(off Attwood St.)
Victoria Ct. *New* 2F **33**
Victoria Ct. *Stoke* 7D **34**
(off Beville St.)
Victoria Hall. 2B **34** (4F **5**)
Victoria Ind. Complex.
Stoke 1F **41**
Victoria Pk. Rd. *Stoke* 1H **27**
Victoria Pl. *New* 5B **26**
(Chesterton)
Victoria Pl. *New* 7G **27**
(Wolstanton)
Victoria Pl. *Stoke* 1H **35**
(in two parts)
Victoria Pl. Link.
Stoke 1E **40**
Victoria Rd. *New* ...5F **33** (4F **7**)
Victoria Rd. *Stoke* 4C **34**
Victoria Row. *Knyp* 6B **14**
Victoria Sq. *Stoke* ...2A **34** (5D **4**)
Victoria St. *C'dle* 3H **45**
Victoria St. *Ches* 5B **26**
Victoria St. *Cong* 5F **9**
Victoria St. *Leek* 3H **17**
Victoria St. *New* 5F **33** (5E **7**)
Victoria St. *Sil* 3K **31**
Victoria St. *Stoke* ...3G **33** (1H **7**)
Victory Clo. *C'dle* 2H **45**
Vienna Pl. *New* 7C **32**
Vienna Way. *Stoke* 1K **41**
Views, The. *N'cpl* 1H **21**
Viggars Pl. *Stoke* 3C **32**
Viking Way. *Cong* 3D **8**
Villa Clo. *Bid* 3B **14**
Village, The. 1K **23**
Village, The. *K'le* 6G **31**
Villas, The. *Stoke* 1K **39**
Villa St. *Stoke* 1K **39**
Villiers St. *Stoke* 5G **41**
Vincent St. *Stoke* 7D **28**
Vine Bank Rd. *Kid* 1D **20**
Vinebank St. *Stoke* 7K **33**
Vine Row. *Stoke* 7K **33**
Viscount Wlk. *Stoke* 7B **42**

Vivian Rd. *Stoke* 7E **34**
Vowchurch Way. *Stoke* 4H **35**

W

Wade Av. *New* 6G **27**
Wadebridge Rd. *Stoke* 4G **35**
Wade Clo. *C'dle* 5G **45**
Wade St. *Stoke* 3A **28**
Wadham St. *Stoke* 6K **33**
Waggs Rd. *Cong* 6E **8**
Wagg St. *Cong* 5F **9**
Wain Av. *New* 5C **32**
Wain Av. *Stoke* 6D **22**
Wain Dri. *Stoke* 7H **33**
(in two parts)
Wain Lea. 6J **13**
Wain St. *Stoke* 3J **27**
Wainwood Ri. *Stoke* 1J **39**
Wainwright Wlk. *Stoke* 3G **5**
Wakefield Rd. *Stoke* 2J **39**
Walcot Gro. *Stoke* 4F **35**
Walfield Av. *Cong* 2F **9**
Walgrave Clo. *Cong* 4C **8**
Walkergreen Rd. *New* 2A **26**
Walker Rd. *Stoke* 7J **21**
Walkers La. *Sch G* 1J **11**
Walker St. *Stoke* 2G **27**
Walklate Av. *Stoke* 2G **33**
Walks, The. *Leek* 4E **16**
Wallbridge Clo. *Leek* 5D **16**
Wallbridge Dri. *Leek* 4D **16**
Wallbridge Park. 5C **16**
Wallbridge Precinct. *Leek* ...5D **16**
(off Wallbridge Dri.)
Waller Rd. *Ful* 7F **49**
Walley Dri. *Stoke* 5G **21**
Walley Pl. *Stoke* 5K **27**
Walley's Dri. *New* ...3G **33** (1G **7**)
Walley St. *Bid* 1B **14**
Walley St. *Stoke* 5K **27**
Wall Hill Ct. *Leek* 5F **17**
(off Junction Rd.)
Wallhill La. *B'lw* 6A **8**
Wallis Pl. *Stoke* 7G **29**
Wallis St. *Stoke* 7E **34**
Wallis Way. *Stoke* 2F **29**
Wallmires La. *Werr* 4E **36**
Wallworth's Bank. *Cong* 5G **9**
Walmer Pl. *Stoke* 1G **41**
Walney Gro. *Stoke* 7B **28**
Walnut Gro. *New* 4A **26**
Walnut Ri. *Cong* 5D **8**
Walpole St. *Stoke* 1J **41**
Walsingham Gdns. *New* 4E **38**
Walton Cres. *Stoke* 1B **40**
Walton Gro. *Tal* 3K **19**
Walton Pl. *New* 6C **26**
Walton Rd. *Stoke* 3J **39**
Walton Way. *Tal* 3K **19**
Warburton St. *Stoke* 5K **27**
(off Warburton St.)
Warburton St. *Stoke* 5K **27**
Wardle Cres. *Leek* 5F **17**
Wardle La. *L Oaks* 3H **29**
Wardle St. *Stoke* 1H **27**
Ward Pl. *Stoke* 6A **22**
Warminster Pl. *Stoke* 3F **41**
Warmson Clo. *Stoke* 7H **35**
Warners Cinema. 5E **32** (4D **6**)
Warner St. *Stoke* 2B **34** (4E **5**)
Warren Pl. *Stoke* 4J **41**
Warren Rd. *Stoke* 5A **22**
Warren St. *Stoke* 4J **41**
Warrilow Heath Rd. *New* 3K **25**
Warrington Dri. *Leek* 4D **16**
Warrington Rd. *Stoke* 4C **34**
Warrington St. *Stoke* 7E **34**
Warsill Gro. *Stoke* 2J **41**
Warwick Av. *C'dle* 4F **45**
Warwick Av. *Stoke* 2F **39**
Warwick Av. *Stoke* 5A **42**
Warwick Clo. *Kid* 7D **12**
Warwick Gro. *New* 2H **33**
Warwick St. *Bid* 3B **14**
Warwick St. *New* 5B **26**

Warwick St. *Stoke* ...2K **33** (5B **4**)
Washerwall. 1B **36**
Washerwall La. *Werr* 1B **36**
Washerwall St. *Stoke* 5J **35**
Washington Clo. *Gil H* 2H **15**
Washington St. *Stoke* 1H **27**
Watchfield Clo. *Stoke* 5A **42**
Waterbeck Gro. *Stoke* 2B **46**
Waterdale Rd. *Stoke* 3K **41**
Waterfall Cotts. *Werr* 5J **23**
Watergate St. *Stoke* 2F **27**
Waterhays Village. 2K **25**
Waterhead Rd. *Stoke* 5A **42**
Watering Trough Bank.
Mad H 5C **30**
Waterloo Gro. *Kid* 1D **20**
Waterloo Rd. *Stoke* ...4K **27** (1D **4**)
Waterloo St. *Leek* 4E **16**
Waterloo St. *Stoke* ...2C **34** (4G **5**)
Waters Edge. *Stoke* 6C **28**
Waterside Clo. *Mad* 2B **30**
Waterside Dri. *Stoke* 7D **40**
Water St. *New* 4F **33** (3F **7**)
Water St. *Red S* 2A **26**
Water St. *Stoke* 1K **39**
Waterworld. 1J **33** (2A **4**)
Watery La. *Stoke* 5J **41**
Watford St. *Stoke* 5B **34**
Watkin St. *Stoke* 1C **40**
Watlands Av. *New* 7F **27**
Watlands Rd. *Big E* 2F **25**
Watlands Vw. *New* 7E **26**
Watson Rd. *Stoke* 2J **39**
Watson St. *Stoke* 5J **33**
Watt Pl. *C'dle* 3G **45**
Waveney Ct. *New* 2E **38**
Waveney Gro. *New* 2E **38**
Waveney Wlk. N. *Stoke* 7K **21**
Waveney Wlk. S. *Stoke* 7K **21**
Waverley Pl. *Stoke* 2D **38**
Waverley Rd. *Stoke* 6K **35**
Wavertree Av. *Sch G* 3B **12**
Wayfield Gro. *Stoke* ...5G **33** (5H **7**)
Wayside. *Als* 1G **19**
Wayside Av. *New* 1F **33**
Wayte St. *Stoke* 7A **28**
Weaver Clo. *Als* 7B **10**
Weaver Clo. *Bid* 1C **14**
Weaver Clo. *C'dle* 1H **45**
Weaver Pl. *New* 2E **38**
Weaver St. *Stoke* 1B **34** (3E **5**)
Webberley La. *Stoke* 3H **41**
Webb St. *Stoke* 3C **42**
Webster Av. *Stoke* 1K **41**
Webster St. *New* 5F **33** (5F **7**)
Wedgwood. 4C **46**
Wedgwood Av. *Big E* 3G **25**
Wedgwood Av. *New* 6C **32**
Wedgwood Ct. *Stoke* ...2K **33** (4A **4**)
Wedgwood Dri. *B'stn* 4B **46**
Wedgwood La. *B'stn* 3D **46**
Wedgwood La. *Gil H* 2H **15**
(in two parts)
Wedgwood Pl. *Stoke* 4J **27**
Wedgwood Potteries Mus. &
Vis. Cen. 3C **46**
Wedgwood Rd. *C'dle* 5F **45**
Wedgwood Rd. *Stoke* 7E **34**
Wedgwood Rd. *Tal P* 4A **20**
Wedgwood's Monument. 1K **25**
WEDGWOOD STATION. RAIL
. . . . .4C **46**
Wedgwood St. *Stoke* 4J **27**
Wedgwood St. *Wol* 7G **27**
Weetman Clo. *Stoke* 4F **21**
Weighton Gro. *Stoke* 4K **35**
Weir Gro. *Kid* 1E **20**
Welbeck Pl. *Stoke* 7H **29**
Welby St. *Stoke* 1C **40**
Welch St. *Stoke* 6A **34**
Weldon Av. *Stoke* 2C **42**
Welland Gro. *New* 3D **38**
Wellbury Clo. *Stoke* 2B **46**
Weller St. *Stoke* 5J **33**
Wellesley St. *Stoke* 3A **34**
Wellfield Rd. *Stoke* 3G **35**
Wellington Clo. *Cong* 3F **9**

Wellington Ct.—Woodhead Yd.

Wellington Ct. Leek 4F 17
Wellington Ct. Stoke . . . 1C 34 (3H 5)
Wellington Rd. Kid 1D 20
Wellington Rd. Stoke 1C 34 (3H 5)
Wellington St. Leek 3F 17
Wellington St. New 7F 27
Wellington St. Stoke . . . 1C 34 (4H 5)
Wellington Ter. Stoke 2C 34 (4H 5)
Well La. Als 7D 10
Well La. Gil H 2H 15
Wells Clo. Bid 2C 14
Well St. Bid 2B 14
Well St. C'dle 3H 45
Well St. For 6H 43
Well St. Leek 4G 17
Well St. Mow C 3G 13
Well St. New 5F 33 (4E 7)
Well St. Stoke 2C 34 (4G 5)
Welsh Clo. Stoke 5J 41
Welsh Row. Mow C 3H 13
Wem Gro. New 2B 26
Wendling Clo. Stoke 4J 35
Wendover Gro. Stoke 4G 35
Wendy Clo. Stoke 4G 35
Wenger Cres. Stoke 7J 39
Wenham Dri. Stoke 7C 42
Wenlock Clo. New 2B 26
Wenlock Clo. Stoke 3A 22
Wensleydale Av. Cong 2J 9
Wensleydale Clo. Stoke 5C 28
Wentworth Dri. Kid 7F 13
Wentworth Gro. Stoke 5E 28
Werburgh Dri. Stoke 7J 39
Wereton. 3D 24
Wereton Rd. A'ly 3E 24
Werrington. 1D 36
Werrington Rd. Stoke 2F 35
Wesker Pl. Stoke 2A 42
Wesley Av. Als 6E 10
Wesley Ct. Cong 5F 9
Wesley Gdns. Kid 1D 20
Wesley Pl. Halm 5E 24
Wesley Pl. New 5C 32 (4A 6)
Wesley St. Big E 3H 25
Wesley St. B Bri 7H 43
Wesley St. Stoke 1G 27
Wessex Dri. Stoke 6K 39
Westacre. Stoke 2E 34
West Av. New 3G 33 (1H 7)
West Av. Stoke 5J 33
West Av. Tal 3K 19
W. Bank. Stoke 7K 33
Westbourne Clo. Leek 3D 16
Westbourne Dri. Stoke 6H 21
Westbourne M. Cong 5D 8
W. Brampton. New 4E 32 (2D 6)
Westbury Cen., The. New 4F 39
Westbury Clo. Stoke 7E 28
Westbury Park. 4E 38
Westbury Rd. New 3E 38
Westcliffe. 4J 21
Westcliffe. Leek . . . . 3E 16 (off Alma St.)
Westcliffe Av. New 3D 38
WESTCLIFFE HOSPITAL. 4J 21
West Cres. Stoke 4D 28
W. End Av. Leek 4E 16
W. End Cotts. Cong 5E 8
Westerby Dri. Werr 2B 36
Westerham Clo. Stoke 7J 39
Westfield Av. A'ly 2D 24
Westfield Rd. Mow C 3F 13
Westfield Rd. Stoke 2G 35
Westfields. Leek 4G 17
West Gro. Als 6F 11
Westhead Wlk. Stoke . . . 2A 34 (5C 4)
West Heath. 5D 8
W. Heath Shop. Cen. Cong 4C 8
Westholme Clo. Cong 4D 8
Westlands. 1D 38
Westlands. Big E 2G 25
Westlands Av. New 6C 32 (6A 6)
Westlands, The. Cong 5E 8
Westland St. Stoke 6K 33
Westmarsh Gro. Stoke 7K 21
Westmill St. Stoke 3C 34
Westminster Pl. Stoke 5K 39
Westminster Rd. Leek 2H 17
Westmorland Av. Kid 4C 20
Westmorland Clo. Stoke 3K 21
Weston Clo. Ash B 2B 36
Weston Clo. New 2C 32
Weston Ct. Stoke 2B 42
Weston Coyney. 2C 42
Weston Coyney Rd. Stoke 3J 41
Weston Dri. Stoke 2B 42
Westonfields Dri. Stoke 3K 41
Weston Rd. Stoke 5B 42
Weston St. Leek 3H 17
Weston St. Stoke 7J 35
Westonview Av. Stoke 7J 35
West Pde. Stoke 1B 40
Westport Greenway. Stoke . . . 2H 27
Westport Lake Rd. Stoke 3G 27
Westport Rd. Stoke 3H 27
W. Precinct. Stoke 2B 34 (4F 5)
West Rd. Cong 4D 8
Westsprink Cres. Stoke 4K 41
West St. Bid 3B 14
West St. Cong 4E 8
West St. Leek 3F 17
West St. Mow C 4E 12
West St. New 5F 33 (4E 7)
West St. Port 5G 27
West St. Sil 4J 31
West St. Stoke 1C 42
West Ter. Kid 2D 20
West Ter. Stoke 5A 22
West Vw. New 7E 26
West Vw. R'gh C 3A 48
Westview Clo. Leek 3D 16
Westville Dri. Cong 5C 8
Westwood Ct. Stoke . . . 1C 34 (3H 5)
Westwood Gro. Leek 3E 16
Westwood Heath Rd. Leek . . . 4D 16
Westwood Pk. Av. Leek 4C 16
Westwood Pk. Dri. Leek 4C 16
Westwood Rd. Leek 4D 16
Westwood Rd. New 6G 27
Westwood Rd. Stoke 4B 42
Westwood Ter. Leek . . . . 3E 16 (off Wellington St.)
Wetenhall Dri. Leek 4C 16
Wetherby Clo. C'dle 1H 45
Wetherby Clo. New 5B 26
Wetherby Rd. Stoke 7A 40
Wetley Av. Werr 1G 37
Wetley Moor. 6K 29
Weybourne Av. Stoke 1G 29
Whalley Av. Stoke 6H 33
Wharfdale Rd. Cong 2J 9
Wharfe Clo. Cong 6H 9
Wharfedale Wlk. Stoke 3F 41
Wharf Pl. Stoke 6B 34
Wharf Rd. Bid 2B 14
Wharf St. New 4G 33 (3F 7)
Wharf Ter. Mad H 5C 30
Whatmore St. Stoke 3B 28
Wheatfields. Stoke 1B 28
Wheatley Bank Cotts. Stoke . . . 2F 35
Wheatly Av. Stoke 7H 33
Wheelock Clo. Als 7B 10
Wheelock Way. Kid 1E 20
Whetstone Rd. Gil H 2H 15
Whieldon Cres. Stoke 1C 40
Whieldon Ind. Est. Stoke 7B 34
Whieldon Rd. Stoke 7B 34
Whimple Side. Stoke 4G 35
Whitaker Rd. Stoke 3D 40
Whitbread Dri. Bid 2D 14
Whitchurch Gro. New 2B 26
Whitcliffe Pl. Stoke 3E 40
Whitcombe Rd. Stoke 4B 42
Whitebeam Clo. New 3A 26
Whitehall Av. Kid 1C 20
Whitehall Rd. Kid 1C 20
Whitehaven Dri. Stoke 7A 28 (1D 4)
Whitehead Rd. Stoke 6A 22
Whitehill. 7E 12
Whitehill Rd. Kid 1D 20
Whitehill Ter. Kid 1E 20
Whitehouse Rd. New 2E 32
Whitehouse Rd. Stoke 7F 29
Whitehouse Rd. N. New 1E 32
Whitehurst La. Dil . . 6K 37 & 1A 44
Whiteridge Rd. Kid 1D 20
Whitesands Gro. Stoke 1C 48
Whitestone Rd. Stoke 1C 48
Whitethorn Av. B'stn 6C 46
Whitethorn Way. New 3B 26
Whitfield. 5C 22
Whitfield Av. New 5D 32 (5A 6)
Whitfield Greenway. Stoke . . . 1J 27 (Greenbank Rd.)
Whitfield Greenway. Stoke . . . 6J 21 (Roseberry St.)
Whitfield Rd. Kid 1E 20
Whitfield Rd. Stoke 4C 22
Whitfield St. Leek 5F 17
Whitfield Vs. Stoke 5C 22
Whitley Rd. Stoke 5C 22
Whitmore Av. Werr 1C 36
Whitmore Rd. But & New 5A 38
Whitmore Rd. New & Tren 6E 38
Whitmore St. Stoke . . . 3K 33 (6B 4)
Whitridge Gro. Stoke 5J 35
Whittle Rd. Stoke 6C 42
Whygate Gro. Stoke 6E 28
Wickenstones Ct. Bid . . . . 3C 14 (off Edgeley Rd.)
Widecombe Rd. Stoke 6E 28
Wigmore Pl. Stoke 7H 35
Wignall Rd. Stoke 5G 21
Wilbraham Rd. Cong 4H 9
Wilbraham's Wlk. A'ly 2E 24
Wilbrahams Way. Als 6E 10
Wild Goose Av. Kid 7G 13
Wilding Rd. Stoke 5C 22
Wileman Pl. Stoke 7D 34
Wileman St. Stoke 7D 34
Wilfred Pl. Stoke 5H 33
Wilkinson St. Stoke 2G 27
Wilks St. Stoke 7H 21
Willatt Pl. Stoke 3F 29
Willdale Gro. Stoke 7E 28
Willeton St. Stoke 2F 35
Willfield La. Brn E 4G 23
William Av. Bid 3C 14
William Av. Stoke 6D 42
William Birch Ct. Stoke 4F 35
William Birch Rd. Stoke 4F 35
William Clo. For 7J 43
William Clowes St. Stoke 4J 27
William Coltman Way. Stoke 6F 21
William Fiske Ct. Stoke 2H 39
William Rd. Kid 1D 20
William Ruston Rd. Stoke 2C 28
Williamson Av. Stoke 5C 22
Williamson St. Stoke 2H 27
William St. Cong 3J 9
William St. Stoke 7D 34
William Ter. Stoke 5A 22
Willmer Cres. Mow C 4E 12
Willotts Hill Rd. New 3A 26
Willoughby St. Stoke 4G 21
Willow Clo. Kid 4D 20
Willow Clo. New 3A 26
Willow Ct. Als 6F 11
Willowcroft Ri. B Bri 6D 42
Willowcroft Way. Har 6H 13
Willowdale Av. Stoke 1B 40
Willow Gro. Stoke 4D 40
Willow La. Stoke 4B 48
Willowood Gro. Stoke 6D 42
Willow Pl. Bid M 1G 15
Willow Row. Stoke 3G 41
Willows Dri. Stoke 3B 48
Willows, The. Leek 4D 16
Willow St. Cong 4G 9
Willow Tree Gro. Rode H 3G 11
Willow Way. For 6H 43
Wilmot Clo. New 2C 32
Wilmot Dri. New 2C 32
Wilmot Gro. Stoke 7H 35
Wilson Rd. Stoke 5J 39
Wilson St. New 4E 32 (2D 6)
Wilson St. Stoke 2A 28
Wilson Way. Stoke 4F 21
Wilton Av. Werr 1G 37
Wilton St. New 3D 32
Wiltshire Dri. Cong 3G 9
Wiltshire Gro. New 2F 39
Wimberry Dri. New 3A 26
Wimborne Av. Stoke 7E 40
Winchester Av. Stoke 3H 35
Winchester Dri. New 2C 38
Windermere Rd. Cong 5C 8
Windermere Rd. New 2E 38
Windermere St. Stoke 7A 28
Windermere Way. C'dle 2J 45
Windmill Av. Kid 3D 20
Windmill Clo. R'gh C 3A 48
Windmill Hill. R'gh C 3A 48
Windmill St. Stoke 1C 34 (2G 5)
Windmill Vw. Werr 1D 36
Windrush Clo. Stoke 2B 46
Windsmoor St. Stoke 1A 40
Windsor Av. Stoke 4J 41
Windsor Dri. Als 6A 10
Windsor Dri. Leek 2J 17
Windsor Pl. Cong 5H 9
Windsor Rd. Stoke 5K 39
Windsor St. New 4F 33 (3E 7)
Windy Arbour. C'dle 2H 45
Windycote La. Dil 3H 37
Wingate Wlk. Stoke 7E 40
Winghay Clo. Kid 1E 20
Winghay Clo. Stoke 4F 27
Winghay Pl. Stoke 6A 22
Wingrove Av. Stoke 5J 41
Winifred Gdns. Stoke 6D 40
Winifred St. Stoke 7A 28 (1D 4)
Winnipeg Clo. Stoke 6A 40
Winpenny Rd. P East 4C 26
Winsford Av. Stoke 4K 41
Winslow Grn. Stoke 4H 35
Winston Av. Als 6D 10
Winston Pl. Stoke 2F 35
Winston Ter. New 6F 27
Winterbourne Gro. Stoke 3K 41
Winterfield La. Hul 5C 36
Winterside Clo. New 3A 26
Wintonfield St. Stoke 6B 34
Winton Sq. Stoke 5B 34
Wise St. Stoke 5H 41
Witchford Cres. Stoke 7E 40
Witham Way. Bid 1D 14
Withies Rd. Stoke 2H 39
Withington Rd. Stoke 4K 21
Withnell Grn. Stoke 4K 21
Withysakes. 1E 36
Withystakes Rd. Werr 1E 36
Witney Wlk. Stoke 7E 40
Woburn Clo. Stoke 2B 46
Woburn Dri. Cong 7K 9
Wolfe St. Stoke 7A 34
Wolseley Rd. New 7E 26
Wolseley Rd. Stoke 2J 39
Wolstanholme Clo. Cong 6H 9
Wolstanton. 7G 27
Wolstanton Retail Pk. New . . . 7G 27
Wolstanton Rd. New 6C 26
Wolstern Rd. Stoke 1J 41
Woodall St. Stoke 7A 28
Woodbank St. Stoke 4J 27
Woodberry Av. Stoke 1H 39
Woodberry Clo. Stoke . . . . 1J 39 (off Woodberry Av.)
Woodbridge Rd. New 4E 38
Woodcock La. Mow C 4F 13
Wood Cotts. Werr 4K 23
Woodcroft. 5D 16
Woodcroft. Big E 3H 25
Woodcroft Av. Leek 5E 16
Woodcroft Rd. Leek 5E 16
Wood Dri. Als 7B 10
Woodend St. Stoke 7E 34
Woodfield Ct. Leek 3H 17
Woodgate Av. Chu L 5H 11
Woodgate St. Stoke 5B 42
Woodhall Pl. New 3G 31
Woodhall Rd. Kid 7F 13
Woodhead Rd. Stoke 5G 29
Woodhead Yd. C'dle 1H 45

A-Z Stoke 75

Woodhouse La.
   Bid & Bid M 2J 15
Woodhouse La. Brn E 5D 22
Woodhouse St. Stoke 7A 34
Wooding Dean Clo. Stoke 1J 41
Woodkirk Clo. Stoke 3K 21
Woodland Av. New 7F 27
Woodland Av. Stoke 7E 22
Woodland Clo. Leek 7G 17
Woodland Ct. Als 5E 10
Woodland Gro. Bur 2A 28
Woodland Hills. Mad 4A 30
Woodland Rd. Rode H 2F 11
Woodlands. Stoke 7J 27
Woodlands Av. Cong 3F 9
Woodlands Av. Tal 1A 20
Woodlands Gro. Stoke 3B 48
Woodlands La. B Bri 2J 49
Woodlands Rd. Stoke 2H 39
Woodlands, The. Stoke 2H 39
Woodland St. Bid 3C 14
Woodland St. Stoke 1H 27
Wood Lane. **3H 25**
Wood La. Cong 3K 9
Woodman St. Stoke 3G 29
Woodpark La. Stoke 1H 47
Wood Pl. Stoke 4C 42
Woodruff Clo. Pac 2J 21
Woodshutts. **2B 20**
Woodshutts St. Tal 2A 20
Woodside. Chu L 6B 12
Woodside. Leek 6G 17
Woodside. Mad 1B 30
Woodside Av. Als 6F 11
Woodside Av. Brn E 5G 23
Woodside Av. Kid 2D 20

Woodside Cres. New 4F 39
Woodside Dri. Stoke 3B 48
Woodside La. Leek 7D 16
Woodside Pl. Stoke 3G 29
Woodside Vs. Stoke 2J 41
Woodstock. **4D 20**
Woodstock Clo. New 2F 33
Woodstock Rd. Stoke 4D 20
Woodstock St. Stoke 3E 20
Woodstone Av. End 5K 23
Wood St. Big E 1F 25
Wood St. Cong 4F 9
Wood St. Leek 4G 17
Wood St. Mow C 3F 13
Wood St. Stoke 2H 41
Wood Ter. Stoke 3A 34 (6D 4)
Wood, The. Stoke 4C 42
Woodvale Cres. End 3K 23
Wood Vw. Big E 3H 25
Woodville Pl. Stoke 4B 42
Woodville Rd. Stoke 4B 42
Woodville Ter. Stoke 4C 42
Woodward St. Stoke 6C 28
Woolaston Dri. Als 7E 10
Woolliscroft Rd. Stoke 2G 35
Woolliscroft Av. New 2G 33
Woolrich St. Stoke 5H 27
Woolridge Ct. Stoke 3C 28
   (off Community Dri.)
Woolston Av. Cong 5H 9
Worcester Clo. Tal 4A 20
Worcester Pl. Stoke 3J 35
Wordsworth Clo. C'dle 4F 45
Wordsworth Way. Als 6E 10
Worrall St. Cong 4G 9
Worsley Dri. Cong 6K 9

Worth Clo. Stoke 2J 41
Worthing Pl. Stoke 3G 41
Wraggs La. Bid M 1G 15
Wrenbury Clo. New 3A 26
Wrenbury Cres. Stoke 4G 35
Wren Clo. Bid 2D 14
Wren Vw. Stoke 4J 41
Wrexham Clo. Bid 1C 14
Wright Av. New 5C 26
Wrighton Clo. Stoke 3E 34
Wright St. Tal 2A 20
Wroxham Way. New 4D 38
Wulstan Dri. New 2F 33
Wulstan Rd. Stoke 6K 27
Wyatt St. Stoke 4F 21
Wycliffe St. Stoke 4J 27
Wye Clo. C'dle 5H 45
Wye Rd. New 2D 38
Wymondley Gro. Stoke 1A 46
Wynbank Clo. Big E 4F 25
Wyndham Rd. Stoke 7E 40
Wynford Pl. Stoke 4G 35
Wynstay Av. Werr 2B 36
Wynstay Ct. New 5F 39

Y

Yale St. Stoke 5H 27
Yardley Pl. Stoke 1E 46
Yardley St. Stoke 6E 22
Yardley Wlk. Stoke 1E 46
Yarmouth Wlk. Stoke 1J 41
Yarnbrook Gro. Stoke 1C 28
Yarnfield Clo. Stoke 4B 42
Yateley Clo. Stoke 3G 35

Yates St. Stoke 2A 34 (5D 4)
Yaxley Ct. New 4E 38
Yaxley Pl. Stoke 1E 46
Yeaman St. Stoke 7A 34
Yeldham Pl. Stoke 1E 46
Yeovil Pl. Stoke 1E 46
Yew Pl. New 4A 26
Yew Tree Av. Stoke 4D 40
Yew Tree Clo. L Oaks 3J 29
Yew Tree Ct. Als 1F 19
Yew Tree Ter. Kid 3D 20
York Av. Ful 6F 49
York Clo. For 6J 43
York Clo. Gil H 2H 15
York Clo. Tal P 4A 20
York Pl. New 4E 32 (3D 6)
York Rd. Stoke 3C 42
York St. Leek 3G 17
York St. New 5F 33 (3F 7)
York St. Stoke 7A 28 (1D 4)
Youlgreave Av. Stoke 3G 35
Youlton Pl. Stoke 3G 35
Younger St. Stoke 7C 34
Young St. C'dle 4H 45
Young St. Stoke 5J 21
Yoxall Av. Stoke 5J 33

Z

Zamenhof Gro. Stoke 3B 28
Zennor Gro. Stoke 3G 35
Zetland Pl. Stoke 1E 46
Zetland Wlk. Stoke 1E 46
Zion St. Stoke 4K 27
Zodiac Dri. Stoke 4H 21